Peace, Détente, and Soviet–American Relations

Peace, Détente, and Soviet-American Relations

LEONID BREZHNEV

A Collection of Public Statements

Harcourt Brace Jovanovich

New York and London

HBJ

Printed in the United States of America

Library of Congress Cataloging in Publication Data

Brezhnev, Leonid Il'ich, 1906–
Peace, detente, and Soviet-American relations.

Includes index.
1. Russia—Foreign relations—1945–   —Addresses,
essays, lectures. 2. Detente—Addresses, essays,
lectures. 3. Peace—Addresses, essays, lectures.
I. Title.
JX1555.B73 1979   327.47   78–22244
ISBN 0–15–185921–3

C D E

Contents

Peace, Détente, and Soviet–American Relations

To My American Reader

Brought together in this book you will find articles and speeches—in full or abridged form—on problems of détente and Soviet-American relations and covering the period from 1973 to June 1978.

Political speeches are sensitive to the test of time and cannot always claim rebirth in book form. The abiding urgency of our theme is due to the longing of billions of people for lasting peace and security, to their concern for the future of détente. The abiding relevance of these statements is due to the consistent and unchanging course of the Soviet Union in foreign policy, a course for the peaceful coexistence and co-operation of states, irrespective of differences between their social and political systems, a course for détente, a course that is unaffected by momentary considerations of expediency.

I do not doubt that the majority of Americans want neither a shooting war between our countries nor the nerve-racking dangerous tensions of a "cold war." At the same time I can grant that some of my American readers may have been conditioned into having doubts and even apprehensions regarding the "real" intentions of the Soviet Union. These doubts and apprehensions certainly do not arise from their own personal experiences. Their only source is belief in the biased statements of journalists, of persons reputed to be "experts" in this field, and even of particular official figures.

Such readers have come under the influence of political forces bent on sabotaging détente. Actively using the means of manipulating public opinion, these forces present their own private interests as the interests of the nation. They are busy creating log jams in the way of agreement between our countries on crucial questions of arms limitation and the preparation of conditions for transition to disarmament. They see danger to their plans and to themselves in any moves conducive to our peoples gaining a better knowledge of each other's life and culture and to their arriving at a greater mutual understanding. They managed to prevent the U.S. government from honoring its promise to end discrimination against the Soviet Union in the fields of trade and credit. As a result the Soviet Union turned to other markets; its trade with other Western countries grew appreciably, while U.S. foreign trade suffered damage that could easily have been avoided.

This book will give you firsthand knowledge of the views of "the other side" in the spirit of "fair play" so respected by Americans.

I hope it will help you to find the answer to the question of Soviet intentions, about which masses of misrepresentations and fantastic inventions have been raised by the opponents of détente. The intentions of the Soviet Union, of its leaders and people, are precisely as set out in this book. There is no other, parallel and secret, "black paper" of our policy. To impute to the Soviet Union insidious designs in Europe, Africa, and the Middle East or with regard to the United States is just a foul tactic of political struggle. It bears no resemblance to the facts.

The reader can trace, chronologically, Soviet efforts to have international relations restructured in the interests of peaceful coexistence, to the benefit of the peoples of our countries and of universal peace. Using the subject index, he will be able to gain a better knowledge of the Soviet view on particular international problems.

Détente has been and remains the subject of a great deal of debate. In this book you will find our understanding of this process of overcoming the "cold war" and moving on to normal, equable, and mutually beneficial relations between states. The need for détente springs from the objective circumstances of the coexistence of states in conditions of a nuclear age. Unless we wish to call in question the very existence of civilization and mankind, there is truly no other way.

To the widely known imperatives of the nuclear age one may add the historical legacy, which favors the development of good relations between the Soviet Union and the United States. Our countries have never waged war against each other, if we discount the brief American participation in foreign military intervention against the young Soviet Republic. We have no territorial claims on each other. The peoples of our two countries possess a tremendous cultural heritage and potential and are keenly interested in each other's cultural life.

True, we are divided by differences in our social systems. The United States is the major capitalist country. (Perhaps you would prefer to say "the major Western country.") The Soviet Union is the major socialist country. There is bound to be an ideological debate between us as to whose world view is more correct and whose way of life is better. Here there is bound to be competition between the two systems. But let us agree that this historical dispute cannot be decided on the battlefield of nuclear war. History will in due course deliver its verdict. In the meantime, attending to our own business in our respective countries, we shall cooperate peaceably on the principles of propriety, mutual respect, and mutual benefit.

In his Farewell Address the founder of your nation, George Washington, advised you to observe good faith and justice toward all nations, and to cultivate peace and harmony with all.

The founder of our Soviet state, Vladimir Ilyich Lenin, put forward and made a persuasive case for the principle of the peaceful coexistence of states belonging to different social and political systems—this was many decades before the word *détente* acquired its present meaning. This principle demands that states not interfere in each other's internal affairs and that they not use force to decide disputed issues, and that normal peaceful and businesslike relations be maintained between socialist and capitalist countries.

Let us follow the behests of the founders of our states.

I hope this book will convince the reader that it is precisely this road which the Soviet Union prefers.

LEONID BREZHNEV

July 1978

From May Day Speech in Red Square

May 1, 1973

May 1, International Workers' Solidarity Day, is an important national holiday in the Soviet Union. On this day Soviet leaders address the working people with words of greeting and sum up the results of the Soviet Union's domestic and foreign policies.

With every year and with every month that passes, with every day, one may say, the active peace-loving policy of the Soviet Union and other socialist countries gives the peoples of the earth ever new, convincing proof that the concepts of socialism and peace are indivisible.

The war in Vietnam, for the ending of which the Soviet Union worked firmly and consistently, has ended. Relying on the powerful moral and material support of the Soviet Union and other socialist countries and on the solidarity of all the progressive forces of the world, the patriots of Vietnam have successfully upheld the just cause of freedom and independence.

Important positive changes have been achieved in Europe thanks to the persistent and constructive policy of the Soviet Union and its socialist allies, and with the support of all peace-loving and realistically minded forces. A turn from the "cold war" and dangerous tension toward rational joint efforts to strengthen peace and develop mutually advantageous co-operation is taking place.

We are calling for Europe's bloody past to be overcome, not in order to forget it, but so that it may never be repeated. This has become a perfectly realistic task now that socialism has become a mighty, irresistible force in the life of Europe. Our aims are clear, constructive, and noble. They are worthy of the Leninist party, they are worthy of the world's first country of victorious socialism.

Lenin's idea of the peaceful coexistence of states with different social systems is scoring ever new victories in the minds of people and in the practice of international relations.

The policy of the Soviet Union in Europe, as in other parts of the world, is first of all a policy of peace. This determines both the development of our relations with France, the Federal Republic of Germany, and other European states and our vigorous activities to prepare an all-European conference.

We also approach relations with countries like the United States of America from the same position. We shall continue to work for the favorable development of Soviet-American relations on the principles of mutual respect and mutual advantage. Our country's approach to relations with Japan is similar.

Our sincere friendship and fruitful co-operation with India, the Arab states, and with all the independent freedom-loving countries of Africa, Asia, and Latin America are growing stronger and deeper. The CPSU and the Soviet state are always true to this friendship; we see in it a mighty source of strengthening the forces of peace and progress.

Comrades, the Soviet Union's international position has never been stronger. The security of the Soviet people is more reliably ensured than ever before. Our people are working under the banner of peace and are carrying on the struggle for peace in the cause of the emancipation of labor.

From Address on West German Television

May 21, 1973

From May 18 to 22, 1973, Leonid Brezhnev visited the Federal Republic of Germany. The visit affirmed the turn toward relations of a new kind, normal for peacetime, and toward mutually advantageous co-operation between the USSR and the FRG.

A change is taking place from a quarter of a century's period of "cold war" to relations of peace, mutual respect, and co-operation between the states of the East and the West. This is precisely the objective of the peaceful-coexistence policy pursued by the Soviet Union in relation to states of the opposite social system. In our days it has found its most complete expression in the now universally known Peace Program approved by the 24th CPSU Congress, as well as in the materials of the Plenary Meeting of the CPSU Central Committee this April. There we find written down, among other things, that our country pursues the aim of effecting a radical turn to relaxation and peace on the European continent. I would like to say that the Soviet Union, its Communist Party, and all our people will vigorously and consistently strive for attaining this aim.

The Europe that has more than once been the hotbed of aggressive wars which brought about colossal destruction and the death of millions of people must forever recede into the past. We want its place to be taken by a new continent—a continent of peace, mutual confidence, and mutually advantageous co-operation among all states.

Among the positive elements of present-day European development is, no doubt, also the gradual improvement of the Federal Republic of Germany's relations with its neighbors in the East—Poland, the GDR, Czechoslovakia, and other socialist states in Europe.

We attach great importance to the businesslike, constructive co-operation we have established with the Federal Republic of Germany, France, the United States, and other states in such an important field as the preparation for an all-European conference on security and co-operation.

There still remain in the world quite a few urgent and explosive problems awaiting solution. For example, the conflict has not yet been settled in the Middle East, where Arab lands continue to be in the hands of invaders, and that is why dangerous tensions remain there. Opponents of détente and of the cessation of the arms race can be found in other areas as well. However, mankind's horizon is brightening. The war in Vietnam has ended. Soviet-American relations continue to develop favorably. On the whole, it can be said that today our planet probably stands closer to a firm and lasting peace than ever before. The Soviet Union uses all its influence to promote this beneficial trend.

Our peaceable foreign policy is an expression of the very essence of our society, an expression of its profound internal requisites. The 250-million-strong Soviet people is engaged in carrying out spectacular projects of peaceful construction. In the north and south of our vast country, in Siberia and in Central Asia, we are building huge power stations, hundreds of plants and factories, and developing irrigation systems in areas that in magnitude could compete with many European states. Our aim is to ensure that tomorrow the Soviet people will live even better than today. Soviet people feel tangibly the results of these collective efforts.

Naturally, all this does not mean that we in the Soviet Union have solved all problems, and have no difficulties. Problems that we still have to tackle exist and apparently will exist always and at all times. Yet, the distinguishing feature of the problems arising before us is that they are connected with the confident growth of the country, of its economic and cultural potential, and that we are looking for a solution to these problems exclusively along the lines of further peaceful construction, of boosting the cultural and living standards of the people, and of developing our socialist society.

I would like to add that our plans are by no means plans with an eye to autarchy. We are not following a policy of isolating our country from the outer world. Quite the contrary, we proceed from the fact that it will develop under the conditions of growing all-round co-operation with the outer world, and not only with the socialist countries, but, in large measure, also with the states of the opposite social system.

Arrival Speech in Washington, D.C.

June 18, 1973

This and the four speeches that follow were made by Leonid Brezhnev during his official visit to the United States. By strengthening and broadening the sound foundation, laid in 1972, for normal development of Soviet-American relations, and for promoting mutually advantageous co-operation between the two countries, the visit was a contribution to détente.

Esteemed Mr. President,
Esteemed Mrs. Nixon,
Ladies and gentlemen,

I am glad to meet you again, Mr. President, and I am grateful for the cordial words you addressed to us, representatives of the Union of Soviet Socialist Republics.

This is my first visit to your country, my first direct acquaintance with America and the American people.

We have covered a great distance coming from Moscow to Washington. Our capitals lie about ten thousand kilometers apart.

But in politics there are notions of relativity not envisaged in Einstein's theory. Distances between our countries are growing shorter not only because we travel in modern planes along a well-charted route but also because we have one great common aim, that of ensuring a lasting peace for the peoples of our countries and of strengthening world security.

A year ago, we together took a big step in this direction. The results of our first meeting have laid a good, sound basis for building peaceful relations between our countries.

Already then we agreed that we must move further ahead on this basis. A good start was made in this respect in the past year. Now we regard our visit to the United States and the forthcoming meetings with you as an expression of our mutual determination to make a new contribution to the work we have begun together.

I and the comrades who have come here with me are prepared to work hard so that the talks we are going to have with you, Mr. President, and with other American statesmen will justify the hopes of our two peoples and serve the interests of a peaceful future for all people.

———

From Speech at White House Dinner

June 18, 1973

First of all, permit me to thank you, Mr. President, for the invitation to visit your country, for the kind words you have said here, and for the hospitality you have extended us on the soil of the United States.

I would like to use this occasion to say that it gives me great pleasure to have the opportunity to continue talks with you for the purpose of further improving Soviet-American relations, a beginning to which was made in Moscow in May last year.

I think that the time that has passed since our Moscow meeting has convincingly proved the correctness of the course we have jointly taken toward improving relations between the USSR and the USA, toward rebuilding them in accordance with the principles of peaceful coexistence, as laid down in the document that we signed a year ago. I think you will agree, Mr. President, that we are on the correct road, for it accords with the vital interests of the peoples of our two countries and of all mankind.

That which has been done and that which is being done to put into practice the principles agreed on in Moscow concerning relations between our countries are of no small importance.

Life is our best teacher. The results of our efforts of the past year show in what direction we should go on. They encourage us to make new big strides during the present meeting, to give greater stability to Soviet-American relations and thereby increase the contribution of our countries to the cause of peace and international détente.

Of course, rebuilding Soviet-American relations is no simple task. This is so not only because the USSR and the USA have different social systems, but also because this requires the overcoming of the inertia of the "cold war" and of the traces it has left in international politics, and in people's minds.

But the development of mankind calls for positive and constructive ideas. It is, therefore, my conviction that the more persistently and the more rapidly we move toward mutually advantageous development of Soviet-American relations, the more tangible will be its great benefits for the peoples of our countries, and the faster the number of supporters of such a development, who, as we know, already today constitute a majority, will increase. That is why we are in favor of building relations between the Soviet Union and the United States on an appropriate scale and on a long-term basis.

We have come here with the firm desire, jointly with statesmen in the United States, to give a fresh, strong impetus to such a development of Soviet-American relations. This fully conforms to the Peace Program adopted by the 24th Congress of our Party.

In its resolution this Congress most definitely emphasized the Soviet Union's readiness to improve relations with the United States. In this it proceeded from the belief that this is in the interests of both the Soviet and American peoples, and in the interests of universal peace.

I would like our American partners in the talks to realize fully that this decision of the supreme forum of our Party—the governing party in the Soviet Union—is an expression of the profoundly principled position of the Soviet state, of our entire people, on questions of relations with the United States of America. It is exactly this that determines the policy we are pursuing.

In my talk with the President today I spoke about the feelings of all our people who support the decisions we took at our meeting last year. Mr. President, the peoples of the world are expecting much from our new meeting. And I believe that it is our duty to justify these expectations. The first talks that we have had with you here at the White House confirm, I think, that this is the desire of the two sides. In this connection I would like to express the hope—indeed, the belief—that our present meeting will play an important role in further strengthening mutually advantageous co-operation between our countries and in improving the international climate as a whole.

And here is another point. It is well known that the process of improving Soviet-American relations, which has begun, has aroused widespread interest around the world. The overwhelming majority of the opinions expressed on the subject indicate that the peoples and governments of other countries welcome this improvement. This is only natural. They regard it as a factor promoting an improvement of the international situation as a whole, as a major contribution of the Soviet Union and the United States to strengthening universal peace.

To all who are aware, if only slightly, of the actual course of events, of the nature of the development of Soviet-American relations, it is absolutely clear that the improvement of Soviet-American relations is in no way detrimental to the interests of any third countries.

Of course, the development of good relations between the USSR and the USA will have, and is already having, a considerable influence on international affairs. But this influence is of a kind that promotes the cause of strengthening peace, security, and international co-operation. In building, through joint efforts, the new edifice of peaceful relations, it is not at all our intention to turn it into a secluded mansion, fenced off from the outside world. We want this spacious building to be open to all who are for peace and for the well-being of people.

Contemporary political practice shows how difficult and strenuous at times are the tasks involved in the implementation of the foreign policy of states. But when our thoughts and practical deeds are aimed at achieving the noble goal of peace, this is a burden that, far from being heavy, imparts strength and confidence.

The beginning of our talks—I mean both their content and the atmosphere in which they are taking place—gives grounds for hope that they will yield good results and will become a new landmark in Soviet-American relations.

From Speech at Soviet Embassy Dinner

in Washington, D.C.

June 21, 1973

It is my pleasant duty to welcome you, Mr. President, your wife, members of the U.S. government, and other esteemed American guests, here at the Soviet Embassy in Washington. . . .

At the same time I would like to express our appreciation to all those Americans who have shown friendly feelings toward us, and a lively interest in our visit and in the talks. We view this as confirmation of the respect that the people of the United States have for Soviet people, as proof of our peoples' mutual desire to live in peace and friendship with each other.

Our entire meeting is imbued with an awareness of our lofty duty and responsibility. Our talks are proceeding at a vigorous pace; they cover a wide range of problems, and are businesslike and constructive. All this yields tangible fruit every day, bringing us closer to our jointly set goals— to ensure a further big stride in the development of Soviet-American relations, to reduce the threat of war, and to strengthen peace and security in the world.

The contribution of both our states to the fulfillment of this paramount task will undoubtedly raise Soviet-American relations to a new level. In May last year, we agreed that in a nuclear age there is no other basis for conducting relations between our countries than peaceful coexistence. Now we can state definitely that the fundamental principle of peaceful coexistence is more and more taking on concrete form.

We are convinced that the results of our negotiations will strengthen still more the relations of peace and mutual trust between the Soviet Union and the United States of America. At the same time still more opportunities will open up for the constructive development of these relations.

One cannot but feel satisfaction over the fact that our mutual efforts have made it possible for us to take a new step forward in the solution of such a vitally important and at the same time difficult question as the limitation of strategic arms of the USSR and the USA. The agreement reached on the basic principles to be followed in further negotiations on this problem contains within it everything needed to give a new stimulus and a clear-cut direction to joint work on the important agreements aimed not merely at curbing, but at reversing the build-up of nuclear-missile armaments—the most dangerous and costly—thereby allowing our countries to channel more funds for creative purposes, for improving the life of people.

Atomic energy, too, must increasingly serve peaceful purposes. The readiness of our countries to facilitate this through joint efforts has found expression in the agreement on co-operation in the field of peaceful uses of atomic energy, also signed by President Nixon and me today.

We attach great importance to the fact that, in pursuance of the line jointly mapped out at last year's Moscow meeting, a series of new agreements on co-operation between the USSR and the USA in other fields of science, technology, and culture have been signed during this visit. This will make Soviet-American relations still more diversified and stable. At the same time we are certain that the development of such co-operation will serve the interests of other nations, since it is aimed at the solution of problems important to all mankind.

Of course, there are still many unsolved problems in the relations between our countries and, I would say, there are also undertakings that still await completion. This, among other things, concerns the sphere of strategic-arms limitation, and also trade and economic questions.

We are optimists and believe that the course of events itself and an understanding of concrete interests will lead to the conclusion that the future of our relations lies along the road of their all-round, mutually advantageous development for the benefit of the present and coming generations.

We are convinced that, on the basis of the strengthening of our mutual trust, we will be able to go forward with confidence. We want the further development of our relations to be as stable as possible, and, moreover, to assume an irreversible character.

Mr. President, in the course of our talks, whose businesslike and constructive character we value, I have already had occasion to say to you, and would like to repeat it here for the benefit of the American guests present, that the Soviet Union's course toward improving relations with the USA is not something temporary. This is a firm and consistent course, reflecting the permanent principles of the Soviet state's foreign policy, which was formulated by its great founder, Lenin. This is a course that has the support of our people.

Soviet people believe that the majority of the American people, too, approve the jointly initiated work to strengthen peace and co-operation between the Soviet Union and the United States of America.

***

Regrettably, the crowded program of our visit left me little time to learn more about your great country, to get better acquainted with the life of the American people. But even the little I was able to see has been very interesting. I hope I will be able to remedy this when, at your invitation, Mr. President, we go to the West Coast of the USA, to California, which has long been famous for its natural beauty and more recently for its rapid industrial development.

For my part, I would like to take this opportunity to reiterate the invitation I extended to you, Mr. President, on behalf of the Presidium of the USSR Supreme Soviet and the Soviet government, to come for an official visit to the Soviet Union in 1974. I am confident that your visit to the Soviet Union will mark a new important stage in the successful development of relations between our countries.

We will also be glad to reciprocate the hospitality extended to us these days by the President, the government, and the people of the United States of America. May I express the hope that on that occasion you, Mr. President, will be able to become better acquainted with our country, its nature, and with the life of the Soviet people.

Progress is being made in the development of Soviet-American relations.

In two years' time Soviet and American cosmonauts will fly into outer space to carry out the first major joint scientific experiment in mankind's history. They know that from there, from outer space, our planet looks still more beautiful, but also small. It is big enough for us to live on it in peace, but too small for us to threaten it with nuclear war.

I do not think I would be wrong in saying that what determines the spirit of our talks and the basic direction of our joint efforts is the realization that everything must be done so that the peoples of the world may live free of war, so that they may live in security and co-operate and have contact with one another. This is the imperative demand of our time. To the achievement of this goal we must devote our concerted efforts.

Speech at Signing of Joint
Soviet-American Communiqué

June 24, 1973

Esteemed Mr. President,

Winding up the official part of my visit to your country, I want to express my thanks to you, Mr. President, to the government of the United States, and to the American people for the hospitality that has been shown to me and to my colleagues who accompanied me to the United States.

It was a great pleasure to visit the United States and to continue the contacts that began in Moscow in May 1972, during President Nixon's visit to Moscow.

At the start of our talks in Washington we declared our determination to work hard for the establishment of a stable peace, for the promotion of the interests of our nations, and for the great objective we have set ourselves.

In the course of our talks in Washington, at Camp David, and here at San Clemente, we did not stay strictly within protocol, but devoted nearly all of our time to business. Here in California, too, the President and I continued our talks late into the night.

And today, summing up the results of our work, we can say honestly that our efforts have not been wasted, that our expectations have been fulfilled. We have reached a number of major and important agreements which meet the interests of our people and the people of other countries.

Most important of all is the Agreement on the Prevention of Nuclear War, which the President and I signed on Friday. This is important not only for our two countries. It will help strengthen peace throughout the world. This is why all the people of the world, all the peace-loving nations welcome it.

During our stay in your country we have met and talked with American senators and congressmen, and a large group of representatives of the American business world. And here, in California, we have had the opportunity of meeting many well-known public figures of this state and other people in different walks of life. My comrades who accompanied me on this trip have had many meetings with Americans. All these contacts and talks have strengthened our conviction that large sections of the

American public are aware of the importance of the steps we have taken toward further development of Soviet-American relations, and that they wholeheartedly approve of these steps.

A few days ago I met a large group of American journalists. They, too, voiced their sympathetic attitude regarding what has been done lately to make the relations between our two countries still more stable. I was pleased to hear this. For my part, I want to assure you that the Soviet people fully support the policy aimed at improving Soviet-American relations in the name of a stable peace, and that they will, without any doubt, approve of the documents signed in the past few days in Washington and San Clemente.

I have no doubt that these documents will meet with the approval of all honest and peace-loving people throughout the world.

That is why we are leaving the United States with light hearts. What has been achieved will give us added strength and new energy to continue our work for peace.

I believe that when President Nixon comes to Moscow next year—and this we have already agreed upon—a number of new agreements will emerge, which will not only consolidate what we began in Moscow and have continued in Washington, but also promote this great cause still further.

Mr. President, now that our visit to your country is drawing to a close I wish to express, on my own behalf, and on behalf of my colleagues in Moscow, thanks to all Americans who support the policy aimed at furthering good relations between our two countries.

We hope that the spirit that prevailed at all our meetings and talks with you, Mr. President, and with other American statesmen will underlie all our future relations as they develop. I also believe that President Nixon and his government will, in their pursuance of this policy in American-Soviet relations, be supported by the majority of Americans, because the improvement of our relations serves the vital interests of both our countries and all other nations as well.

In conclusion, I want again to thank you, Mr. President and Mrs. Nixon, and all your colleagues for the hospitality that has been extended to us.

Good-bye, until we meet again!

Address on American Television

June 24, 1973

Dear Americans,

On my visit to your country I highly value this opportunity of addressing you directly with the help of American television.

I would like first of all to convey to all of you the greetings and friendly feelings of the millions of Soviet people who have been following my journey to your country and talks with President Nixon with keen interest, and are hoping that this new Soviet-American summit meeting will be fruitful in improving relations between our countries and strengthening universal peace.

The talks with President Nixon and other members of the United States government continued for several days in a row, and were very intense. We traveled here knowing that these would be very responsible negotiations, devoted to crucial questions concerning the development of Soviet-American relations and a search for ways in which both countries could further improve the entire international atmosphere. We now have every reason to say that these hopes have been justified. We are satisfied with the course taken by the talks and the results that have already been achieved. The new agreements signed in Washington greatly expand the sphere of peaceful and mutually advantageous co-operation between the United States of America and the Union of Soviet Socialist Republics. A new, big stride has been made along the road that we opened up together a year ago, during the meeting in Moscow.

Personally, I am also pleased that this visit has afforded me an opportunity to gain a firsthand impression of America, to become acquainted with some aspects of American realities, to meet your country's noted statesmen and public figures, and to come into contact with the life of Americans.

You are well aware of the fact that, in the past, relations between our countries have developed very unevenly. There have been periods of stagnation, and there have been ups and downs, but perhaps I will not be mistaken in saying that the most farsighted statesmen have always clearly realized the significance of good relations between the Soviet Union and the United States of America. We may recall in this connection that it was forty years ago when, on the initiative of President Franklin Roosevelt, our countries established diplomatic relations.

In the Second World War the Soviet Union and the United States were allies. They fought together against Nazism, which threatened the freedom of nations, threatened civilization itself. The jubilant meeting of Soviet and American soldiers on the river Elbe at the hour of victory over Hitlerism is well remembered in our country.

It might have been expected that this wartime alliance would usher in a new era of broad, peaceful co-operation between the Soviet Union and the United States. Certainly our country sought this; we wanted to consolidate and develop good relations, the foundations of which were laid during the war.

But something different happened. Instead of peace there came the "cold war"—a sorry substitute for genuine peace. For a long time the relations between our countries, and international relations as a whole, were poisoned. Unfortunately some of the sinister influence of the "cold war" survives to a certain extent to this day.

In these circumstances it was, of course, no easy matter to effect a change from mutual distrust to relaxation, normalization, and mutually advantageous co-operation. This took courage and political foresight, and required a lot of painstaking work. We appreciate the fact that President Nixon and his administration united their efforts with ours in order to lead Soviet-American relations onto a really new road.

I have heard that the American political vocabulary contains the expression "to win the peace." I feel that this is a historical moment when this expression can perhaps be used most appropriately. We jointly won the war. Today our concerted efforts must help mankind win lasting peace. The possibility of a new war must be excluded.

The results of the two summit meetings between the Soviet Union and the United States and all that has been accomplished in the year between these two meetings demonstrate convincingly that important progress has already been achieved. It transpired that a reasonable approach, acceptable to both sides, could be found to many questions that had seemed unresolvable. Only recently it was perhaps difficult even to imagine that such progress was possible.

The agreements signed last year are being successfully implemented, on the whole. There is tangible progress in nearly every sphere, and this advance is ensured by our mutual efforts. The inauguration of a regular passenger shipping line between Leningrad and New York, the establishment of consulates general in Leningrad and San Francicso, the initiation of friendly ties between cities in the USSR and the USA, the further promotion of sports exchanges—all this, already today, is becoming part of the life of the peoples of our countries.

The best proof that Soviet-American relations are not standing still, but are developing, is the important document that President Nixon and I signed the other day—the Agreement between the Union of Soviet Socialist Republics and the United States of America on the Prevention of Nuclear War. I don't think I will be accused of exaggerating if I say that this is a document of historic importance.

The Union of Soviet Socialist Republics and the United States of America have concluded an agreement aimed at preventing the outbreak of nuclear war between them, an agreement to do all in their power to prevent the outbreak of nuclear war in general. The tremendous importance of this for the peace and tranquillity of the peoples of our two countries and for improving the prospects for a peaceful life for all humanity is obvious.

Even if this, our second, meeting had no other results than this, it can be said in all justice that it will occupy a worthy place in the history of the development of Soviet-American relations and international life as a whole. Now the whole world can see that both our states, after signing last year the fundamental document on the Basic Principles of Mutual Relations Between the Union of Soviet Socialist Republics and the United States of America, regard it not as a mere declaration of good intentions, but as a program of vigorous and consistent action—a program that they have already started to implement and firmly intend to continue implementing.

Nor is it of small importance that our countries have agreed on basic principles of further work to prepare a new, wider agreement on limiting strategic armaments, and for a much longer term. This means that this exceptionally important work, which began in May 1972 in Moscow, is moving ahead. It means that political détente is being matched by relaxation in the military sphere. This will benefit all peoples and the cause of peace generally.

Representatives of our two states have also just signed new agreements on Soviet-American co-operation in a number of specific fields. Together with the agreements signed earlier in the course of the past year, they constitute an impressive body of documents dealing with the co-operation of our two states, of two great nations, in most diverse fields—from the peaceful uses of atomic energy to agriculture, from the expanses of space to the depths of the ocean.

———

Of course, the Soviet Union and the United States are self-sufficient countries, so to speak. And this, in fact, has been the case up to now in our relationship. But at the same time both we and many Americans realize well that rejecting co-operation in the economic, scientific, technological, and cultural fields means a rejection of considerable additional benefits and advantages that could be derived by both sides. What is more, this would be an absolutely purposeless rejection, which could not be justified on any sensible grounds.

This particularly concerns economics. Now, I think we all agree that it isn't sufficient merely to overcome the anomaly, generated by the "cold war," of the complete freezing of Soviet-American trade. Today life faces us with much bigger questions. I have in mind, first of all, such forms of economic relations as stable, large-scale ties in a number of economic branches, and long-term scientific and technological co-operation, something that in our age is of great importance. The contacts we have had with officials and businessmen of your country confirm that it is precisely along these lines that there is the main prospect for further development of economic co-operation between our two countries.

One occasionally hears the allegation that the development of such co-operation is of a one-sided nature, and is to the advantage of the Soviet Union alone. But such a thing could be said only by one who is entirely ignorant of the actual situation, or who has deliberately turned a blind eye to the truth.

The truth of the matter is that from the development and deepening of economic co-operation in general and the long-term, wide-scale deals about which talks between Soviet organizations and major American firms are either under way or have been successfully concluded both sides must derive real and tangible benefits. We have had clear confirmation that this is so, as far as they are concerned, from representatives of U.S. business circles with whom I happened to talk, both here in the United States and earlier in Moscow. President Nixon and I also discussed this very point in our talks.

To this I would like to add that the leadership of the Soviet Union, just as, I understand, the government of the United States, is attaching great importance to the fact that the development of long-term economic co-operation will also have favorable political consequences: it will consolidate the turn for the better that has become apparent in Soviet-American relations as a whole.

There are also good prospects, as we see it, for a broad development of Soviet-American exchanges in the cultural field. Both our countries have much to give each other in this respect. To live in peace it is necessary to trust one another, and to trust, each must know the other better. We, in any case, want Americans to know, as fully as possible, and truthfully, our way of life and our way of thinking.

On the whole we can say that much has already been accomplished in the development of Soviet-American relations. But we are still standing at the very beginning of a long road. We must show constant concern to protect and nurture the fresh shoots of good relations. Tireless work is needed to determine the most necessary and most suitable forms of co-operation in various spheres. Patience is needed to understand this or that specific feature of the other side and to learn to do business with each other in a good spirit.

I think that those who support a radical improvement in relations between the Soviet Union and the United States may look ahead with optimism, for this goal is in the interests of our two peoples and in the interests of peace-loving people throughout the world.

The general atmosphere in the world depends in great measure on the climate prevailing in the relations between our two countries. Neither economic and military might nor international prestige confers upon our countries any additional rights, but, instead, invests them with special responsibility for the fate of world peace, for preventing war. In its approach to its ties and contacts with the United States, the Soviet Union is fully aware of this responsibility.

We regard the improvement of Soviet-American relations not as an isolated phenomenon, but as an integral and very important part of the wide process of a radical clearing of the international atmosphere. The world has outgrown the rigid armor of the "cold war," in which attempts were made to confine it. Man wants to breathe freely and peacefully. And we shall welcome it if our efforts to improve Soviet-American relations help draw into the process of détente more and more states, be they in Europe or Asia, in Africa or Latin America, in the Middle or the Far East.

We consider it a highly positive fact that the normalization of Soviet-American relations will make it easier to carry out such a big and important task as strengthening peace and security in Europe, including the holding of an all-European conference.

The improvement of Soviet-American relations has undoubtedly played a part in helping to end the long Vietnam war. Now that the agreement on ending the Vietnam war has come into force and both our countries, together with other states, have signed the agreement reached at the Paris

Conference on Vietnam, we deem it especially important that this success be consolidated, and that all the peoples of Indochina be given the opportunity to live in peace.

There are still areas of dangerous tension in the world. In our talks, President Nixon and I touched on the Middle East situation, which is still very acute. We believe that justice must be ensured in the area as soon as possible and that a lasting peace settlement must be achieved—a settlement that will restore the legitimate rights of those who suffered in the war and ensure the security of all the peoples of this vast area. This is important for all the peoples of the Middle East, and it is important for ensuring universal peace.

In a word, the elimination of conflicts that have flared up and the prevention of new crisis situations are essential for the creation of truly reliable guarantees of peace. And our two countries are called upon to make a worthy contribution to this. The President and I gave these questions much attention during our talks of the last few days.

I would like to stress here that, when discussing questions of bilateral relations and general international problems alike, we invariably took into account the fact that both the Soviet Union and the USA have allies and commitments concerning some other countries. It should be made quite clear that both the spirit of our talks and the letter of the agreements signed take this fully into account.

The main point of our discussions and agreement in the field of international affairs is the firm resolve of both sides to make the good relations between the USSR and the USA a permanent factor of international peace.

Even today, as you of course know, there are still too many people who prefer to shout about military preparations and the arms race, rather than discuss the question of détente and peaceful co-operation in a constructive spirit.

What can be said about this? The Soviet people, perhaps better than any other people, know what war is. In the Second World War we achieved a victory of world-wide historical importance. But more than 20 million Soviet citizens died in that war, 70,000 of our towns and villages were razed. One-third of our national wealth was destroyed.

Now the wounds of war have been healed. Today the Soviet Union is stronger and more prosperous than ever before. But we remember well the lessons of the war. And it is precisely for this reason that the people of the Soviet Union so highly value peace and wholeheartedly approve of the peace-oriented policy of our Party and government.

To us peace is the supreme achievement, for which people must strive if they want to have a life worth living. We believe that reason must prevail and feel sure that this belief is shared also by the people of the United States of America and other countries. If this belief were to be lost, if it were to be replaced by a blind reliance on force alone, on the might of nuclear weapons or some other weapon, then it would be a sorry outlook for human civilization and for humanity itself.

The historical path we have traversed has not been an easy one. Our people take pride in the fact that in a short historical period following the victory of the socialist revolution a backward Russia was transformed into a major industrial power which has achieved outstanding success in scientific and cultural fields. We take pride in the fact that we have built a new society, a stable and confidently developing society, which has brought to all the citizens of our country social justice, and in which the wealth of modern civilization is owned by the whole people. We take pride in the fact that the many formerly oppressed nations and nationalities of our country have attained genuine equality and are living in a friendly family of peoples, successfully developing their own economies and cultures. We have great plans for the future. We want to raise considerably the living standards of the Soviet people. We want to achieve further success in the spheres of education and medicine. We want to make our towns and villages more convenient for living in and more beautiful. We have outlined programs for developing the remote areas of Siberia and the North and the Soviet Far East, with their incalculable natural resources. And every Soviet person knows full well that the realization of these plans requires peace above all, and peaceful co-operation with other states.

Of course, just as any other country, we have our own difficulties and problems. But the solution of all the problems facing us, just as of those facing other peoples, requires not war, or the artificial building up of tension, but peace and creative labor. We are certain that this alone can secure the well-being of our people and supply all the needs, both material and spiritual, of every member of society.

I have tried to describe here briefly the thoughts and plans of the Soviet people in order to explain the nature of the Soviet Union's foreign policy. Its peaceful orientation stems from the very essence of our society. The very notion of peaceful coexistence, which is these days increasingly becoming the generally recognized foundation for developing relations between states with differing social systems, was formulated by the founder of the Soviet state, Vladimir Ilyich Lenin.

You probably know that two years ago the 24th Congress of our country's governing party—the Communist Party of the Soviet Union—approved a Peace Program which is a concrete embodiment of the policy of peaceful coexistence in modern conditions. This is a program that provides an active contribution to international détente, to securing truly lasting peace throughout the world for many generations to come. It expresses not only the convictions and intentions of the citizens of our state, but also, we are sure, the aspirations of millions and millions of peace-loving people all over the world. We are implementing this program, working hand in hand with our friends and allies, the socialist countries. On the basis of this program we seek to build relations of good will and mutually beneficial co-operation with all countries that have a similar desire. And the improvement of Soviet-American relations occupies its rightful place in that program.

Dear friends, the importance and complexity of the problems on the agenda of my talks with President Nixon, of our meetings and discussions with members of the Senate Foreign Relations Committee, headed by Senator Fulbright, and with prominent representatives of the American business community—all this inevitably called for a tight work schedule on this visit. As I have already mentioned, these were fruitful discussions, held in a good atmosphere, and this cannot but give us cause for satisfaction.

At the same time, I personally regret that the pressure of business has not given me, and my colleagues who accompanied me and took part in our joint work, a chance to see more of your country. But in Moscow, and here in the United States, I have received many warm letters from various American cities, organizations, companies, and private citizens kindly inviting me to visit towns, to see factories, farms, and universities, and the private homes of Americans. I would like to take this opportunity to express my sincere thanks to all the writers of these letters. I regret that, for the reasons just mentioned, I have been unable to take up those invitations. Of course, it would have been most interesting to visit New York and Chicago, Detroit and Los Angeles, to see industrial enterprises and farms, and to talk to the American working people, for whose achievements our Soviet people have great respect. Perhaps the future will offer such an opportunity, especially since President Nixon and I have agreed that our contacts from now on should be on a regular footing. We are looking forward to President Nixon's visit to the Soviet Union next year.

But, even though this brief visit has not given me the chance to see as much of America as I would have liked, I nevertheless have every reason, when I return home, for telling my colleagues and the Soviet people both about the important political results of the visit and about the atmosphere of good will and the trend in favor of peace, détente, and improved relations between our two countries. This is a trend that we have felt during our stay in the United States and during our contacts with government and public leaders of your country, and with many American citizens. I can assure you that these feelings are fully shared by the Soviet people.

I do not think I will be giving away any secrets if I tell you that in our talks over the last few days President Nixon and I not only addressed ourselves to current political problems but also tried to look ahead and to take into account the future interests of the peoples of our two countries. In so doing we proceeded from the assumption that in politics those who do not look ahead inevitably find themselves left behind, among the stragglers. A year ago, in Moscow, we laid the foundations for improving Soviet-American relations. Now we have achieved a measure of success in this great and important objective. It is our hope that this trend will continue, for it meets the interests of our two great peoples and of all mankind.

In conclusion, I want to express my sincere thanks to the American people and to the President and the government of the United States for their hospitality, and for their kindness and numerous expressions of warm feelings toward the Soviet people and us, their representatives.

Dear citizens of America, please accept my good wishes to each of you for your well-being and happiness.

Thank you.

From Speech at Luncheon in
Rambouillet, France

June 26, 1973

Between June 25 and June 27, 1973, Leonid Brezhnev had meetings in Paris with Georges Pompidou, then President of France. They discussed the prospects of Soviet-French relations and urgent problems of world politics. The discussions were important for strengthening détente in Europe and throughout the world.

Allow me to thank you, Mr. President, for the invitation to visit your country, and for your friendly greetings and warm words about the Soviet Union and our relations.

We are glad to have had this opportunity of having another meeting with you. It continues the dialogue between us, an important element of which was our meeting in Zaslavl early this year. High-level contacts and consultations are a normal feature of the present-day relations between the Soviet Union and France, and each meeting gives a fresh impetus to the cause of mutual understanding and co-operation between our countries.

Our current meeting is taking place at a dynamic time in world developments. Relations between a number of states having different social systems have been revitalized. An active search is under way for solutions to the greatest and most important problems facing the world. This refers not only to Europe, but also to other regions of the world. It has been possible to settle one of the most acute problems—that of ending the war and restoring peace in Vietnam. Realization is growing of the necessity for a settlement in the Middle East.

If we try to make a general assessment of all this, we may say that international relations are entering a new stage in their development. Whereas, only recently, the ideas and policy of the "cold war" formed a general background to the international situation, now the picture is different. However difficult it is to overcome the inertia of the "cold war," there is every reason to regard it as something receding into the past. Quite a lot has already been done to overcome the consequences of this dangerous period in man's history. The state of tension that the world has known has been abolished. We have, so to speak, stepped over an area of dangerous tension. Practical possibilities now exist to begin to develop relations of peace and mutually advantageous co-operation between East and West in real earnest, to start freeing mankind from the threat of nuclear war.

The results of the visit we have just ended to the United States speak in favor of such a conclusion. It may be confidently said that the constructive and businesslike exchange of views we had with President Nixon and the agreements signed in Washington make it possible to advance further along the road of USSR-U.S. co-operation in the interests of both peoples, security, and universal peace.

I would particularly like to stress the importance of the Agreement on the Prevention of Nuclear War, concluded the other day between the Soviet Union and the USA. The purport of this agreement is not only to prevent a nuclear clash between these two powers but also to lessen to a considerable extent the threat of nuclear war for other countries. Therefore, it is our deep conviction that this agreement meets the vital interests of all nations. And this is the reason why the agreement has been met with such approval by the world public.

At such a turning point as now, one sees particularly clearly how timely and fruitful were the steps taken by the Soviet Union and France, which, with mutual accord, have directed their efforts toward the achievement of détente, co-operation, and peace. Our relations have set a good example. I would like to stress this particularly here, in Paris, because the growing Soviet-French co-operation, in our opinion, serves as a model of peaceful coexistence, of the promoting of relations of friendship and good-neighborliness between big powers having different social systems. It is important, in our opinion, that constructive ideas should continue to present themselves, ideas that can inspire peoples, and open before them reliable and firm prospects for a peaceful life.

Soviet-French co-operation has been extensive in European affairs. At the present time the all-European conference which will begin in a few days is in the forefront of attention in European politics. For the first time in the history of Europe responsible representatives of the European states, the USA, and Canada will gather in Helsinki. This fact in itself is of immense significance. But the main thing is that at this conference its participants will have to look at the future of our continent and map out ways for the development of mutual relations between the states concerned in conditions of peaceful co-operation. This is a problem of

---

truly historic scope. And solving it will mean not only taking a new approach in Europe, but also providing an example having wide international importance. In our opinion, the similarity of the positions of the Soviet Union and France on the key issues of European security is an excellent promise of further co-operation of our two countries in ensuring the success of the conference. We are convinced that in the future as well the Soviet Union and France will be able to play a leading part in establishing peaceful co-operation over the entire Continent—of course, taking due account of the fact that the Soviet Union and France have their own friends and allies.

The Communist Party of the Soviet Union and the entire Soviet people put a high value on friendly relations with France and the French people. The development of these relations in the political, economic, scientific, and cultural fields is one of the major trends of Soviet foreign policy. Such was the approach of our Party's 24th Congress to the question of relations with France, an approach that was once again confirmed at the April Plenum of the CPSU Central Committee, which considered the basic issues of Soviet foreign policy.

Esteemed Mr. President,

During the present exchange of opinions we concentrated our attention on a number of key issues of contemporary international development and on assessing their importance on a European and world scale. As formerly, we found a close correspondence in our viewpoints. The meeting and the talks with you were a fresh confirmation of the viability and stability of Soviet-French co-operation. The trust between our two countries, a trust established in the difficult years of the war and further strengthened subsequently, is growing stronger, to the benefit of the peoples of our two countries and European and international security.

Speech on Receiving the International
Lenin Peace Prize

July 11, 1973

Esteemed members of the International Committee,

Dear comrades and friends,

I am deeply moved in accepting today the Lenin Prize for Strengthening Peace among Peoples.

For me, a Communist, there can be no higher assessment of one's work than the award bearing the name of the great Lenin, our teacher, a brilliant theorist, and a skillful and farsighted statesman. Allow me to express my sincere gratitude to the International Committee for conferring such a high honor on me.

The foreign policy of the Soviet Union is the fruit of the collective thinking and effort of our Communist Party. I therefore regard the award of the Lenin Prize to me as an honor conferred on the entire Party for its work, as international recognition that the policy pursued by its Central Committee is correct. And I am happy that, as a member of the Party and as one who has been reared and steeled by the Party, I can participate in the struggle for the great goals of a durable peace and the lasting security of nations—goals that working people everywhere are striving to achieve.

For us Soviet people the active struggle for peace is not a temporary task dictated by the moment. It is our principled, deliberate, and consistent policy, which we pursue in fraternal unity with all the countries of the socialist community.

With great insight into the future of social development Marx wrote that when the working class builds its own, socialist, society, its "international rule will be *Peace,* because its national ruler will be everywhere the same —*Labor.*"

The Soviet people have built a socialist society and today are building communism, a system that will most fully reveal man's creative potentialities. It is therefore understandable why our Party, which is leading an effort, unparalleled in history, to build the future, and why our people, who have utter trust in the Party and are carrying out that constructive work with their own hands, consistently denounce war and aggression and call for a reliable, lasting peace for all people in the world.

It is entirely understandable that for Soviet people the concept of a just peace and of a policy of peace is inseparably linked with the name of our great leader and teacher, the founder of our Party and state, Vladimir Ilyich Lenin. Lenin was the first in history to unite the theory of scientific communism with the conduct of state foreign policy. This union of Leninist theories and Leninist practice gave rise to the principles and methods underlying the socialist policy in the international arena by which we, his pupils and followers, are and shall always be guided.

Today the principles of Soviet foreign policy are known to the whole world. It is a policy of promoting the fraternal unity of the countries of the socialist community, a policy of consolidating the alliance with peoples fighting for national and social liberation, a policy of peaceful coexistence of states with different social systems, and a policy of resolute action against aggression. It is a policy of active, straightforward diplomacy, of strict and unfailing fulfillment of commitments. This policy is consistent with the interests of socialism, and it fully accords with the interests of all peoples, with their aims and vital requirements.

In fulfillment of the behests of the great Lenin the 24th Congress of our Party put forward a realistic and, as developments have shown, fruitful Peace Program. This program is inspired by a lofty aim—to keep the skies always clear, to make guns silent forever, and to use rockets solely for peaceful purposes, and to employ the inexhaustible forces of nuclear energy to promote only constructive efforts, only goodness and the happiness of the working people. That is why our Peace Program enjoys great esteem and recognition among workers and peasants, among all who are engaged in peaceful work, and is winning their growing and increasingly more effective support.

It has always been the position of Communists that the masses and their political parties and organizations should be active in solving questions relating to war and peace, and that in world politics they should be an active force and not passive onlookers. The voice of the people can be a detriment only to those who want to preserve international tension. And at the same time the authority of public opinion and its active support can only help those governments which consistently pursue a policy of peace.

I would like to take this opportunity, with the presence here of people prominent in public life—representatives of peace-loving forces—to point out that the Soviet Union wholeheartedly welcomes the increasing participation of these forces in the struggle for international security. We are confident that the World Congress of Peace Forces to be held in Moscow this year will mark an important stage in the public movement in defense of peace. As regards us, you may be certain, dear friends, that the Congress and its noble aims and tasks will have our full support.

The ranks of those who are resolutely and consistently working for peace among nations and peaceful co-operation between all countries and peoples have been steadily growing every year. This is a very good sign and it fills us with optimism. Today I should like to extend my sincere congratulations to my colleagues in the struggle for peace, to our friends who have also been awarded the Lenin Peace Prize this year. I refer to the President of Chile, Salvador Allende, the well-known English writer James Aldridge, and the prominent leader of the Uruguayan and international working-class movement and Chairman of the World Federation of Trade Unions, Enrique Pastorino. We wish all of them, all the laureates of the Peace Prize that bears the name of Lenin, further successes in their work for humanity.

It has been correctly said that experience is, above all, memory, the memory of generations. Our experience teaches us that peace does not come of itself. It has to be fought for. Sometimes the heaviest sacrifices have to be made in order to uphold a country's independence and honor, to defend the very right to live and to be the complete master of one's own land and destiny.

Fifty-five years ago the first generation of Soviet people started the revolutionary transformation of Russia. Today the Soviet Union is a powerful and free country confidently advancing toward communism. But can one ever forget that for every eighteen months of peaceful construction in our history there was one year of war or of postwar rehabilitation?

It is now midsummer, a time when blossoming nature reveals all her wealth, her inexhaustible creative power. And together with nature we rejoice in life and feel the fullness of happiness in work. But Soviet people have not forgotten, nor will they ever forget, that on a summer day just like this, thirty-two years ago, the explosions of Nazi bombs and shells darkened the sunrise.

From the very first to the very last day of the war I, like millions of my compatriots, passed over many roads of the front, or, to be more exact, over the roadless battlefields. My heart swells with great pride for the immortal feats of the courageous Soviet people during the Patriotic War. At the same time, I grieve over the memory of those who died the death of the brave on the battlefield, of those who were killed in Nazi prison camps or perished under enemy bombs in their own homes.

It was not only the destiny of our people and the future of our country that were at stake in those years, but also the destiny of many countries and hundreds of millions of people in those countries. Nobody has the right to forget that our contemporaries largely owe their very existence and their freedom to the valiant Soviet people, to the Soviet state, and to the great socialist system.

Last year I visited many parts of the country: the Novosibirsk region, the Altai, Uzbekistan and Kazakhstan. This was a business trip connected with current tasks of the national economy. The matter in hand concerned the harvest, the fulfillment of plans and how to resolve various economic problems better and more effectively. But wherever and whatever the talk was about—whether at meetings of people holding executive positions in the economy, at research institutes, in the fields, or at factories—one short, meaningful word, peace, figured prominently.

The Soviet citizen associates many things with this word: his love of life and his Motherland, and his achievements in creative labor for the building of a communist society in his country, and for the common ideals of the working people of the whole world. Struggle against aggression and defense of peace are the people's injunction to our Party, and in faithfully fulfilling it the Party is aware of its responsibility to the present and future generations of Soviet people.

Today we are witnesses to—and not only witnesses to but active participants in—the most momentous event in the whole of postwar history. This is the transition from the period of hostile confrontation in international life, when the dangerous tension could break and plunge the world into the holocaust of war, to a period of more stable peaceful coexistence, of reasonable, peaceful co-operation between socialist and capitalist states on a basis of mutual benefit and equal security.

The road from confrontation to co-operation is not an easy one. It requires both effort and time. The major landmarks along this road were the treaties signed in recent years in Europe between the USSR and the FRG, between Poland and the FRG, between the German Democratic Republic and the FRG, and between socialist Czechoslovakia and the FRG, and the series of agreements on West Berlin. It is not possible to overestimate the importance of the Paris Agreements on the restoration of peace in Vietnam, which record the triumph of the just cause of the heroic Vietnamese people. Important international acts, such as the treaty banning bacteriological (biological) weapons, or last year's Soviet-American agreements on limiting strategic arms, have likewise played their role.

As you all know, we have recently had talks with representatives of leading capitalist countries, such as the United States of America, the Federal Republic of Germany, and France. We devoted these talks to exploring ways to settle extremely important matters—the consolidation of the favorable changes that have taken place in world affairs and the establishment of interstate relations based on the principles for which we have struggled since the October Revolution, since the days of Lenin. It must be said that the work that was done has yielded real, tangible results that are valuable both for our people and for all the peoples of the world.

Let us consider the following. For almost thirty years after the nuclear explosions in Hiroshima and Nagasaki mankind has been living with the awareness that somewhere, beyond the horizon, or perhaps somewhere rather close, the threat of a nuclear catastrophe was lurking. All these years peace-loving people have been demanding the removal of that threat from the life of mankind. Today, at last, we have made real progress in that direction.

Indeed, is it possible to overestimate the fact that the USSR and the USA, the two powers holding most of the world's stocks of nuclear weapons, have agreed to refrain from the threat or use of force against each other, against each other's allies, and against other countries, and that they have agreed to act in such a way as to exclude the possibility of a nuclear war breaking out between them or between either of them and other countries? It is really impossible to overestimate this!

I have already said that if we had limited ourselves only to one agreement with the USA, the Agreement on the Prevention of Nuclear War, we would, even in that case, have accomplished a great deal.

Imperialism's forces of aggression will evidently not lay down their arms for a long time yet. There are still adventurers who are capable of kindling another military conflagration in order to further their own mercenary interests. We therefore consider that it is our sacred duty to conduct our policy in such a way as to avoid being caught unawares by any emergency and firmly to counter any attempt at returning the world to "cold war" days.

The best way of defending peace is to continue actively pursuing our policy of peace, to continue our—as people now call it—peace offensive.

At its Plenary Meeting in April, the Central Committee of the Communist Party of the Soviet Union instructed the Politburo to carry on its vigorous efforts to implement the Peace Program in its entirety and to make irreversible the favorable changes that are now being increasingly felt in the international situation. On behalf of all my comrades in the Politburo and in the Central Committee I should like to state: We shall spare no effort to carry out this "peace mandate" given to us by the Party and by the entire Soviet people.

A feature of the present situation is that some provisions of the Peace Program have been, in effect, carried out, and the fulfillment of others is proceeding at a fairly rapid pace. This compels us to take a new view of some issues. We are now working to determine new objectives and new horizons of our policy, and by advancing toward them we can more effectively secure the main goal—the consolidation of peace and the establishment of peaceful coexistence as an indispensable norm of interstate relations.

Of course, comrades, as has been the case hitherto, our main concern is to strengthen our friendly relations with the socialist countries.

Our Party and all our people derive profound satisfaction from the fact that the fraternal Parties and peoples of the countries of the socialist community are working actively side by side with us to strengthen the present turn in world affairs.

Our militant co-operation and our combined support have helped the heroic Vietnamese people to achieve victory. Our joint actions predetermined the dynamic developments in Europe that have led to the holding of the all-European conference. We are convinced that the strengthening of our unity is a major prerequisite for further progress along the entire front of international relations. We are currently working out concrete steps to strengthen further the unity of the socialist countries.

Moreover, as we have done in past years, we shall pay great attention to promoting our relations with the national-liberation forces, and with the new states of Asia and Africa that, having taken the path of freedom, are now endeavoring to consolidate their independence and promote their economic and social development.

As we see it, one of the most important tasks at the present time is to eradicate the hotbed of aggression in the Middle East. The aggressors, the adventurers can no longer be permitted to continue holding that huge region in a state of explosive tension. The rights of the Arab peoples, who have been made the victims of aggression, must be fully secured. Israeli troops must be withdrawn from all occupied Arab territories. Peace, security, and the state frontiers of all the countries of the Middle East must be guaranteed. For our part, we shall continue to adhere firmly to precisely this policy.

We consider it important that new steps should also be taken to strengthen friendly relations with the Latin-American states, notably with those of them that are actively working for peace and the freedom of peoples.

We know full well and always bear in mind that, together with the peoples of the socialist countries, the peoples of the Asian, African, and Latin-American states form an important contingent, so to say, of the standing army of peace in international relations. Together we have accomplished a great deal, and we are convinced that our ways will not part. The Soviet Union, for its part, is prepared to take all the measures necessary to strengthen and develop our co-operation.

In the immediate future there is much that we shall have to do to promote relations with the USA, France, the FRG, Japan, and other countries of the capitalist world. It is necessary to consolidate what has been achieved in the sphere of improving our relations and to take new effective measures to deepen and widen the framework of our mutually beneficial co-operation on the basis of the principles of peaceful coexistence. Of course, first and foremost, we shall have to occupy ourselves with the practical and full implementation of all the treaties and agreements that have now come into force. Actually, this is both the condition and the prerequisite of further progress.

In Europe the truly immediate task is to bring to a conclusion the work of the all-European conference, which has gotten off to a successful start. We consider that this must be done within the shortest possible time, without any unjustified delays. Moreover, we are convinced that the draft "General Declaration on the Foundations of European Security and the Principles of Relations Between States in Europe" submitted in Helsinki by the Soviet Union in agreement with the fraternal countries, and the proposals made by our friends and allies in agreement with us, can become an effective vehicle for the achievement of the historic aim of turning Europe into a continent of lasting peace.

We are devoting due attention, comrades, also to questions linked with various aspects of the policy of disarmament. We are firmly convinced that political détente in Europe must be augmented with military relaxation. The Soviet-American talks on limiting and then reducing strategic arms are to be continued. We hope that progress will be achieved also at the United Nations talks in Geneva over a wide spectrum of disarmament issues.

In short, there is a great deal of work, important work, to be done, important not only for the Soviet people but also for all mankind.

As Soviet people we cannot help feeling proud that it was our Soviet country that, translating Lenin's behests into life, has become the state that is showing all mankind the road to lasting peace.

This feeling rests on a deep and solid foundation. The CPSU's foreign policy of peace is, after all, the expression of the will, and the result of the efforts, of the millions whose name is the Soviet people. A contribution to the historic successes of that policy has been made by all Soviet people—men and women, old and young; those who make steel and those who grow grain; those who work in laboratories and those who wear army greatcoats; those who teach our children and those who look after the health of our great people. Each one of these people is a dedicated toiler, devoted to his work, and merits the most profound gratitude for his accomplishments in labor and battle.

Our work on the international scene is creating the peaceful conditions needed for the constructive labor of Soviet people. In turn, the results of this labor are embodied in the multiplication of the country's wealth and might, in the rise in the standard of living and in the cultural level of the Soviet people, and they serve as a firm foundation for the Party's foreign-policy activities.

Marching with us in the same rank are our true friends—the peoples of the socialist countries, our class brothers—the Communists of the whole world, those who are fighting for freedom and independence, and all who uphold the ideals of peace and progress on earth. We are sincerely grateful to all our friends for their solidarity and support, for this gives us strength and the confidence that we have chosen the right road.

We would like to assure our friends that our policy will always consistently combine the national interests of the Soviet country with the interests of the working people of all countries, and with the interests of all who champion freedom, independence, democracy, and socialism. Today, as in the past, we consider that it is our sacred duty, a duty springing from our communist convictions, from our socialist morality, to give all possible support to the peoples fighting for the just cause of freedom. This has always been so, and it will remain so in future.

Dear comrades and friends, this day is an important and joyous occasion in my personal life. It is true, as you have seen, that I have spoken today not of my personal feelings but of our common affairs, of our common past and future. I could not do otherwise, because my whole life, from my early youth, has been dedicated to the Party, to its work, and to its concerns.

After I was awarded the Lenin Prize I received congratulations from many people. With all my heart I thank everyone who sent me those greetings. With all my heart I say thank you for the kind wishes and the warm words spoken here in this hall. I am deeply touched and encouraged by the sincerity of the feelings expressed in them.

In accepting the Lenin Peace Prize I would like to assure our Party, the Soviet people, and people of good will everywhere that I will continue to do everything in my power to achieve the most wonderful and most humane objective—the objective implicit in the very name of the award conferred upon me, namely, that of strengthening peace among nations.

Speech at the World Congress
of Peace Forces

October 26, 1973

The World Congress of Peace Forces was held in Moscow from October 25 to October 31, 1973. It was attended by over 3,000 delegates from 143 countries, including members of many national and international organizations of diverse political trends that are working for peace and co-operation among nations.

Dear friends, dear guests, comrades,

I am sincerely glad of this opportunity to extend heartfelt greetings to you, representatives of the world's peace forces, on behalf of the Communist Party of the Soviet Union and the entire Soviet people.

Yesterday, our friend Romesh Chandra and delegates representing a number of authoritative international organizations expressed from this rostrum kind and warm sentiments about our country and its foreign policy. For this we are deeply grateful. The selection of Moscow, our capital, as the venue for the Congress will be an incentive for all Soviet people to intensify their efforts for peace and the freedom and security of nations.

The history of the mass peace movement offers many inspiring examples. But I should like to join in the view already expressed here that there has never been an international forum on such a scale, and as representative an assembly, as this World Congress of Peace Forces.

Gathered in this hall are delegations of peace fighters from the socialist countries, the capitalist countries, and the developing countries.

In this hall are representatives of various political trends: Communists, our brothers in the struggle for a better future on the globe; Social-Democrats; representatives of revolutionary-democratic parties and national-liberation movements. Also present here are leaders of some other political parties. Politically unaffiliated men and women deeply concerned for the future of their nations are also present. Atheists and religious people have gathered here together.

Among those present we find workers, farmers, scientists, artists, representatives of all sections of the intelligentsia, that is, men and women whose hands and minds and whose creative inspiration produce all the material and cultural values of the world. Peace and labor have always been linked, since time immemorial. Wars have bred exploitation and oppression, but peace has always ultimately depended on the workingman. Peace is what man, the worker, needs most of all, whether operating a machine tool or a smelting furnace, whether driving a tractor or erecting a building, whether lecturing in a university auditorium or doing research in a laboratory.

Among those taking part in the Congress there are also businessmen from the capitalist countries representing groups that advocate mutually advantageous economic co-operation by all the countries of the world. This provides fresh evidence of the broad base on which the great movement of the peace forces rests.

I should like to make special mention of a new and, in our opinion, welcome development, namely, the participation in the Congress of Peace Forces of representatives of the United Nations and also of its committees and specialized agencies. This, we believe, is a natural development, because the main purposes and tasks of the United Nations, as written into its Charter, are identical with the purposes and aspirations of this Congress: in every way to promote world peace and fruitful co-operation among states and nations.

Dear friends, for many centuries men—at least the wisest among them—have never tired of condemning and cursing war. The peoples have had visions of lasting peace, but almost every page in the history of mankind is marred by the sinister reflection of the flames of wars, big and small.

Neither the lessons of history nor what would appear to be man's natural aversion to killing his like has ever prevented new blood baths, because the forces of war, the role of those who stood to gain from war, were too great.

In our epoch this state of affairs has changed fundamentally. Today, the struggle against war has a reliable basis in the strength of the forces of peace and the forces of democracy, and in the freedom and independence of nations.

Esteemed participants of this Congress, on behalf of the 250 million Soviet people, on behalf of their Communist Party and the Soviet government, I assure you that it is one of the principal concerns of our state to consolidate peace.

"Peace for the peoples!" was one of the main slogans under which the working people of this country accomplished the October Revolution at the height of the First World War fifty-six years ago. Indeed, the Decree on Peace, written by Lenin, was the first legislative act of the world's first socialist state.

Addressing that historic document not only to the governments but also to the peoples of all countries, the worker-peasant government of Soviet Russia expressed our country's firm desire for a just and democratic peace. I emphasize, a peace that is just, a peace that is democratic, that is, a peace based on respect for the rights and interests of all peoples. And in the years since the Great October Revolution we have always steadily and consistently worked to bring about the triumph of just such a peace in the world.

The Soviet people, who lost more than 20 million of their fellow-citizens in the fight against fascism, are well aware of what war is like and of the incalculable suffering it entails for the people. For the Soviet people the Great Patriotic War was not only a struggle for our country's freedom and independence. It was also a battle to save world civilization, a battle for a just peace in the future. Throughout the postwar period, the Soviet Union has tirelessly worked for lasting peace and the security of nations.

The consistently peaceable policy of the CPSU and the Soviet state is epitomized at the present stage by the Peace Program of the 24th Congress of our Communist Party. Putting forward this Program, we felt that it was our task to help eliminate seats of tension, to assist mankind in ridding itself of the specter of a thermonuclear holocaust, and to promote a relaxation of tension in every possible way. And we have been working and will continue to work ceaselessly for these noble goals, for the benefit of all working people.

I

Dear friends, your Congress has met at a most important and highly responsible time in history.

In the past few years, the people's long and persistent struggle against the outbreak of another world war, and for lasting peace and international security, has achieved significant successes.

The most important of these is that the danger of a world-wide nuclear-missile war, which first loomed over mankind in the second half of the 1940s, has begun to recede, while the prospects for maintaining world peace are becoming better and more reliable than they were ten or twelve years ago. That is something we can say quite confidently.

The principles of the peaceful coexistence of states with different social systems are winning ever broader recognition. They are becoming more and more specific in content, and are gradually becoming generally accepted as a standard of international relations.

In particular, significant changes have come about of late in the relations of the socialist countries with the West European countries—with France, which was one of the first to adopt the course of constructive co-operation among states with different social systems, the Federal Republic of Germany, Italy, and some other countries. Among the most significant indications of the change for the better in international relations are the treaties concluded by the Soviet Union, Poland, and the German Democratic Republic with the Federal Republic of Germany. As you all know, these treaties are based on the recognition of the inviolability of the existing frontiers and contain commitments to refrain from the use of force in international issues.

All this has unquestionably improved the situation in Europe, the continent where both world wars broke out. And the European Security Conference is a concentrated expression of the positive changes. The fact that this Conference, for which the progressive forces of the Continent worked for so long, has met, that practically all the European countries and also the United States and Canada are taking part in it, and that matters relating to European peace and security and to peaceful co-operation are being jointly discussed is in itself a considerable gain.

As we know, the past two years have seen positive changes in the relations between the Soviet Union and the United States of America. The agreements concluded during our meetings with the U.S. President in Moscow in May 1972 and in Washington in June 1973 have opened the way to transition in Soviet-American relations from confrontation to détente, normalization, and mutually beneficial co-operation. We are deeply convinced that this accords with the interests of the peoples of the Soviet Union and the USA, and of all other countries, because it serves to strengthen international security.

In recent years, much has changed in areas that are also important in terms of international security, such as Southeast Asia and the Far East. The ending of the war in Vietnam was an event of world-wide significance. It was first and foremost a victory for the heroic people of Vietnam. It was also a victory for the socialist countries, which had rendered unfailing and effective aid to Vietnam in its just struggle. Furthermore, it was a victory for all the forces of peace that had worked actively to end the imperialist aggression in Indochina. The public circles working for peace sincerely welcome the normalization of relations in South Asia, that is, the relations between such countries as India, Pakistan, and Bangladesh. In many spheres, good relations are developing between the Soviet Union and other socialist countries, on the one hand, and Japan, on the other. One indication of this is the results of the recent visit to Moscow of the Prime Minister of Japan.

The elimination of some seats of war, the first steps to limit the arms drive, the conclusion of a series of important acts having the force of international law, and the regular political consultations between states with different social systems are all visible features of the deep-going changes in international affairs. These changes are also highlighted by the ever larger scale of international economic, scientific, technological, and cultural co-operation. In brief, the struggle for international security has many successes to its credit, and the peoples welcome this heartily.

To be sure, we are realists and cannot help seeing facts of a different order as well. We know all too well that wars and acute international crises are by no means over. There are still acts of aggression in the world, and not all nations are able to feel secure. And we fully share the concern expressed here in this context by prominent spokesmen for world opinion.

But acts of aggression and violence have never before generated such universal indignation, protest, and active resistance as they do today. Never before have such powerful governmental and public forces been set in motion in such cases in order to stop the aggressor, extinguish the flare-ups of war, and consolidate peace. And this, also, is a major achievement.

We are deeply convinced that the current change-about from "cold war" to détente, from military confrontation to a more solid security and to peaceful co-operation is the main tendency in present-day international relations.

How has this become possible?

The main factor, we are certain, is the general change in the correlation of world forces—a change that is against the exponents of "cold war" and the building up of arms and those who fancy diverse military ventures, a change in favor of the forces of peace and progress.

It would be hard to exaggerate the role played by the socialist forces, the socialist community, in the positive changes now under way. The Soviet Union is working for a better and more solid peace together with the other countries of the socialist community, its good friends and associates. The world is aware of the great contribution made by Bulgaria, Hungary, the German Democratic Republic, Poland, Romania,

---

46

and Czechoslovakia to the consolidation of peace and the growth of international co-operation, and in particular to the consolidation of European security. Socialist Yugoslavia, too, is an active champion of peace.

The consistently peaceful policy of the Mongolian People's Republic is a substantial factor of peace and security in Asia. The Democratic Republic of Vietnam displayed supreme courage in combating the armed intervention of U.S. imperialism and has made a notable political contribution toward eliminating a dangerous seat of war in Southeast Asia. The initiative of the People's Democratic Republic of Korea, designed to bring about the peaceful reunification of Korea, has met with wide response throughout the world.

Revolutionary Cuba, the first socialist country in Latin America, is doing much to establish in international relations the principles of peace, and the freedom and independence of peoples.

From the rostrum of this Congress I should like to express the heartfelt and deep respect of the Communists of the Soviet Union, of all Soviet people, for the fraternal socialist countries and for their principled and consistently peaceful foreign policy.

Frequent dialogues between the leaders of different states have been a typical feature of international relations in recent years. In our time, the statesman's true role and political weight depend largely on the extent to which he appreciates the importance of safeguarding and consolidating peace and on what he does in practice to solve this most crucial problem of our time.

In this sense we must give due credit to those Western statesmen who are striving to overcome the inertia of the "cold war" and embark on a new course, that of a peaceful dialogue with states belonging to a different social system. We are also aware of the struggle in the Western countries between the supporters and opposers of international détente, and of certain inconsistencies in the attitudes of some states on various issues. This means that considerable efforts are still required to ensure further progress toward a more durable peace. Speaking for ourselves, we are prepared to make them.

In analyzing the main causes and reasons for the present turn in the world situation it is necessary to underscore the big role played in this process by the countries that have thrown off the colonial yoke and won national independence.

The entire course of postwar development has proved convincingly that colonialism and aggression, the policy of colonial tyranny and the policy of force, are essentially two sides for the same coin. There is therefore every justification for the fact that in the very name of your

---

Congress the struggle for peace is associated with the struggle for national liberation.

This connection is most clearly seen in the example offered by the long years of the heroic Vietnamese people's struggle for their freedom. I think that we all agree that it is this success of the people of Vietnam in rebuffing aggression and their successful defense of their freedom and independence that create a basis for just and lasting peace. We are convinced that only on the basis of respect for the freedom, independence, and sovereignty of all nations in the area can peace and security in Southeast Asia be finally ensured.

Is it not obvious that the struggle of the Arab peoples for the eradication of the consequences of Israeli aggression is simultaneously a struggle for a lasting and just peace in the Middle East?

The seat of tension in that region of the world has given rise to war for the fourth time. This month's hostilities reached unparalleled intensity, with heavy casualties on both sides, including loss of life among the civilian population during barbarian bombing raids on peaceful towns and villages in Egypt and Syria. The latest developments have very strikingly shown the whole world the danger of the situation in the Middle East and the pressing need for changing it.

You are, of course, well aware of the actual course of events. I should therefore like to say a few words about the essence of the issue. What are the basic causes of the military conflicts that have periodically broken out in that region, including the present war? From our point of view they are self-evident: Israel's seizure of Arab territories through aggression, Tel Aviv's stubborn refusal to reckon with the legitimate rights of the Arab peoples, and the support this policy of aggression is getting from forces of the capitalist world that are seeking to hinder the free and independent development of progressive Arab states.

In recent years the Soviet Union has time and again—and I stress this —warned that the situation in the Middle East is explosive. Our stand on this issue has been clear and consistent from beginning to end. In keeping with the general principles of socialist foreign policy and in view of the fact that this region is in direct proximity to our frontiers, we are interested in seeing that a really durable and just peace is established in the Middle East and that the security of all the countries and peoples of that region and their right to build their life peacefully and in a manner of their own choosing are ensured. For that very reason the Soviet Union has always insisted that the territories seized by Israel should be returned to the Arab states and that justice should triumph in respect to the

Palestinian people. This has been and will remain the policy of the Soviet Union.

From the moment hostilities resumed in the Middle East early this month the Soviet Union maintained close contact with friendly Arab states and took all the political steps in its power to help end the war and create the conditions under which peace in the Middle East would be really lasting for all the countries of that region.

As is known, acting on the proposal of the Soviet Union and the United States of America, the UN Security Council twice, on October 22 and 23, passed a resolution calling for a cease-fire. On both occasions, Israel, while proclaiming compliance with the Security Council resolutions, in fact violated them treacherously, and continued its aggressive actions against Egypt. Capturing more and more of that country's territory, Israel completely ignored the Security Council's demand that the troops be withdrawn to the positions they occupied on the evening of October 22.

It is difficult to understand what the Israeli rulers are counting on by following this rash course, flouting the resolutions of the UN Security Council, and defying world public opinion. Apparently, outside patronage has something to do with it. But the people of Israel are paying a heavy price for this policy of the Israeli government. Hopes of ensuring peace and security for one's own state through the forcible seizure and retention of the lands of others are wild hopes that are doomed to inevitable failure. Such a course will yield neither peace nor security for Israel. It will only result in Israel's still greater international isolation, arousing still greater hatred for it among the neighboring peoples. The Arabs' courageous struggle and the growing solidarity of the Arab states show very well that they will never be reconciled to Israeli aggression and will never give up their legitimate rights. The Soviet Union supports the Arab peoples' just demands firmly and consistently.

The collective will of those who demand the establishment of peace in the Middle East must prevail over the recklessness of those who violate the peace. The experience of the past few days compels us to be vigilant. Urgent and firm measures are required to assure implementation of the cease-fire and troop-withdrawal resolutions.

President Sadat of Egypt addressed a request to the Soviet Union and the United States of America to send their representatives to the area of military operations in order to supervise the fulfillment of the Security Council cease-fire resolution. We expressed our readiness to meet Egypt's request and have already sent such representatives. We hope that the U.S.

government will act similarly. At the same time, we have been considering other possible measures, whose adoption the situation may require.

In view of the continuing violations of the cease-fire, the UN Security Council decided on October 25 forthwith to form a special United Nations force, which will be sent to the area of the hostilities. We hold that this is a useful decision and hope that it will serve its purpose in normalizing the situation.

In the matter of normalizing the Middle East situation, the Soviet Union is prepared to co-operate with all the interested countries. But, surely, co-operation is not benefited by such moves of the past few days, by certain elements in the NATO countries, as the artificial whipping up of sentiment with all kinds of fantastic rumors about the intentions of the Soviet Union in the Middle East. As we see it, a more responsible, honest, and constructive approach would be much more appropriate in the present situation.

I would like to stress that the Security Council's resolution of October 22 envisages more than a mere cease-fire: it envisages important measures aimed at eliminating the very causes of war. And this makes it especially valuable. The parties concerned are to begin immediately the practical fulfillment of all the provisions of the Middle East resolution adopted by the Security Council on November 22, 1967.

Let me remind you that this resolution, which stresses the "inadmissibility of the acquisition of territory by war," provides for the withdrawal of Israeli armed forces from territories occupied during the 1967 conflict. It demands respect for and recognition of the sovereignty, territorial integrity, and political independence of all states in the region, and their right to live in peace. It also emphasizes the necessity for a fair settlement of the "refugee problem," that is, of ensuring the legitimate rights of the Arab people of Palestine.

It is not difficult to see that had all these provisions adopted in 1967 been translated into life there and then, there would already have been peace in the Middle East for six years. However, this did not take place. It did not take place because of the same shortsighted policy of Israel's ruling circles, encouraged by external forces.

In accordance with the letter and spirit of the resolution adopted by the Security Council on Monday, October 22, the parties concerned are to start immediately, under the appropriate auspices, negotiations aimed at establishing a just and lasting peace in the Middle East. It is impossible to overestimate the importance of such negotiations. A historical responsibility devolves on their participants. Let me say that the Soviet Union is prepared to make and will make a constructive contribution to this matter. Our firm stand is that all the states and peoples in the Middle East—I repeat, all of them—must be assured of peace, security, and inviolability of borders. The Soviet Union is prepared to take part in the relevant guarantees.

We feel that one of the most urgent tasks before all peace fighters and all peace forces in present-day conditions is to work for the immediate and full implementation of the Security Council resolution of October 22, 1973. This is necessary for the free and independent development of all states and peoples in the Middle East. This meets the interests of many states in Europe and Asia, Africa and America, for whom normalization of the political and economic life in this key area of the world is of considerable importance. Finally, the acute situation that has arisen in the Middle East over the last few days and the risk of an extension of the conflict quite clearly show how important it is to settle this problem also for the sake of stronger world peace.

Esteemed participants in the Congress, the peoples of countries that have thrown off the colonial yoke face gigantic economic and social tasks. These can be successfully carried out only on the basis of peace founded on reliable security and the broad, mutually beneficial co-operation of all countries.

The Republic of India is setting an example of a consistent peace policy combined with democratic solutions of internal problems. By urging a just and peaceful settlement of existing international issues, it creates favorable conditions for the solution of its own internal problems. And by gradually resolving their domestic socioeconomic problems, the Indian people are substantially strengthening the foundations of their peace-loving foreign policy.

The decisions of the Non-Aligned Nations' Conference in Algiers, attended by the leaders of many countries, are of great international importance. The Conference reaffirmed these countries' determination to fight purposefully against imperialism, war, and aggression, and for peace and the independence and freedom of nations.

In a word, the active policy of the peace-loving states of Asia, Africa, and Latin America is making a tangible and considerable contribution to the relaxation of international tension.

One of the key factors in the current international development is the active participation of the broad public and public organizations and political parties in the settlement of issues of war and peace. This is, of course, the result of the historical experience accumulated by mankind. The memory of the bitter lessons of the First and Second World Wars and knowledge of the terrible consequences that would ensue from the use of nuclear weapons imperatively demand that the people of our planet take vigorous action to prevent a tragedy unprecedented in the annals of mankind.

In this nuclear age the peoples are showing a new and deeper sense of solidarity in the struggle for peace and, at the same time, a keener sense of their common responsibility for the future of the world. This sense serves as a powerful stimulus in the mounting struggle for the consolidation of peace, for reliable international security.

One can say with confidence that present changes in the world situation are largely the result of the activities of public forces, of the hitherto unparalleled activity of the people, who are displaying sharp intolerance of arbitrary rule and aggression and an unbending will for peace.

This is seen also from the recent World Trade Union Congress in Bulgaria, which unequivocally expressed the will for peace of more than 200 million organized factory and office workers and intellectuals.

Indeed, the convocation of your Congress and its breadth and representative character are convincing and striking evidence of the power of world public opinion and of the role that it can play in the struggle for peace and security, and for the democratization of international relations.

II

Dear friends, we can thus note with satisfaction that through the concerted efforts of all the peace forces the international climate has grown, on the whole, healthier in recent years, and the policy of peaceful coexistence, of peaceful co-operation between countries, is yielding tangible results.

However, this is obviously only the beginning of the advance toward an objective that, I understand, unites all those present in this hall and all whom they represent, only the beginning of the advance toward a reliably peaceful future for humanity. We are only building the conditions for the attainment of that objective. Our common duty is to move tirelessly forward along the chosen path, to move steadily, perseveringly along a wide front, resolutely breaking down the resistance of the adversaries of détente and the proponents of "cold war." As we in the Soviet Union see it, the task is to make the détente achieved in the decisive areas of international relations stable, durable, and, what is more, irreversible.

And in this respect, of course, much can be done, above all, in Europe. The peoples of that continent, more than of any other, have suffered from past wars, including the most terrible of all, the Second World War. Because of the present-day character of productive forces, closed economic life in each of the "rooms" of the "European house" has become too crowded and uncomfortable. Besides, due to the modern means of mass destruction, the house has become an acute fire risk. As a result, maintenance of peace in Europe has essentially become an imperative necessity; and the utmost development of diverse peaceful co-operation among the European states, the only really sensible solution. A contributing factor is that an increasingly more active and important role in European life is being played by the socialist countries, which are profoundly and sincerely devoted to the cause of peace and international co-operation, while in the western part of the Continent there is a growing appreciation of the political realities, and the circles favoring these goals are winning ever more influence.

That is why we have faith in the ultimate success and the historic role of the European Conference, despite all the difficulties that are still to be overcome by those participating in this unique forum, which is now at a perhaps not very spectacular but extremely important stage of its work.

What do we expect from this Conference and what are we hoping for? To put it in the most general terms, we want to see well-defined principles of relations between European states formulated unanimously, sincerely, with heart and soul, as they say, without "diplomatic" equivocations and misconstructions, approved by all the participants in the Conference and endorsed by all the peoples of the Continent. I have in mind, for instance, such principles as the territorial integrity of all the European states, the inviolability of their frontiers, the renunciation of the use or threat of force in relations between countries, noninterference in each other's internal affairs, and the promotion, on such a basis, of mutually beneficial co-operation in diverse fields.

We would like these principles to become accepted as a sacred and indisputable part of the day-to-day fabric of European life and of the psychology of the European peoples. We would like these principles to be adopted by the governments and the peoples in order that they become reality.

We would like to see a dense all-European network of economic, scientific, and cultural co-operation between states flourishing on the basis of these principles.

Trade has linked peoples and countries from time immemorial. The same is true of our day. But today it is disadvantageous and unreasonable to confine economic co-operation solely to trade. Broad international division of labor is the only basis for keeping pace with the times and abreast of the requirements and potentialities of the scientific and technological revolution. This, I should say, is now axiomatic. Hence the need for mutually beneficial, long-term and large-scale economic co-operation, both bilateral and multilateral. Of course, this applies not only to Europe, but also to all continents, to the entire system of present-day international economic relations. Another reason why we advocate such co-operation is that we regard it as a reliable means of materially consolidating peaceful relations among states.

We hope and believe that the political foundation worked out at the European Conference and the day-to-day peaceful co-operation will be supplemented and reinforced with measures aimed at achieving military détente on the Continent. This, as you know, will be the subject of the talks scheduled to open in Vienna in five days' time.

These talks are of considerable importance for Europe and for the entire world situation. The Soviet Union's attitude to them is serious, responsible, constructive, and realistic. Our stand is clear and comprehensible. We hold that agreement must be reached on a reduction, in the region of Central Europe already specified, of both foreign and national land and air forces belonging to the states party to the talks. The security of any of the sides must not be prejudiced and none of them should gain any unilateral advantages. Moreover, it must be recognized that the reduction should also apply to units equipped with nuclear weapons.

How exactly the cutback is to be effected and what method is to be applied—whether the reduction should be by equal percentages or by equal numbers—still remain to be settled by those participating in the talks. In our view it is important that the future reduction should not upset the existing balance of strength in Central Europe and on the European continent generally. If attempts are made to violate this principle, the entire issue will only become an apple of discord and the subject of endless debate.

How soon a start can be made to the actual reduction of armed forces and armaments also remains to be decided in Vienna. The Soviet Union would be prepared to take practical steps in this direction as early as 1975. A specific agreement on this score could be concluded in the immediate future. Such an agreement would unquestionably be a further major step in improving the political situation in Europe and helping to foster an atmosphere of trust, good will, and peaceful co-operation.

We have repeatedly stated that détente and interstate co-operation cannot be the privilege of any particular region of the world. Peace is truly indivisible. We believe that the norms of peaceful coexistence and peaceful co-operation must prevail in Europe and in Africa, and in South and North America. And for a number of concrete historical reasons this matter has probably a special significance for Asia.

It is common knowledge that the Soviet Union is advocating the consolidation of peace on the Asian continent by collective effort. We conceive of this as the progressive development of all aspects of mutually beneficial and mutually enriching relations and peaceful co-operation between all the Asian states, as the consolidation in these relations of the well-known principles proclaimed by the Asian states at Bandung of peaceful coexistence with strict observance of the sovereignty and independence of each country. The peoples of Asia most certainly need lasting peace and constructive co-operation no less than, say, the peoples of Europe. It is probably safe to say that the people of Tokyo and Tashkent, of Hanoi and Teheran, Peking and Rangoon, Delhi and Colombo—all the hundreds of millions of inhabitants of the world's largest continent—have an equal stake in lasting peace and tranquil peaceful labor. This, I am convinced, is in the interest of them all.

It is often said that the idea of creating and ensuring security in Asia by collective effort is directed against China and all but pursues the perfidious aim of "surrounding" or "isolating" China. But these contentions are either the product of morbid suspicion or a reluctance to face the facts.

And the facts are that the Soviet Union and the other states favoring collective efforts to ensure peace and security in Asia have always maintained that all the states of the Asian continent without exception should take part in this big and important undertaking if they so desire. Nobody has ever raised the question of China's nonparticipation or, much less, "isolation"—not to speak of the fact that it would be ludicrous to think of "isolating" such a big country. As for the Soviet Union, it would welcome the participation of the People's Republic of China in carrying out measures aimed at strengthening Asian security.

Dear friends, of course we would be going against the facts if we pretended that China's present actions on the international scene are consonant with the task of strengthening peace and peaceful co-operation between countries. For reasons they alone know, China's leaders refuse to halt their attempts to poison the international climate and heighten international tension. They continue to make absurd territorial claims on the Soviet Union, which, naturally, we reject categorically. They doggedly repeat the timeworn inventions of anti-Communist propaganda about a "Soviet threat," about "a threat from the north," and, while dismissing all reasonable proposals for a settlement and for a treaty of nonaggression, continue to keep their people in an artificially created feverish atmosphere of war preparations. And all this is accompanied by the dissemination of preposterous, slanderous accusations against the USSR and other countries, by brazen attempts to interfere in our—and, in fact, not only our—internal affairs.

What strikes one is the total lack of principle in the foreign policy of the Chinese leaders. They say that they are working for socialism and peaceful coexistence, but in fact they go out of their way to undermine the international positions of the socialist countries and encourage the activity of the aggressive military blocs and closed economic groups of capitalist states. They style themselves proponents of disarmament, but in fact try to block all the practical steps designed to restrict and slow down the arms race and, defying world public opinion, continue to pollute the earth's atmosphere by testing nuclear weapons. They assert that they support the just struggle of the Arabs for the return of the territories seized by the aggressor and for the establishment of a just peace in the Middle East, but at the same time are doing their utmost to discredit the real assistance rendered to the victims of aggression by their true friends, the Soviet Union and the other countries of the socialist community. They call themselves revolutionaries, but cordially shake the hand of a representative of the fascist junta of Chilean reactionaries, a hand stained with the blood of thousands of heroes of the revolution, the sons and daughters of the working class, of the working people of Chile.

Of course, a policy of this kind does not help to strengthen peace and security. It injects an element of dangerous instability into international affairs. But the possibility of changing this policy depends wholly and entirely on the Chinese leaders. As regards the Soviet Union, we, I repeat, would welcome a constructive contribution by China to improving the international atmosphere and promoting true and equitable peaceful co-operation between states.

Esteemed delegates to the Congress, the development of relations of peaceful co-operation between the Soviet Union and the United States of America is an important factor in solving the problems vitally important for the peoples of the earth of averting another world war and ensuring universal peace.

In the past two years the development of these relations has been marked by the conclusion of a number of important treaties and agreements, such as the Basic Principles of Mutual Relations Between the Union of Soviet Socialist Republics and the United States of America, the treaty and agreement on the limitation of antiballistic-missile systems and of strategic offensive arms, and the agreement between the USSR and the USA on the prevention of nuclear war. We are faithfully fulfilling our obligations under these treaties and agreements and intend to continue to do so in future. Naturally, we expect the other side to do likewise.

In our view, the prospects for the development of peaceful, mutually beneficial co-operation between the Soviet Union and the United States in the various spheres are good, provided, of course, that this question is approached with a sense of responsibility and in good faith, that the principles of mutual benefit and mutual respect are applied in practice, and that no attempt is made to distort them and to interfere in the internal affairs of the other side, dictating one's own terms, the way some irresponsible politicians in the United States are trying to do, in spite of the official policy of their own government.

As for the Soviet Union, we are convinced that the documents adopted in 1972 and 1973 have created a good basis for mutually advantageous co-operation which greatly benefits the cause of peace.

In 1974, the President of the United States, as you know, is to pay an official visit to the Soviet Union. We would like it to be marked by fresh major steps in the development of peaceful relations between our two states and the improvement of the international situation.

Successful completion of the new phase of negotiations between the USSR and the USA on the further limitation and possible reduction of strategic armaments can have a considerable role to play. You will appreciate that this is no simple task, but we have agreed to do our utmost to carry it out.

All of us, dear friends, love peace, want a lasting peace, and work to ensure peace as far as our abilities and the opportunities open to us allow. We are gladdened by the current relaxation of international tension and the growth of peaceful co-operation among states. But I would like to stress most emphatically that neither peace nor détente will descend on the world in the manner of some divine blessing. Peace and détente can only be the result of persistent and tireless struggle by all peace forces—the states, political parties and tendencies, public bodies and individuals—against everything resisting détente, imperiling peace, and creating the danger of war.

We must not forget that wars still keep breaking out, people are still being killed, and cities, factories, villages, and objects of cultural value are being destroyed in various parts of the world. These are what politicians have become accustomed to calling "local wars," that is, wars confined to the relatively narrow boundaries of some geographical region. Past experience shows that, as a rule, in modern conditions these break out wherever and whenever the forces of imperialism and reaction attempt to put down liberation movements, or to obstruct the free and independent development of states that have opted for progressive internal development and the anti-imperialist line in foreign policy.

For millions of people of our planet peace has yet to come; arms in hand they are forced to fight against imperialist aggressors and their accomplices, against arbitrary acts by invaders. They are forced to fight for their freedom and independence, and for the elementary right to be masters in their own home. And the fighters for peace cannot but draw their own conclusions from this situation.

Nor must we forget that in an atmosphere marked by a relaxation of international tension, the process that does in fact constitute a material preparation for world war is continuing and in fact quickening.

The military budgets of the NATO countries are being increased by two to three billion dollars a year, and these are figures indicative of ever newer types of weapons of destruction: new and ever more destructive nuclear bombs and warheads, new and ever more powerful missiles, tanks and planes, warships and submarines. The qualitative improvement of weapons has assumed unprecedented proportions.

Attempts are being made to justify this kind of activity by claiming that it could allegedly help secure success at the arms limitation talks by creating "bargaining counters." Quite obviously, these bargaining counters will in fact yield nothing except an intensification of the arms race. As for the arms limitation talks, their success does not require any new military programs, but a sincere desire, backed by mutual restraint, to check the arms race.

Even today, almost three decades since the Second World War, the farmer's plow and the builder's excavator frequently unearth shells and mines. These are a reminder of war, and they jeopardize human life again today, in peacetime. But is there not a thousand times greater danger in the vast stockpiles of means of mass annihilation unequaled in all human history, which today, at this very moment, stand primed on launching pads, are carried on board patrolling planes and submarines, and fill to overflowing the underground silos at military bases all over the globe? Is it possible to build a lasting and durable peace with any confidence when these modern "powder magazines" remain beneath its foundation and can blow up the entire globe?

The military preparations of the capitalist states are compelling the socialist countries to allocate the necessary funds for defense, diverting them from civilian construction, to which we would like to dedicate all our efforts and all our material resources. Dozens of newly independent countries are also being drawn into the orbit of the arms race, which, of course, is prompted by the threat to their independence posed by imperialism now in one part of the world, now in another.

It goes without saying that the further extension of the arms race by the aggressive circles of imperialism, on the one hand, and the relaxation of international tension that has set in, on the other, are two processes running in opposite directions. The two cannot develop endlessly along what might be called "parallel" lines. If we want détente and peace to be sound, the arms race must be stopped.

That is precisely the idea behind the numerous initiatives of the Soviet Union and other socialist states aimed at implementing the UN-approved program of general and complete disarmament. The same purposes are served by the proposals for partial steps along this way, including the Soviet proposal, now under consideration by the UN General Assembly, for a reduction of the military budgets of the permanent member states of the UN Security Council by ten percent and for the use of a part of the funds so saved for assistance to developing countries.

I would like to draw your attention to yet another point. The Soviet Union and the United States have been taking definite agreed measures to limit what government documents describe as "strategic arms." But we live in a world in which everything is closely interconnected. Clearly, the struggle to avert nuclear war cannot long be confined to the efforts of only two states, especially if in the meantime other states—and in particular the nuclear powers—continue to build up their armaments.

We believe that like the process of détente, the process of limiting and arresting the arms race should spread ever wider, involving new states and areas of the globe. Equally, there should be more and more states acceding to existing international agreements, such as the convention on the prohibition of bacteriological weapons, and the treaties on the nonproliferation of nuclear weapons and the prohibition of nuclear-weapon tests. It is the prime duty of all sincere peace fighters to demand that this be so, to work vigorously for this.

Some tend to regard the arms race as something habitual or even as something fatalistically inevitable. This dangerous mental inertia must be broken, and the peace-loving public forces of the world have here a big part to play.

It should be clearly seen that the threat to peace is posed by quite concrete social groups, organizations, and individuals. Thus, even on the testimony of the top-ranking leaders in the major Western countries, the sinister alliance of the professional militarists and the monopolies making fortunes out of weapons of war, usually known as the military-industrial complex, has become something of a "state within the state" in these countries and has acquired self-sufficient power. Militarism cripples not only the society that has produced it. The exhaust gas emitted by the war-preparation machine poisons the political atmosphere of the world with fumes of hatred, fear, and violence. To justify its existence, myths are created about a "Soviet menace" and the need to defend the so-called Western democracies. But the militarist robot fosters as its cherished progeny the most reactionary, tyrannical, and fascist regimes, and devours the democratic freedoms.

The previous speakers have justly dwelt on the events in Chile. I also want to touch upon this subject. The monstrous and blatant outrage against the country's constitution, the gross contempt for the democratic traditions of a whole nation, the abuse of elementary legality, the shootings, the tortures, and the barbarous terror, the bonfires of burning books —such is the junta's truly fascist snarl, such is the true face of reaction, domestic and external, which is prepared to commit any crime in order to regain its privileges in defiance of the clearly and freely expressed will of the people.

The tragedy of Chile has echoed with a pang in the hearts of millions of people and in diverse sections of the democratic public all over the world. We shall always cherish the memory of Salvador Allende and of the other heroes of that country who gave their lives for freedom and peace. Allow me from the rostrum of this Congress to express our complete solidarity with Chile's democrats and patriots and our firm conviction that the just cause for which they have fought and are now fighting in such difficult conditions—the cause of independence, democracy, and social progress—is invincible and indestructible! The defense of these lofty values, their realization in life, the struggle against those who threaten them and seek to destroy them are closely connected with the struggle to ensure lasting peace throughout the world.

When it comes to the policy of peaceful coexistence and peaceful co-operation between states, regardless of their social systems, we Communists are frequently asked: Is this policy compatible with the revolutionary outlook?

Let me remind you that Lenin, that greatest of revolutionaries, used to say: Revolutions are not made to order or by compact. And we might add that neither can revolution, class struggle, nor the liberation movements be abolished to order or by agreement. No power on earth is capable of reversing the inexorable process of the resurgence of social life. Wherever there is colonialism, there is bound to be struggle for national liberation. Wherever there is exploitation, there is bound to be struggle for the emancipation of labor. Wherever there is aggression, there is bound to be resistance.

The popular masses are striving to change the world, and they will change it. As for the Soviet Union, it will always side with the forces of social progress. We oppose "export of revolution." At the same time, the Communist Party of the Soviet Union, our government, and the entire Soviet people openly and unequivocally express their solidarity with their class brothers fighting in other countries and their solidarity with the liberation and anti-imperialist movements. This attitude does not contradict the struggle for peace and for peaceful co-operation between states.

By promoting the principles of peaceful coexistence, we are working for something that billions of people all over the world cherish most of all: the right to life itself, and deliverance from the danger of its destruction in the flames of war. At the same time, we are thereby also working to ensure favorable international conditions for the social progress of all countries and peoples. This means recognition of each people's right to choose the social system it wants. This means simple and clear rules of intercourse between states. Breaches of these rules tend not only to undermine equality in relations between countries, but also to produce armed conflicts, for nowadays the peoples of the world refuse to tolerate any *diktat*. And they are perfectly within their rights in rebuffing aggression. With the world split into two systems, the only basis for international security is full and scrupulous observance of the principles of peaceful coexistence, and, in particular, noninterference in the internal affairs of states.

In this connection one cannot help noting that in the recent period some Western circles have been in effect trying to circumvent these principles by proposing something like a new edition of the "cold" or, if you prefer, "psychological" war. I am referring to the campaign conducted under the hypocritical slogan "defending human rights" in the socialist countries.

Some of those who have initiated this campaign claim that détente is impossible unless some changes are effected in the internal order of the socialist countries. Others leave the impression of not actually opposing détente, but declare with amazing frankness their intention to use the process of détente to weaken the socialist system, and, ultimately, to secure its destruction. For the public at large this tactic is presented as concern for human rights or for a so-called liberalization of our system.

Let us call a spade a spade, dear friends. With all the talk of freedom and democracy and human rights, this whole strident campaign serves only one purpose: to cover up attempts to interfere in the internal affairs of the socialist countries, to cover up the imperialist aims of this policy. They talk of "liberalization," but what they mean is elimination of socialism's real gains and erosion of the sociopolitical rights of the peoples of the socialist countries.

We have no reason to shun any serious discussion of human rights. Our revolution, the victory of socialism in this country, has not only proclaimed but has secured in reality the rights of the workingman whatever his nationality, the rights of millions of working people, in a way capitalism has been unable to do in any country of the world.

From the bourgeois standpoint such human rights as the right to work, education, social security, free medical aid, rest and leisure, and the like, may be something secondary or even unacceptable. Just one figure: nearly a hundred million people are at present unemployed in the nonsocialist countries. Many capitalist states violate the rights of national minorities and foreign workers, and the right of women to equal pay for equal work. This is probably why many Western powers have not yet subscribed to international covenants establishing the social and political rights of man.

The staggering socioeconomic changes that have taken place in our country are the result of the far-reaching and conscious political creativity of the masses, and also of their will to safeguard the system they themselves have created from every possible incursion. For this reason, Soviet people will not tolerate any encroachment on the sovereignty of our state, the protector of their sociopolitical gains. This sovereignty is not an obstacle to contact and exchanges; it is a reliable guarantee of the rights and freedoms hard won by our people.

Soviet laws afford our citizens broad political freedoms. At the same time, they protect our system and the interests of the Soviet people from any attempts to abuse these freedoms. And this is in full conformity with the International Covenants on Human Rights ratified by the Soviet Union, which say that the rights they enumerate "shall not be subject to any restrictions except those which are provided by law, are necessary to protect national security, public order, public health or morals or the rights and freedoms of others. . . ." We subscribed to this.

And what kind of freedoms are those who are attacking us talking about?

For example, we have a law banning war propaganda in any form. There is legislation prohibiting the dissemination of ideas of racial or national strife and hatred, and of those that degrade the national dignity of any people. There are laws combating immoral behavior, laws against the moral corruption of society. Are we expected, perhaps, to repudiate these laws in the name of free exchange of ideas and information? Or are we to be prevailed upon to believe that this would serve the cause of détente and closer international ties?

We are being told: "Either change your way of life or be prepared for cold war." But what if we should reciprocate? What if we should demand modification of bourgeois laws and usages that go against our ideas of justice and democracy as a condition for normal interstate relations? Such a demand, I suspect, would not improve the outlook for sound development in interstate relations.

It is impossible to fight for peace while impinging on the sovereign rights of other peoples. It is impossible to champion human rights while torpedoing the principles of peaceful coexistence.

To put it in plain language, no one is any longer able to subvert the socialist world, but regrettably it is still possible to subvert peace. For peace depends on multilateral efforts, and not least of all on mutual— and I stress—mutual respect for the principles of sovereignty and non-interference in internal affairs. As concerns the Soviet Union, our ship of state, cutting through the ripple of propaganda campaigns directed against socialism, will continue on its course, seeking constructive solutions to the problems of international life that are facing the world today.

III

Dear friends, humanity is in need of a durable peace. But when it will come and what it will be like depend on how fully all the peace-loving forces use the already available opportunities.

I do not think that any of us would be satisfied with a peace that is based, as before, on a "balance of fear." That kind of peace would differ but little from the "cold war." It would be a "cold peace" that could easily revert to a situation of tense confrontation oppressive to the consciousness and life of the peoples, and fraught with the danger of a world-wide conflict.

The peoples want a dependable and irreversible peace, based, if one may say so, on a balance of security and mutual trust, a peace that opens up possibilities for broad international co-operation in the name of progress.

Peace is a precious thing. To live in the knowledge that blood is not being shed anywhere, and to be confident that no bombs or shells will fall tomorrow on one's roof, and that children can grow up without the tragedy and suffering experienced by older generations—this is the greatest of boons.

But peace is not only a question of security. It is also the most important prerequisite for solving the most crucial problems of modern civilization. And here the very future of humanity is involved—yes, the future of the entire world, which it is no longer possible to ignore when tackling the problems of the present day, no matter how complicated and difficult they may be. You, who represent the world public in all its variety, must feel this keenly.

Here it will be sufficient to mention but a few of the problems that are beginning to cause many people concern: energy supply, environmental protection, elimination of such blights as mass hunger and dangerous diseases, and development of the resources of the world's oceans.

Solution of these problems requires comprehensive, sincere, and effective co-operation among governments, representatives of economic and scientific circles, and, of course, the most diverse political, professional, and cultural organizations. The peoples must come to know one another, and there must therefore be a lively and varied exchange between many of their representatives.

Clearly, peace is the most important condition for such co-operation. It is impossible to make a good start in resolving the problems that affect the future of all mankind or to fulfill the many urgent tasks of today without a system of international relations based on peaceful coexistence.

The concrete directions of further advance toward the kind of peace we all want are clear. I have spoken about them earlier. They are suggested by the existing international situation. And we are deeply convinced that the vital tasks that are of foremost importance today in the struggle to consolidate peace can be accomplished through joint effort.

This means, above all, taking steps to settle, on a fair and just basis, the armed conflicts that are still taking place.

This means creating a system of collective security in Europe, and then also in Asia; this would enable us gradually to eliminate the present division of the world into political-military blocs.

This means ending the race of nuclear and other armaments through faithful observance by states of the commitments they have voluntarily accepted, and—this is especially important—involvement of the world's major powers in this process. This would mark the beginning of a gradual reduction in the material basis for a military confrontation.

This means development of economic, scientific, technical, and cultural co-operation based on complete equality, mutual advantage, without any discrimination and without attempts at interference in each other's internal affairs.

These we regard as the main objectives in the struggle for peace in present-day conditions. Of course it will take time to achieve some of these objectives, while others demand prompt and immediate action right now. But persevering, energetic and active efforts are required on the part of states, and also of political and broad public forces interested in consolidating peace, to attain both these sets of objectives.

The long years of "cold war" have left their imprint on the minds not only of professional politicians; they have resulted in prejudice, suspicion, and poor knowledge—even a reluctance to acquire knowledge—of the real position held by others and their possibilities. Certainly, it is not easy to turn over a new leaf. But this has to be done; it is essential to learn to co-operate.

Our philosophy of peace is a philosophy of historical optimism. Though the present situation is complicated and contradictory, we are confident that the broad peace offensive now under way will be successful. What are the grounds for our optimism?

Our optimism is based, above all, on the fact that there exists such a permanent, powerful, and dynamic factor of peace as real socialism, whose peace-loving policy stems from the very nature of this social system. Our optimism rests on the unity of views and actions of the majority of the socialist countries.

Our optimism is based on the profound interest in a just and democratic peace of many of the Asian, African, and Latin-American states and peoples, including the nonaligned countries.

Our optimism is based on the successes already achieved by the policy of peaceful coexistence, on the fact that the ruling circles in some of the capitalist countries are showing a growing appreciation of the real correlation of world forces and are coming to realize that war is unacceptable as a means for solving international problems.

Our conviction that the cause of peace is invincible is based on our profound belief in the great life-affirming force that springs from the peace-loving nature of the workingman—whether he is a worker, a peasant, or an intellectual. And these constitute the vast and overwhelming majority in the world.

Finally, we associate our optimism with regard to the question of peace with the activity of all the public movements working for peace, which are broadly represented here at this world-wide forum, and with the further development of joint action by Communists, Socialists, Social-Democrats, and Christians.

All this is a source of hope and confidence.

However, the achievements on the way to peace must be tirelessly developed. Further progress will not be easy. We will have to surmount

---

many obstacles, and repulse many counterattacks by the enemies of peace. The complexity of the struggle also stems from new conditions, the new phase in international relations that we have now entered. As before, it will require not only a great degree of consistency, firmness, and energy, but also better forms of work, new methods, timely and precise formulation of concrete initiatives that can forestall the appearance of seats of tension and relapses in the process of détente. Much still remains to be done to invigorate each of the peace-loving streams and, at the same time, to merge them into a single channel. The imperative of the present moment in history, or, if you like, the imperative of the epoch, is to unite all the peace-loving forces of the world and secure the peaceful development of all countries, all peoples.

Dear friends, millions of people throughout the world expect much of the World Congress of Peace Forces. They are awaiting answers to burning questions that trouble the broad masses, and guidelines for the world-wide public movement whose aim is to help solve one of the most important problems of the twentieth century—the problem of ensuring a lasting peace. This is a great responsibility, and, as I see it, it is also a great and inspiring challenge.

Allow me to assure you that in your activity to consolidate peace you will have the fullest and most effective support of the Communist Party of the Soviet Union, the Soviet government, of all Soviet people.

You can depend on the Soviet people, who have always—in the early years after their great revolution, in the years of building socialism, in the battle against fascism, in the postwar decades, and at the present time—stood and will continue to stand in the front line of the struggle for the interests of humanity.

In conclusion I would like to thank the organizers of the Congress and all of you, dear friends, for this opportunity to speak from this high rostrum.

Esteemed participants in this Congress, allow me, in conclusion, to wish you every success in your fruitful joint work, which will, I am sure, find a ready response in the hearts of people on all continents.

From Speech to the Electors in the
Bauman District of Moscow

June 14, 1974

Leonid Brezhnev addressed his constituents on the eve of elections to the USSR Supreme Soviet. In his speech he summed up the results of the development of Soviet society since the previous elections, in 1970, and discussed a number of major international problems.

Comrades, in recent years the Party has carried out exceptionally intensive and strenuous activities on the foreign-political front. And you understand what that was connected with. The situation in the world and concern for the vital interests of the Soviet people, for the maintenance of peace on earth, have led us to concentrate our efforts on the solution of acute international problems.

Let us recall what we had been faced with in the international arena in the comparatively recent past. Fierce battles raged in Vietnam. The situation in the Middle East was fraught with the danger of outbreaks of military conflicts. The "cold war" weighed heavily upon the minds and life of peoples. Relations with the United States, the FRG, and many other big states of the capitalist world remained tense.

Our Party had never regarded such a state of affairs as inevitable, let alone normal. An appraisal of the general alignment of forces in the world led us several years ago to this conclusion, namely, that a real opportunity existed for bringing about a fundamental change in the international situation. The important thing was to furnish a broad basis for constructive discussion and solution of the problems that had accumulated. Those considerations and our policy were summed up in the Peace Program proclaimed by the 24th Congress of the CPSU.

There is not a single person in the Soviet Union who would not regard this program as an embodiment of his thoughts about the destinies of his country, about the present and the future. There is not a single person in the Soviet Union for whom war would not be hateful. All our projects, all our plans are connected with the maintenance of peace.

At present the first generation of Soviet people who did not have to live through war, to experience the hardships and sorrows of wartime, is in the prime of life. To put it simply, what we would like very much, comrades, is that our children and grandchildren will never know what war is. It is for the sake of this that the Party has put forward the Peace Program and launched a struggle for a genuine normalization of the entire system of international relations.

The results of our efforts are a matter of common knowledge. The main thing is that the foundations of peace and security of peoples have been consolidated to a significant extent, and the danger of nuclear war has been lessened. The Soviet people, all peoples of the world, regard this as a triumph of truly historic importance.

The favorable changes in the world situation are first of all due to the impact of the world of socialism, its achievements, its might, and its example, on international developments. This is a result of the purposeful and concerted policy of the community of socialist countries. . . .

In many ways owing to the policy of the Soviet Union and the socialist countries, owing to the change in the climate in international relations, there have emerged more favorable conditions for the struggle against imperialist aggression and for the elimination of the hotbed of war in the Middle East. Agreements on the disengagement of troops in the Sinai Peninsula and the Golan Heights areas have been reached. At the same time it is necessary to realize that only the first steps have been made. The main questions of settlement are still to be considered at the Geneva Conference. This is an extremely complex task. It can be accomplished only through the combined efforts of the states participating in the conference.

The Soviet Union contributes and will continue to contribute to this cause. Our stand with regard to a final settlement of the Middle East crisis is well known. Progress toward a settlement will create conditions for the development of relations between the Soviet Union and all the countries of the Middle East. A durable and just peace should at last be established in the Middle East.

Thus, there is every reason to say that a major point of the Peace Program concerning the elimination of the most dangerous hotbeds of war is being successfully implemented. Much has also been achieved in other directions of our foreign policy.

The tendency toward relaxation of tension has now become a dominant feature of the development of the international situation. This is particularly noticeable in Europe, which is now justly referred to as a continent that may become an important link in the system of interstate relations, based on the principles of peaceful coexistence, effective security, and equitable co-operation.

The growth of realistic tendencies in the policy of France and later of the FRG has played an important role in bringing about a change in the European climate. The credit for this undoubtedly belongs to such political leaders as De Gaulle, Pompidou, Brandt, and the forces that supported them. They realized that a system of international relations oriented to the "cold war" presented a dangerous impasse, that it ran counter to the basic national interests of their countries. Their striving to develop constructive links with the East enhanced the prestige of the countries they represented in the European and world political arena.

At present there is new leadership in France and the FRG. In their first speeches, President Giscard d'Estaing and Chancellor Schmidt said that they would preserve and carry on what was started by their predecessors. This policy of France and West Germany meets with understanding and reciprocity in the Soviet Union.

Tens of states—both large and small, those that belong and those that do not belong to military-political groupings—have now been drawn into the orbit of peaceful coexistence. Possibilities have emerged for a broadening of our relations with Italy. We are co-operating successfully with Finland, the Scandinavian countries, Austria, and other states. Certain changes are beginning to take place in our relations with Britain.

The process now under way of turning Europe into a zone of stable peace and fruitful co-operation among nations should be supported in every way and continued. With this aim in view it is necessary first of all to bring the all-European conference to a successful completion. . . .

We are convinced that given the desire, decisions that are satisfactory and beneficial for all can be found with regard to issues that remain to be settled. Only one thing is necessary for this: to preserve a sense of realism, to be guided by a concern for the peaceful future of Europe. We are also convinced that owing to the importance and the scope of the problems with which the conference deals, participation by top leaders at its concluding stage is necessary.

One of the most important foreign-policy events in recent years has been the serious turn in relations between the Soviet Union and the United States of America. Guided by the decisions of the 24th Congress, we have approached this question from a principled position, taking into consideration the significance that Soviet-U.S. relations have for the preservation of peace and the improvement of the international climate.

It is obvious that progress has been achieved in this matter. The Soviet Union and the USA have signed a number of documents of tremendous importance—those on the basic principles of our relations, in conformity with the principles of peaceful coexistence, on the prevention of nuclear war, and on the first steps in the limitation of strategic arms.

Agreements have been also concluded on mutually beneficial co-operation in many fields. These documents and agreements have created a good basis for the development of broad contacts and links not only in the diplomatic but also in many other fields—between business circles of the two countries, scientists, cultural workers, and representatives of the public. The Soviet Union has been visited by many prominent members of the U.S. Congress. In its turn our parliamentary delegation has recently visited the USA. All this is of great significance, both for resolving problems of today and for the future of Soviet-U.S. relations.

As you know, President Richard Nixon of the United States will soon again be in Moscow. The third meeting of Soviet and U.S. leaders will be held. Understandably, it is awaited with interest not only in our two countries, but also all over the world. One can read in the foreign press pessimistic forecasts of the possible outcome of the meeting in Moscow. We are of a different opinion. The improvement of Soviet-U.S. relations can and must continue. Nobody, of course, is going to decide hastily questions that have not yet matured. Nor should we mark time.

While fully acknowledging what has already been achieved, we must not close our eyes to the difficulties and problems that remain to be solved. They do exist. And it is all the more important that we should make full use of all the existing possibilities for advancing further.

This applies to political relations between the USSR and the USA. This also fully applies to economic relations between the two countries. But perhaps the most important and most complex problems are in the field of limitation of the arms drive. They have become the subject of heated debate.

Those circles in the USA and the countries allied to it which oppose détente are striving to spur on the arms drive and to put the responsibility for this drive on the Soviet Union. This is an obvious misrepresentation of facts. It is, perhaps, not always necessary to recall the past. But in the present instance it is quite appropriate. Well-known facts show that the arms drive, the rivalry in the development of the most dangerous weapons of mass destruction, was forced on us. It is not we who started the making of atomic bombs, submarines with strategic missiles, multiple warheads, and many other weapons.

We believe that the Soviet-U.S. agreements on arms limitation concluded in 1972 and 1973 have paved the way toward a worthy goal, and we must go further along this way. Our wish is that the United States and the Soviet Union would agree to exercise maximum restraint in building up their arms and would reach an agreement making it possible to prevent the development of ever new systems of strategic arms.

We are also prepared to reach agreement now with the United States on the limitation of underground nuclear tests, including their complete cessation on the basis of a co-ordinated timetable.

In a word, if the government of the United States adheres to the principles of equal security and renunciation of attempts to gain unilateral advantages, as set down in our agreements, the Soviet Union will always be a conscientious and active partner in such an important cause as the limitation and reduction of strategic arms.

We want Soviet-U.S. relations to become truly stable and not be dependent on temporary considerations. It is our wish that the future development of Soviet-U.S. relations should benefit our countries and the world as a whole.

Favorable changes are taking place in the Soviet Union's relations with Japan. At our meeting with Prime Minister Tanaka last October both sides stated that they were for achieving a meaningful improvement in the relations between their two countries, and they reached a common opinion as regards the necessity to expand economic co-operation considerably.

Large contracts beneficial to both sides have already been concluded, and there are good prospects. It may be hoped that Soviet-Japanese relations will develop simultaneously in the political sphere. We are convinced that the positive development of Soviet-Japanese relations meets the requirements of both countries. It also meets the interests of peace and security on the Asian continent.

In this respect, of great significance also is our country's fruitful co-operation with India, Afghanistan, Bangladesh, and other Asian countries. The past years have been marked by many successes in the conduct of relations with these countries. The same can be said about the Soviet Union's relations with a number of Arab states, and with many countries of Africa and Latin America.

In a word, comrades, much in the world has begun to change in recent years. But there must be no stopping halfway in this field. The easing of tensions must become irreversible, and we will work for it.

We are also for supplementing political détente with military détente. In the field of arms limitation, as is known, a number of international agreements have been concluded, and without them the international situation would probably be graver, but, regrettably, the arms drive has not been stopped.

In these conditions the Party Central Committee and the leading bodies of our state continue to devote utmost attention to the strengthening of our socialist homeland's defense capacity.

And I can assure you, comrades, that our defense is reliable, that it will remain at an adequate level.

At the same time we are working tirelessly for real progress in the field of disarmament. The advocates of the arms drive argue that limiting arms, to say nothing of reducing them, means taking a risk. But as a matter of fact, it is an immeasurably greater risk to continue unrestrained stock-piling of arms. Proceeding from this we have again and again called on all states, all governments to put an end to the arms drive and to begin to advance to the great goal—universal and complete disarmament.

Being aware of the complexity of this task, which is of tremendous scope, we are ready to agree to partial measures on the limitations and reduction of arms. This determines in particular our position at the talks on the reduction of armed forces and arms in Central Europe. We think that there is a possibility of achieving in this field the first concrete results at an early date, if, of course, good will is displayed by all the participants in the talks.

An important factor in consolidating the positive political changes in the international arena and in creating a material basis for a lasting peace is the all-round development of economic and scientific-technical links. It meets the interests of all states and all peoples. However, there are circles in the West that hope to obtain from us, in exchange for such links, political and ideological concessions. That is a futile undertaking.

We are for the participation of every state in the international division of labor on an equitable basis and under conditions that are advantageous for all and that do not permit violation of sovereignty and interference in internal affairs.

This contributes to the general development of world economic ties, whose significance is steadily increasing.

Another factor—the great activity of the general public—has acquired tremendous significance in the efforts to consolidate the positive changes in international relations. The policy of détente is acquiring at present a genuinely mass basis. We shall continue to pay constant heed to the development of contacts with the public of other countries, the development of links along parliamentary, trade-union, and other lines, the all-round extension of the front of peace champions.

The struggle for the triumph of reason in international relations can hardly be an easy one. Every gain on the road to lasting peace comes about through struggle, through fierce clashes with the most reactionary circles of imperialism and their accomplices.

A struggle between representatives of aggressive forces and supporters of realism is taking place in practically all the bourgeois countries. But whatever acute forms the struggle may assume, we are confident of one thing: the future is not with the advocates of "cold war," not with those who would like to push peoples into the abyss of war.

The leadership of the People's Republic of China is acting contrary to the over-all positive changes in the international arena. Whipping up militaristic, chauvinistic passions in that country, they have subordinated their foreign policy to the tasks of struggle against the Soviet Union and the other socialist countries, to attempts at frustrating relaxation. The PRC leadership has recently gone so far as to team up openly with representatives of arch reaction, the Chilean junta, the leaders of the right-wing imperialist bourgeoisie in Britain, the FRG, the USA, and other countries. These deeds, more than any words, reveal the real essence of Peking's policy.

As far as our relations with China are concerned, we will naturally continue to rebuff anti-Soviet slander, firmly to protect the interests of our state and our security. At the same time we continue to advocate normalization of relations with China, restoration of friendship with the great Chinese people on the reliable basis of proletarian internationalism. In other words, in this important issue we will consistently pursue the line of the 24th Congress of our Party.

The main mandate of the electorate is to protect the peaceful work of the Soviet people, to strengthen peace in the world. The Party constantly bears this in mind and works persistently to solve this big and complex task. The election platform of the CPSU is a platform of peace. This is precisely why all the working people of our country so ardently support it.

From Speech at Kremlin Dinner for
U.S. President Richard Nixon

June 27, 1974

Leonid Brezhnev made this and the following speech during the official visit to the Soviet Union by Richard Nixon, then President of the United States. This visit took place from June 27 to July 3, 1974.

This is already the third meeting between the leaders of our countries in just a little over two years, since a cardinal turn became evident in Soviet-American relations toward normalization and the development of peaceful co-operation.

On the firm basis of the fundamental agreements that were signed in 1972 and 1973 and are known all over the world, we have made tangible progress.

Probably never before have ties and contacts between the Union of Soviet Socialist Republics and the United States of America in different areas of political, economic, and cultural activity been as lively as they are today. Nowadays thousands of people annually travel from America to the Soviet Union and from the Soviet Union to America.

Mutual visits of ministers, contacts among businessmen, meetings between scientists and public figures, concert tours, various exhibitions and tourist trips have become customary events. Parliamentary ties are beginning to develop. We have been glad to welcome in the USSR senators and congressmen belonging to the two biggest parties of the United States, and a delegation of the USSR Supreme Soviet recently visited America.

The material foundation of our good relations is becoming stronger as well. The volume of trade has increased several times over during the last two years and several important long-term contracts have been signed. At the same time, we all know that much remains to be done here, both in the sense of making economic ties more balanced and stable and in the sense of clearly establishing the principles of equality and respect for each other's interests in this area of relations.

Credit is certainly due to those farsighted members of the business community of the United States who correctly understood the mutually advantageous nature of the development of economic ties between our countries and their importance to both our peoples and who actively support their government's line in this matter.

The biggest contribution, however, that we, Soviet and U.S. statesmen of the seventies of the twentieth century, can make to the cause of greater well-being and happiness for our peoples and for all mankind is undoubtedly the reduction and subsequently the complete removal of the possibility of war between our two states.

To ensure stable peace between the USSR and the USA is the chief task in the development of Soviet-American relations, and the leaders of both countries are continuing to devote unflagging attention to its solution. For all the useful things that we can achieve in this direction future generations will remember us with kind words. If we fail to solve this task, however, all other achievements in the development of mutual relations may lose their significance.

The new Soviet-American summit meeting, as it is usually called, is a new step in the great endeavor we jointly initiated with you, Mr. President, two years ago, and which we resolutely intend to pursue, for it meets the fundamental interests of the peoples of the two countries and the interests of world peace.

Experience shows that progress along this path requires effort. Sometimes quite a bit of it. The relaxation of tension in Soviet-American relations, as in international relations generally, comes up against rather active resistance.

There is no need for me to dwell on this subject, since our American guests know better and in more detail than we about those who oppose international détente, who favor whipping up the arms race and returning to the methods and procedures of the "cold war." I just want to express my firm conviction that the policy of such individuals—whether they themselves know it or not—has nothing in common with the interests of the peoples. It is a policy that, rather, attests to the unwillingness or inability of its proponents to take a sober look at the realities of the present-day world.

We are confident, however, that the peoples will support those who seek to assure their peaceful future and a tranquil life for millions of people, not those who sow enmity and distrust.

That is why we believe that the good results it has proved possible to achieve in Soviet-American relations in the last two years will not be erased, particularly since their improvement has already justified itself and has in many respects given practical proof of its usefulness for both sides and for the world as a whole.

Today the task, as we see it, is to consolidate the successes already achieved and to advance further along the main road that we have jointly chosen to follow.

The third round of Soviet-American summit talks has begun. We shall be discussing both the further development of bilateral relations and a number of international problems. Although we have different viewpoints on several matters, we shall seek, and I feel not unsuccessfully, agreed ways toward the further consolidation of peace and mutually advantageous co-operation.

I believe it can definitely be said that our talks will proceed in a businesslike and constructive spirit. We, for our part, express the hope that this time as well our meeting will be as fruitful as the preceding meetings in Moscow and Washington.

From Speech at U.S. Embassy Dinner

for Soviet Leaders

July 2, 1974

The Soviet people . . . entertain feelings of respect and friendship for the American people.

We are confident that mutual good feelings will grow and strengthen as the relations between our countries develop further along the road of peace and co-operation.

Your visit, Mr. President, as well as our talks, is drawing to a close. You and we already have every reason to say that the results of this meeting, like the outcome of the two previous ones, can be described as constructive and weighty.

I am referring first of all to the new steps in a field that may rightfully be called central in Soviet-American relations—the field of lessening the risk of war and restraining the arms race.

The signing of several important agreements and of the joint communiqué on the talks between the leaders of the USSR and the USA is still to come. Without anticipating the concrete content of those documents, I would just like to stress that agreement on such matters as a new, considerable limitation of the antiballistic-missile systems of the two countries, the agreed limitation of underground nuclear tests, new efforts aimed at the further limitation of strategic offensive arms, and several other measures all mean a substantial advance along the jointly charted path of consolidating peace and mutual confidence.

This complex could perhaps have been still broader, but what has been agreed upon this time tangibly strengthens and deepens the relaxation of international tension and serves the cause of peace throughout the world.

A further progressive development of Soviet-American relations is also betokened by the agreements on expanding commercial and economic, scientific and technological co-operation between the USSR and the USA, signed during our meeting.

Ahead lie new horizons and new spheres of co-operation to the benefit of both our great peoples and of peace-loving people in the entire world. In large-scale economic projects and in the development of new sources

of energy, on transportation lines, in scientists' laboratories and in archi-
tects' designing rooms, everywhere new shoots of fruitful mutually beneficial co-operation between our countries will spring forth in the name of
peace and a better life for man.

I trust you will agree with me, Mr. President, that these days have once
more convincingly proved the significance that meetings at the highest
level have for the development of Soviet-American relations in a good,
constructive direction. They facilitate the possibility of approaching, on
a broader basis and with due account of the historical perspective and
the lasting interests of the peoples, the solution of many problems, including the most difficult and complicated ones, and they give an impetus
to all the links of state machinery and to the representatives of both sides
at different levels.

In this connection, I feel we should express our gratitude to all the
officials of our diplomatic, foreign-trade, and other departments, agencies, and organizations who on the instructions of their superiors took
part in the great and painstaking work of preparing this meeting and the
appropriate agreements.

I would like to say a few words more about our talks on international
problems. As during our previous meetings with President Nixon, they
were thorough, quite frank, and useful.

Given all the differences of views and positions of our two countries
on a number of specific questions, both the Soviet and evidently the
American participants in the talks have treated, and continue to treat,
as a matter of paramount importance joint or parallel efforts by the
Soviet Union and the United States to strengthen universal peace and
create conditions for the peaceful co-operation of all states in the spirit
of the well-known principles of peaceful coexistence and the provisions
of the United Nations Charter.

The last two years have already shown the useful influence that the
improvement of Soviet-American relations may have in this sense. It
has certainly played a positive role in ending the war in Vietnam and in
creating conditions for certain progress toward a peaceful settlement in
the Middle East and in convening the all-European conference.

Now the task, as we see it, is successfully to complete what has been
started and to ensure that the development of Soviet-American relations
continue to be beneficial for universal peace and for the security of
nations.

I feel it will be no exaggeration to say that the political results of our
talks will be a new confirmation of the determination of both sides to go
on developing and deepening ties and co-operation between our two

countries in many fields, and to act on the international scene in favor of détente and peace. This is exactly what we expected from the talks, and that is why we express our satisfaction with their results.

We appreciate the contribution that you have made, Mr. President, to the achievement of these results and we wish you and the entire administration and the Congress of the United States every success in giving effect to the good initiatives of peace, growing mutual confidence, and useful co-operation embodied in the documents signed in the days of this meeting, as well as in those Soviet-American documents that were signed last year and the year before last.

You may rest assured that the leadership of the Soviet Union, fully supported by the entire Soviet people, will do all in their power in this direction.

Speech at Kremlin Dinner during the

Second Moscow Session of the U.S.–USSR

Trade and Economic Council

October 15, 1974

Established in 1973, the U.S.-USSR Trade and Economic Council is a public organization whose purpose is to promote trade and economic co-operation and develop ties in science and technology between Soviet and U.S. organizations and firms. Prominent leaders and business executives from both countries are members of the Council.

Esteemed gentlemen,

Comrades,

It was with pleasure that I accepted the invitation to meet personally the participants in the second session of the U.S.-USSR Trade and Economic Council. Allow me, first of all, sincerely to welcome the American guests who have come to our capital on this occasion. Many of you I have met before, here in Moscow and during my visit to the USA last year. It is always pleasant to see good old acquaintances and to make new ones.

I think it augurs well that such authoritative representatives of our governments and of the American business community and their Soviet counterparts are taking part in the work of the Council and in this session. I particularly want to greet and extend best wishes for success to the dynamic cochairmen of the Council, Mr. Kendall and Comrade Alkhimov.

We appreciate the fact that Mr. Simon, the U.S. Secretary of the Treasury and Honorary Director of the Council, a man who does so much to promote trade and economic relations between our countries, is here with you. His participation in this session is, to us, a concrete manifestation of the intention of President Ford's administration to contribute to the development of these relations, as was recently stated in the President's message to Congress.

The participation in the Council's session of the USSR's Foreign Trade Minister, Comrade Patolichev, signifies that the Soviet side also attaches due importance to the work of this organization for Soviet-American business co-operation. Allow me personally to reaffirm this to you, on behalf of the leadership of our Party and the Soviet state.

We feel that the U.S.-USSR Trade and Economic Council is making a substantial and constructive contribution to the development of a very important field in the relations between our states and peoples.

Without further advances in this area, which represents the material foundation, as it were, for the vast edifice of Soviet-American peaceful co-operation and good-neighborliness, much of what has been accomplished through joint efforts in 1972, 1973, and 1974 stands the risk of being weakened.

We by no means underestimate the significance of what has been achieved. Much has been done in the past two or three years to normalize and develop trade and economic relations between the USSR and the USA. A number of government agreements have been signed on various aspects of these relations, and their consistent implementation will create a sound basis for further advance.

What is especially valuable is that we are increasingly moving from abstract interstate documents to real practical action in the field of economic ties. Soviet economic organizations have signed the first sizable and mutually advantageous contracts with American firms, as well as some agreements on scientific and technical co-operation. Comrade Patolichev has told me that Soviet organizations are already trading or discussing new agreements and contracts with hundreds of American firms, making possible a considerable expansion in the over-all volume of trade between our countries. Whereas three years ago trade turnover stood at about $200 million, the indications are that this year it will amount to about $1 billion.

It is significant that along with the conventional, so-called traditional forms of trade, new and promising ways and methods of co-operation are being introduced in our trade and economic relations. I am referring, in particular, to joint implementation of long-term, large-scale projects on a compensation basis. There are quite a few examples of such co-operation. These include the $20 billion deal to build a major chemical complex in the USSR and for mutual deliveries of fertilizers, initiated by Dr. Hammer, who is present here and whom we all respect, as well as active co-operation in various projects connected with automobile and machine-tool production, chemistry and petrochemistry, and the production of a number of consumer items.

I have already had occasion to note the importance of these new forms of economic relations; I remember talking about it during meetings with American businessmen. We believe that co-operation of this kind holds great promise because it accords in the best possible way with both the present status of industrial, economic, scientific, and technological development of our states and their potential.

Esteemed American guests, I would like you to understand clearly that we in the Soviet Union value highly what the U.S. government has already done to promote stable, long-term, mutually advantageous economic relations between our two countries. We think highly of the agreements that have been signed in this field, and of President Ford's stated intention to continue the course of promoting relations between the USA and the USSR along that line.

For my part, I would like to assure you that the course of building stable and productive economic relations for the mutual benefit of the Soviet and American peoples is the long-standing, immutable policy of our Party and of the Soviet state, a continuation of the policy formulated by Lenin, their founder. I would like to quote the words he spoke fifty-five years ago: "We are decidedly for an economic understanding with America—with all countries but *especially* with America." We intend to advance consistently along this course, to which we attach not only economic but, I would say, to an even greater degree political significance. However, it goes without saying that this calls for reciprocity, for the only possible solid basis—the complete equality of both sides and the absence of any discrimination.

However, you are all well aware that it is precisely in this area that a number of negative factors still impede the further successful development of Soviet-American relations.

It is a fact, for instance, that in some transactions with American firms our planning and foreign-trade bodies derive less economic benefit than firms in some Western countries do. This is because there are still a number of laws in the United States that discriminate against the USSR, a carry-over from the "cold war" epoch. These discriminatory laws impede the export of our goods and, to some extent, limit the possibilities of financing the exports of your American goods to the USSR. Credit for financing American deliveries to the USSR is at times granted, at times frozen for an indefinite period. Needless to say, this kind of inconsistency does not contribute to stable business ties. The net result of all this is that it makes U.S. firms less competitive than our organizations' other trade partners. I do not know who stands to benefit from this but I believe it is not the peoples of either of our countries.

Finally, attempts to use the development of trade and economic ties as a means of making demands on the Soviet Union with regard to matters that have absolutely nothing to do with trade and economics and are fully within the domestic competence of states are utterly irrelevant and unacceptable. It is high time to understand clearly that such attempts at interference in internal affairs can do nothing but harm, affecting, among other things, the trade and economic relations between our countries.

Unless timely concern is shown for eliminating such negative factors, the further development of co-operation may be seriously impeded. Of course, both the USSR and the USA are sufficiently large states, with rich resources, a vast internal market, and extensive foreign-trade relations. In this sense, we both could very well do without developing trade and economic relations with each other any further. But one would think that this would hardly be desirable or useful, either from the point of view of practical good sense, the immediate economic usefulness for either side, or, especially, from the point of view of the political climate of our relations, which, as we know, is of great significance for the cause of universal peace and international détente.

We remain optimistic and assume, as before, that the prospects for business relations between our countries will be determined by the realistic economic, as well as political, interests of both states, and not by the egoistic calculations of certain individuals or narrow political groups whose thinking still bears the imprint of the archaic "cold war" legacy.

Your Council is holding its second session in autumn, but the economic relations between our two countries are, I would say, in their early spring, the season when the sun shines brighter, but there is as yet not enough warmth and the temperature still vacillates. But we believe that, as in nature, summer will inevitably come in these relations. What is important is that the process should not be delayed too much.

Much work has yet to be done in normalizing trade and economic relations, and to this both government and business circles can make a contribution.

I can tell you frankly, our esteemed guests, that there is great awareness and understanding in the Soviet Union of the full significance of the farsighted and active stand taken by many prominent U.S. businessmen, including those who are present here, to develop Soviet-American economic ties. It is our conviction that this activity goes beyond purely commercial matters: objectively, it accords with the deeper long-range national interests of both our countries and the interests of strengthening peace on our planet.

The work of your Council is one instance of our joint efforts on that worthy road. Allow me to wish all of you great success. I would like to say on behalf of the leadership of the Soviet Union that the activities of the Council will have our full support. There will be no lack of good will.

From Speech at Vladivostok Dinner for
U.S. President Gerald Ford

November 24, 1974

On November 23 and 24, 1974, Leonid Brezhnev and Gerald Ford, then President of the United States, met near the city of Vladivostok. They issued a statement confirming the intention of both countries to conclude a new strategic arms limitation agreement based on the principles of equality and equal security. The participants in the meeting worked out the basis for such an agreement.

This is our first meeting, Mr. President, and we are pleased with the fact that it is held in the Soviet land, so we have an opportunity to show, to some extent, hospitality to President Ford. Though, of course, you are just starting to familiarize yourself with our country, Mr. President, we are sure you will be able to learn still more about it.

The fact that our first meeting has a purely working nature and is held less than six months after the previous Soviet-American summit meeting is indicative of many things. Meetings and talks of the leaders of our two countries become regular. Without losing their great significance in essence, they are no longer anything extraordinary. They are becoming, as it were, a norm of development in Soviet-American relations. And this, to my mind, is a substantial achievement in itself.

Over the past two or three years, quite a lot has been done by joint efforts to rebuild relations between the Soviet Union and the United States of America on the basis of peaceful coexistence, in the interests of the peoples of both countries and universal peace.

Our states have pledged themselves to act in such a way as to prevent an outbreak of nuclear war. This is a great undertaking. The first steps have been made to arrest the strategic-arms race. The transition of our countries to a constructive dialogue in this extremely important field has become a serious factor in the consolidation of international security and universal peace.

Versatile bilateral relations and co-operation between our countries are expanding quite well on the political and legal basis created by the joint efforts. These relations encompass the sphere of economy, various branches of technology, ever more lively exchange of cultural values, and reciprocal visits of representatives of various state and public organizations. These relations, undoubtedly, are useful by themselves, in a purely practical way in every specific field. But they are even more valuable due to the fact that they create better conditions for mutual understanding and growth of trust between our peoples. And this is especially important.

The time is ripe for outlining jointly the new steps that will enable us to move forward, relying on the basis we have created. It is precisely in this, as I understand it, that both of us see the main task of our meeting, Mr. President. Certainly, in the first place our attention was attracted by such a vitally important problem as achievement of an agreement on further limitation and then reduction of armaments, especially such armaments as it is now customary to call "strategic" ones. This is necessary if we really wish to promote elimination of the threat of an outbreak of a nuclear-missile war, with all its disastrous consequences. To make international détente really firm, it is necessary to consolidate it by détente in the military field. Further progress in this direction will be of great importance for universal peace. I think we have done a good job in this respect here in Vladivostok. If it is carried through and a new agreement is signed, you, Mr. President, and I will be thanked for this not only by the Soviet and American peoples, but also by all the peoples of the world.

And one more important point. We in the Soviet Union are convinced that the USSR and the USA, being guided by the interests of peace and acting jointly with other peace-loving states, can and must actively promote settlement of acute international problems that still remain unsolved, promote liquidation of dangerous seats of tension and conflicts. Certain things have been done in this respect in the past. But, we believe, the co-operation of our two countries for the consolidation of peace and the security of peoples could be much more effective.

It is known that much yet remains to be done to really clear the way for development of commercial and economic relations between our two countries on the basis of equality. This is needed even more so since it means not merely mutual material benefit, but also the creation of a sort of material basis for the steady improvement of Soviet-American relations as a whole.

As I understand it, Mr. President, we have established the common view that it is necessary to exert all efforts to ensure the steady progressive development of Soviet-American relations, to make this process irreversible. It is worthwhile to work for this purpose, sparing no efforts, and we are glad that our meeting enabled us to take new essential steps in this direction.

From Speech to the Electors in the

Bauman District of Moscow

June 13, 1975

Leonid Brezhnev made this speech before his constituents of Moscow's Bauman District on the eve of elections to the Supreme Soviet. He touched upon many aspects of Soviet life, as well as pressing international issues.

The line of our Party and state in international affairs is well known. It stems from the very nature of socialism and is wholly subordinated to the interests of the peaceful constructive labor of the Soviet people and our brothers in the socialist countries. Being consistently a class policy, it serves the cause of peace, freedom, and security of all peoples, the cause of their national independence and social progress, and meets the interests of the broadest masses throughout the world. The Soviet people enthusiastically and unanimously support this policy. We shall continue to pursue it vigorously and persistently in future as well.

Over the last few years belief in the possibility of and, moreover, the need for peaceful coexistence has been rooted in the consciousness of both the broad popular masses and the ruling circles of the majority of countries. The relaxation of international tensions has become possible because a new correlation of forces now exists on the world scene. Today the leaders of the bourgeois world can no longer seriously expect to decide the historical dispute between capitalism and socialism by force of arms. The senselessness and the extreme danger of the further fanning of tensions are becoming increasingly obvious in conditions where both sides possess weapons of enormous destructive power.

The norms of peaceful coexistence between states have already been recorded in many binding official documents of a bilateral and multilateral character, as well as in political declarations. Of course, all this did not come about by itself. An enormous amount of political work had to be accomplished to do away with the "cold war" and reduce the threat of a new world war. And it may be said that of decisive significance in attaining détente was the joint activity of the Soviet Union and the other countries of the socialist community, their consistent struggle against the forces of aggression and war.

Now the world is entering a period when the task of translating the principles of peaceful coexistence and mutually beneficial co-operation into daily practical actions is coming to the fore.

This is a crucial period. Those to whom the destinies of states and peoples have been entrusted should show that their deeds match their words. For politicians can be found who use the slogan of peace and pay lip service to the principles of peaceful coexistence and détente while actually hoping to return to the policy of the "cold war" period, calling for a build-up of the arms race and displaying open animosity toward the socialist countries.

The efforts of these politicians run counter to the aspirations of the peoples. For, in fact, they can offer nothing but new economic burdens and a revival of the threat of a new world war. But they are capable of impeding the consolidation of universal security and the development of peaceful co-operation between peoples unless they are given a timely rebuff.

Experience teaches us that for peace to become genuinely durable, it is necessary for statesmen and politicians to make consistent and purposeful efforts, to be able to counter the enemies of détente and, of course, not to be led along by them.

One can only be surprised at hearing certain apparently responsible Western leaders speculating on whether détente is useful or harmful, that is, whether it is useful or harmful to live in conditions of a more stable peace and a reduced threat of war.

Sometimes we are told that attempts to question the benefit of détente are being made for purely internal political, tactical considerations, in order to win the sympathies of the right-wing circles in the country concerned. But, frankly speaking, we are convinced that the strengthening of peace is too serious a matter for the present and future generations of people to be subordinated to considerations of expediency or to one's mood.

Of course, we have our own ideology, our own convictions, but we proceed from the assumption that peace is equally needed by all peoples and that all states have a stake in removing the threat of a world nuclear war. Herein lies the main foundation for joint efforts to strengthen peace and security. Speaking of Soviet-Amercan relations, U.S. President Ford stressed recently that détente is advantageous to both sides. One cannot, it seems to me, but agree with this.

We firmly adhere to the view that détente can and must be further deepened. For this it is necessary that states should take due account of mutual, precisely mutual and not unilateral, interests, and assume treaty obligations on a basis of reciprocity. Properly speaking, it was on this basis that international détente started, and on this basis it continues to develop.

Permit me, comrades, once again to declare from this rostrum that the Soviet Union, its Communist Party, and the entire Soviet people are firmly and consistently coming out and will continue to come out for the invigoration of the international climate, for the strengthening of peaceful relations between states, for the consolidation of security in Europe, for the further improvement of relations with France, the United States, the FRG, Britain, Italy, Japan, and indeed all countries that reciprocate in this matter.

We consider that in the nearest future it is quite possible to make further big and real steps toward a more stable and sound peace in Europe and elsewhere on the planet.

This concerns the all-European conference, where the overwhelming part of the work has already been done and its completion is within sight.

This also concerns the Vienna talks on the reduction of armed forces and armaments in Central Europe—if only to approach them honestly and objectively and not try to use them as an instrument for strengthening one's military positions with regard to the other side, as the NATO countries are still trying to do.

This also concerns the relations between the Soviet Union and the United States of America.

The steps for their further development, which are now being mapped out in connection with the new forthcoming Soviet-American summit meeting, which is to take place this year, including the signing of a new agreement on the limitation of strategic arms on the basis of the Vladivostok accord—all these are very necessary and important steps. We, however, by no means think that this exhausts all that can be done in the struggle against the arms race.

It is well known that, as a result of the agreements concluded in recent years, we have succeeded in checking, to some extent, the arms race in some sectors, and that the socialist states played a very important part in this matter. However, we cannot say, unfortunately, that an end has been put to the build-up of armaments.

Some Western powers are boosting military budgets. Their military establishments are making tremendous efforts to push ever new appropriations through legislative bodies. The Soviet Union considers that things should proceed in a different direction. We stand for the reduction of military budgets and we urge other powers to do the same. Our country has been and remains a staunch champion of the limitation and reduction of armaments, a champion of disarmament. We shall not slacken our efforts in this field in the future as well.

In this connection I would like to emphasize the significance of one important matter. It has not yet received a reflection in agreements between states but, in our belief, it is becoming increasingly acute and pressing with every passing day. This is that all states, the big powers in the first place, should sign an agreement banning the development of new types of mass-annihilation weapons and new systems of such weapons.

The level of contemporary science and technology is such that there is serious danger of the development of even more dreadful weapons than the nuclear ones. The common sense and conscience of mankind dictate the necessity of putting up an insurmountable barrier in the way of the emergence of such weaponry.

Of course, this task requires the efforts of a broad circle of states, big powers in the first place. However, acting in one direction, the Soviet Union and the United States could, we consider, make their weighty contribution to this cause.

Message to Soviet Cosmonauts
Alexei Leonov and Valeri Kubasov and
American Astronauts Thomas Stafford,
Donald Slayton, and Vance Brand

July 17, 1975

Leonid Brezhnev sent this telegram in connection with an important event—the docking of the Soviet spaceship Soyuz and the American spacecraft Apollo.

On behalf of the Soviet people and on my own behalf I congratulate you on a remarkable event, the first link-up of the Soviet spaceship Soyuz 19 and the American spaceship Apollo.

The whole world is following with close attention and admiration your joint work in carrying out the complex program of scientific experiments. The successful docking has confirmed the correctness of the technical solutions worked out and realized in creative harmony by Soviet and American scientists, designers, and cosmonauts. It may be said that Soyuz-Apollo is the prototype of future international orbital stations.

Since the launching of the first man-made satellite of the Earth and man's first space flight, outer space has become an arena of international co-operation. The relaxation of tension, the positive shifts in Soviet-American relations have made possible the first international space flight. New possibilities are opening up for extensive fruitful development of scientific ties between countries and peoples in the interests of peace and the progress of all mankind.

Upon you, courageous conquerors of outer space, has fallen the great honor of opening a new page in the history of space exploration. I wish you the successful realization of your program and a safe return to Earth.

Message to U.S. President Gerald Ford

July 25, 1975

Esteemed Mr. President,

On the occasion of the successful conclusion of the joint flight and docking of the Soviet spaceship Soyuz and the American spaceship Apollo, the first in history, I extend on behalf of the Soviet people and on my own behalf heartfelt congratulations to you and to the people of the United States of America. Please convey our congratulations and best wishes to the courageous American cosmonauts Thomas Stafford, Vance Brand, and Donald Slayton and to the American scientists, designers, specialists, and workers who have taken part in the preparation and implementation of the Soyuz-Apollo program.

The compatible gear of the spaceships, worked out to enhance the safety of manned space flights, has been tested in practice, and the possibility of joint work in space by representatives of different countries has been demonstrated as a result of the flight of the Soyuz and Apollo spaceships, their docking in orbit, and the crew transfer. Being a major landmark in Soviet-American co-operation in the exploration and utilization of outer space for peaceful purposes, the joint flight that has been carried out lays the foundation for possible further Soviet-American work in this field.

The success of this outstanding experiment has been ensured by the faultless implementation by the Soviet and American crews of the complex program of the flight; it is a result of the close and effective co-operation of scientists and specialists of our countries at all stages of its preparation and realization. This experiment is a major scientific and technical achievement, opening new pathways for the further development of outer space for the good of all mankind.

The Soyuz-Apollo flight is of historic significance as a symbol of the current process of relaxation of international tension and improvement of Soviet-American relations on the basis of the principles of peaceful coexistence. At the same time, it is a practical contribution to the further development of mutually advantageous co-operation between the Soviet Union and the United States in the interests of the peoples of both countries, for the benefit of world peace.

Speech at the Helsinki Conference on

Security and Co-operation in Europe

July 31, 1975

Leonid Brezhnev headed the Soviet delegation to the Helsinki
Conference, in which the leaders of thirty-three European
states, the United States of America, and Canada took part.
The Conference adopted a fundamental document for the
development of peaceful co-operation in Europe. He made
this speech at the conclusion of the Conference.

Esteemed Comrade Chairman,

Esteemed Conference participants,

All of us who take part in the final stage of the Conference on Security
and Co-operation in Europe feel the unusual character of this event, its
political scope. It can be said with confidence that the same feeling is
shared by millions upon millions of people in all the countries participating in the Conference—and not only in those countries. Together with
us they are in the process of comprehending what is taking place these
days in the capital of Finland.

What has made the top political and state leaders present in this hall
adopt such an attitude to the Conference?

The answer seems to be that the results of the Conference are linked
with expectations and hopes never before engendered by any other collective action during the period following the well-known allied decisions
of the postwar period.

The people who belong to the generation which experienced the horrors of the Second World War most clearly perceive the historic significance of the Conference. Its objectives are also close to the hearts and
minds of the generation of Europeans which has grown and is now
living in conditions of peace and which quite justly believes that it
cannot be otherwise.

The soil of Europe was drenched with blood in the years of the two
world wars. Top political and state leaders of thirty-three European

states, of the USA and Canada have assembled in Helsinki in order to contribute by joint effort to making Europe a continent that would experience no more military calamities. The right to peace must be secured for all the peoples of Europe. We stand, of course, for securing such a right also for all the other peoples of our planet.

Being a focus of multiple and distinctive national cultures and one of the peaks of world civilization, Europe is in a position to set a good example of building interstate relations on the basis of durable peace.

The Soviet Union regards the outcome of the Conference not merely as a necessary summing up of the political results of the Second World War. This is at the same time an insight into the future in terms of the realities of today and the centuries-old experience of European nations.

It was here, in Europe, that aggressors crowned themselves with questionable laurels many a time, only later to be cursed by the people. It was here, in Europe, that a political doctrine was made of the claims to world domination which ended in a collapse of states whose resources had been used to serve criminal and inhuman purposes.

This is why the hour has struck for the inevitable collective conclusions to be drawn from the experience of history. And we are drawing these conclusions here, being fully aware of our responsibility for the future of the European continent, which must exist and develop under conditions of peace.

One could hardly deny that the results of the Conference represent a carefully weighed balance of the interests of all participating states and, therefore, should be treated with special care.

Not an easy road has been traveled from the advancement of the very idea of the European conference to its culmination, the conclusion at summit level. In assessing soberly the correlation and dynamics of various political forces in Europe and in the world, the Soviet Union firmly believes that the powerful currents of relaxation and co-operation on the basis of equality, which in recent years have increasingly determined the course of European and world politics, will gain, due to the Conference and its results, a new strength and an ever greater scope.

The document we are to sign, summing up the results of the past, is oriented, in its content, to the future. Understandings that have been reached cover a wide range of most topical problems, that is, peace, security, co-operation in various fields.

Relations between participating states have been placed on the solid basis of fundamental principles that are to determine rules of conduct in their relationships. These are the principles of peaceful coexistence for which the founder of the Soviet state, V. I. Lenin, fought with such conviction and consistency and for which our people are fighting to this very day.

The Conference has also determined directions and specific forms of co-operation in the fields of economy and trade, science and technology, environmental protection, culture, education, and contacts between individuals, establishments, and organizations.

Possibilities of co-operation now extend also to areas where it was unthinkable in the years of the "cold war," for instance, broader exchanges of information in the interests of peace and friendship among nations.

It is no secret that information media can serve the purposes of peace and confidence or they can spread all over the world the poison of discord between countries and peoples. We would like to hope that the results of the Conference will serve as a correct guideline for co-operation in these fields as well.

The Conference has adopted a number of important agreements supplementing the political relaxation by a military one. This is also a qualitatively new stage in building up confidence among states.

The Soviet Union has consistently supported the idea that the Conference should be followed by further developments in the sphere of military relaxation. In this regard, one of the first-priority objectives is to find ways of reducing armed forces and armaments in Central Europe without prejudicing the security of anyone—on the contrary, to the benefit of all.

The special political importance and moral force of the agreements reached at the Conference lie in the fact that they are to be certified by signatures of the top leaders of the participating states. To make these agreements effective is our common, most important objective.

We proceed from the assumption that all the countries represented at the Conference will translate into life the agreements reached. As regards the Soviet Union, it will act precisely in this manner.

In our view, the sum total of the results of the Conference consists in the fact that international détente is being increasingly invested with concrete material content. It is precisely the materialization of détente that is the essence of everything that should make peace in Europe truly durable and unshakable. Therefore, uppermost in our mind is the task of ending the arms race and achieving tangible results in disarmament.

It is very important to proclaim correct and just principles of relations among nations. It is no less important to see that these principles are firmly rooted in present-day international relations, are put to practical use, and are made a law of international life, which is not to be breached

96

by anyone. This is the aim of our peaceful policy and this is what we declare once again from this lofty rostrum.

The very meeting of the leading figures from thirty-three European states, from the United States and Canada, unprecedented in history, should, of course, become a key link in the process of relaxation, of strengthening European and world security, and of the development of mutually advantageous co-operation. All that is so.

But if the hopes of peoples, pinned on this meeting and on the decisions of the Conference, are to be fully justified, and not frustrated at the slightest change of weather, what is required are common efforts and day-to-day work by all the participating states in furthering détente.

The success of the Conference has become possible only because its participants continuously took steps to meet each other halfway and, often overcoming great difficulties, succeeded in working out, in the final analysis, mutually acceptable agreements on each of the issues before them. These agreements were conceived and reached not by way of imposing the views of some participants in the Conference upon others, but on the basis of accommodating the views and interests of each and every one and with general consent.

If there are compromises here, then these compromises are well grounded and of the kind that benefit peace without obliterating the differences in ideologies and social systems. To be more precise, they represent an expression of the common political will of the participating states in a form that is feasible today, in conditions where states with different social systems exist.

The experience of the work of the Conference provides important conclusions for the future, too. The main conclusion, which is reflected in the Final Act, is this: no one should try, on the basis of foreign-policy considerations of one kind or another, to dictate to other peoples how they should manage their internal affairs. It is only the people of each given state, and no one else, who have the sovereign right to decide their own internal affairs and establish their own internal laws. A different approach is flimsy and perilous ground for the cause of international co-operation.

The document that we are signing is a broad but clear-cut platform to guide unilateral, bilateral, and multilateral actions of states in the years and, perhaps, the decades to come. What has been achieved, however, is not the limit. Today, it is the maximum of the possible and tomorrow it should become a starting point for making further headway along the lines mapped out by the Conference.

Aspiration for continuity in endeavors and deeds is inherent in mankind. This is also true of the great cause that is now being initiated by the thirty-five states represented in Helsinki. This finds its reflection in the fact that further steps following the first conference on Security and Co-operation in Europe have been outlined to implement and develop its objectives.

Before this exceptionally competent audience we would like to stress most emphatically one of the inherent features of the foreign policy of the Soviet Union, of the Leninist policy of peace and friendship among nations—its humanism. The decisions of the 24th Congress of our Party are imbued with ideas of humanism, as is the Peace Program, a plank of which called for the convocation of an all-European conference.

We note with deep satisfaction that the provisions drawn up by the Conference with respect to the main problems of strengthening peace in Europe serve the interests of peoples, serve the interests of men and women regardless of their occupation, nationality, and age: industrial and agricultural workers, working intelligentsia, each and every individual and all people together. Those provisions are imbued with respect for man, with care, so that he can live in peace and look into the future with confidence.

Agreements we have reached expand the possibilities of peoples to increase their influence upon so-called big politics. At the same time they also touch upon worldly problems. They will contribute to better living conditions for people, providing them with work and improving conditions for education. They are concerned with care for health, in short with many things related to individuals, families, youth, and different groups of society.

Like many of those who have spoken from this rostrum, we view the Conference on Security and Co-operation in Europe as a common success of all its participants. Its results can be of use also outside Europe.

The results of the prolonged negotiations are such that there are neither victors nor vanquished, neither winners nor losers. This is a victory of reason. Everyone has won: countries of East and West, peoples of socialist and capitalist states; parties to alliances and those who are neutral, big and small. This is the prize of all people who cherish peace and security on our planet.

We are convinced that successful implementation of what we have agreed upon here not only will have a beneficial effect on the life of European peoples, but will also become a major contribution to the cause of strengthening world peace.

And one more thought, which is, perhaps, shared by many of those present here. The Conference has proved to be a useful school of international politics for the participating states, particularly useful in our time, when incredible means of destruction and annihilation are in existence.

The powerful impetus provided by the meeting of leaders of thirty-five states participating in the Conference is intended to help everyone inside and outside Europe to live in peace.

In conclusion I would like to express profound gratitude to the people and government of Finland, personally to President U. Kekkonen for the excellent organization of the proceedings of the third stage, for exceptional cordiality and hospitality.

From Speech at Kremlin Dinner for
French President Valéry Giscard d'Estaing

October 14, 1975

President Giscard d'Estaing was in the Soviet Union on an official visit from October 14 to October 18, 1975. The top-level talks and the signing of agreements on Soviet-French co-operation in various fields were a substantial contribution to strengthening relations between the USSR and France and the process of détente in general.

My personal impression and the impression of my colleagues who have visited your country is that the French people clearly see the peaceful role of the Soviet Union, of the Soviet people in international affairs. We in the Soviet Union, for our part, believe that France and the French people are impelled by a desire for peace. Such mutual confidence is a firm foundation for the development of Soviet-French co-operation now and in the future.

The strong point of this co-operation consists in the fact that, apart from the friendly sentiments and sympathies that the peoples of the two countries have toward each other, it is permeated with political, state, realism. What I have in mind is, above all, the fact that both our countries proceed in their policy from a recognition of the situation that had arisen in postwar Europe, from the need for peaceful coexistence between states with different social systems, from the principle of the impermissibility of interference in the internal affairs of other countries. It is quite logical that much of what has been developed in the process of Soviet-French co-operation was later accepted in wider international practice.

A decade in international affairs is both little and much. It is not much if viewed in terms of history. But it is a great deal if it is measured in terms of the concentration of effort to promote peace and relaxation of tension and in terms of all that is good that has been done during the period.

Indeed, important positive changes have taken place in relations between states, in the general political climate, and in the sentiments of broad public circles.

This was clearly manifested at the Conference on Security and Co-operation in Europe. At this Conference there were outlined tasks of truly historical scope. Those who would like to call into question the realities of present-day Europe—territorial realities, realities of postwar development, realities of relaxation of tension—had the ground cut from under their feet. An extensive program of co-operation in the name of the noble goals of peace and progress of the peoples was worked out.

I think that you and I and all those who sat at the conference table in Helsinki and signed the Final Act of the Conference see more clearly than others the responsibility that rests on the participating states for the implementation of the agreements reached. It will take, of course, much effort, mutual and constant efforts, to further reshape relations between states in accordance with the principles approved in Helsinki, to deepen economic, scientific, and technical ties, to intensify co-operation in the fields of culture, education, and information, and to widen contacts between peoples.

Materialization of détente is now becoming the most vital demand in international relations. We believe that our countries, our peoples can actively facilitate the attainment of this aim. The businesslike, constructive nature of the contacts between political leaders and statesmen, systematic consultations, close economic co-operation, various joint scientific-technical projects, including those in the most advanced spheres of human knowledge, and the great scope of cultural contacts—all these are the tangible results of the work of recent years. At the same time, undoubtedly, there are possibilities that have not yet been explored for the further deepening and enrichment of Soviet-French relations. And we are convinced that the deepening and widening of Soviet-French co-operation, the drawing of ever broader sections of the population into it, would meet with a favorable response on the part of the Soviet and French peoples.

Materialization of relaxation is simply inconceivable without détente in the military sphere, too. I think that the conditions for this have become more favorable.

A lessening of military confrontation in Europe, limitation of armaments, and disarmament are a sphere of international relations where the good will and initiative of the states are now particularly necessary. Ever more urgent, in our view, is the reaching of a broad international agreement envisaging strict commitments of states not to develop new types of weapons of mass destruction or new systems of such weapons. Life itself confronts the states with the necessity of defining their role in the solution of these problems, which are of vital importance for all peoples.

From Report to the 25th Congress of the Communist Party of the Soviet Union

February 24, 1976

The 25th Congress of the CPSU, held from February 24 to March 5, 1976, was attended by 4,998 delegates representing 15,694,000 members of the Communist Party. Also present at the Congress were representatives of 103 Communist, Workers', National-Democratic, and Socialist parties of 96 countries. The Congress heard and discussed the main report, delivered by Leonid Brezhnev, entitled "Report of the CPSU Central Committee and the Immediate Tasks of the Party in Home and Foreign Policy." The report contained a profound analysis of the economic, social, and political development of the USSR and the Party's political, ideological, organizational, and educational work, and defined further tasks in these areas for the period 1976 to 1980. The report featured an analysis of the world situation and CPSU activity on the international scene. The Congress unanimously approved the program of further work for peace and international co-operation, for the freedom and independence of nations, outlined in the report.

Development of Relations with the Capitalist States

Struggle to consolidate the principles of peaceful coexistence, to assure lasting peace, to reduce, and in a longer term to eliminate, the danger of another world war has been, and remains, the main element of our policy toward the capitalist states. It may be noted that considerable progress has been achieved in this area in the past five years.

The passage from "cold war," from the explosive confrontation of the two worlds, to détente was primarily connected with changes in the correlation of world forces. But much effort was required for people—especially those responsible for the policy of states—to become accustomed to the thought that not brinkmanship but negotiation of disputed questions, not confrontation but peaceful co-operation, is the natural state of things.

A big part here was played by the fact that our Party succeeded in accurately defining the main practical tasks of consolidating international security, and presenting them at its 24th Congress in the Peace Program. The very first foreign-political actions of Soviet power, based on the platform of the peaceful coexistence of states with different social systems, showed the peoples of the world, as Lenin put it, "the only correct way out of the difficulties, chaos, and danger of wars" (*Collected Works,* vol. 33, p. 357). Invariably mindful of this platform, and acting on Lenin's behest and the half-century's experience of its foreign policy of peace, our Party advanced the Peace Program at its 24th Congress. This Program showed the realistic way to end the "cold war" and set clear objectives in the struggle to replace the danger of wars with peaceful co-operation.

Facts have borne out the program's timeliness and realism. And though world peace is by no means guaranteed as yet, we have every reason to declare that the improvement of the international climate is convincing evidence that lasting peace is not merely a good intention, but an entirely realistic objective. And we can and must continue to work tirelessly in the name of achieving it!

Permit me to dwell on the concrete directions of the work done by our Party to put the Peace Program into practice.

First of all about Europe. Here the changes toward détente and a more durable peace are, it seems, especially tangible. And, of course, this is not accidental. It is in Europe that socialism's positions and the impact of the agreed policy of the socialist states are the strongest. The 24th Congress set the objective of assuring European security through recognition of the territorial and political realities that resulted from the Second World War. And that was the direction in which our Central Committee worked.

The co-operation of the Soviet Union and other socialist countries with France developed successfully on this basis. Since the negotiations with President de Gaulle, Soviet-French summit talks have become a tradition. In the course of a series of meetings—first with President Pompidou and then with President Giscard d'Estaing—the positions of the two countries drew closer on a number of foreign-political questions, and diverse Soviet-French ties and contacts became more active. This was broadly supported by the French people, the majority of the French political parties. We highly value our relations with France and are prepared to extend the areas of accord and co-operation.

A significant shift occurred in USSR-FRG relations on the basis of the 1970 treaty. They have been normalized, and this on the only possible basis—abandonment of the ill-founded intentions to tear down the existing European frontiers. Now the FRG is one of our major partners in our mutually beneficial business co-operation with the West. Our talks with Chancellor Brandt in Oreanda and Bonn, and likewise the negotiations in Moscow during the visits of Chancellor Schmidt and President Scheel, made it possible to improve mutual understanding and enabled us to further co-operate with the FRG in the economic and other fields.

The settlement with regard to West Berlin was one of the complicated questions. It will be recalled that crises upsetting the situation in Europe erupted over that city. But the four-power agreement concluded in the autumn of 1971 together with the agreements and understandings reached on a number of issues by the governments of the GDR and the FRG and the West Berlin Senate have, essentially, relieved the tension. We value the co-operation achieved in the matter with the United States, France, and Britain. Conditions have been created to turn West Berlin from a source of disputes into a constructive element of peace and détente. All sides must only show true respect for the agreements reached. Unfortunately some of their signatories are doing far too little in this respect. We shall insist on strict and complete observance of all understandings. The Soviet Union favors a tranquil and normal life for West Berlin.

On the whole, our relations with the West European countries may be described as positive. This also applies to our relations with Britain and Italy. We value and also want to develop and enrich our traditional good-neighbor relations with Finland, and our ties with the Scandinavian countries, Austria, Belgium, and other West European states. The restoration of relations with Portugal and improved relations with Greece were, of course, a reflection of the big and welcome changes in the political climate on the Continent. By and large, no state in the West of Europe has stayed out of the broad process of normalizing relations with the socialist countries.

Comrades, in the interests of détente and lasting peace in Europe the 24th Congress of the CPSU called for ensuring the convocation and success of a European conference. Now this has become reality. Last August in Helsinki the leaders of thirty-three European states and those of the United States and Canada signed the Final Act of the Conference, whose work had lasted two years, and the political preparations for which took ten years.

The results achieved are well worth the expended energy. The participants in the Conference have collectively reaffirmed the inviolability of existing frontiers. A set of principles has been worked out for governing interstate relations, conforming fully—in letter and spirit—with the requirements of peaceful coexistence. Favorable conditions have thus been created for safeguarding and consolidating peace on the entire continent.

In many ways, the results of the Conference are projected into the future. Perspectives for peaceful co-operation have been outlined in a large number of fields—economics, science, technology, culture, information, and development of contacts between peoples. Some other measures, too, have been defined to promote confidence between states, covering also military aspects. The main thing now is to translate all the principles and understandings reached in Helsinki into practical deeds. This is exactly what the Soviet Union is doing and will continue to do. Recently we made certain proposals for expanding all-European co-operation in a number of important spheres. We will continue to apply our efforts in this direction, and expect the same approach from all the other participants in the European Conference.

Thus, comrades, there are gains, and substantial ones, in the matter of building peaceful relations in Europe.

But we should not overlook the negative aspects. There still exists in Europe, for instance, such a complex and dangerous source of tension as the Cyprus problem. We are convinced that sensible consideration of the interests and rights of both communities in Cyprus will—given unconditional respect for the independence, sovereignty, and territorial integrity of the Republic of Cyprus and barring attempts to impose outside solutions alien to Cypriots—pave the way to a settlement of this acute problem to the advantage of peace, security, and tranquillity in Europe.

There are also certain difficulties in our relations with a number of capitalist European states. They evidently derive from the reluctance of influential circles in these states really to reject "cold-war" psychology and consistently follow a policy of mutually beneficial co-operation and non-interference in the internal affairs of other countries.

In the FRG, for example, the course of normalizing relations with the socialist countries is being attacked by right-wing forces who essentially cling to revenge-seeking positions. And, evidently, their pressure is affecting certain aspects of the Bonn government's policy. Far from promoting mutual confidence and international co-operation, a considerable section of the mass media in Western countries is inciting distrust and hostility toward the socialist countries. Certain quarters are trying to emasculate and distort the very substance of the Final Act adopted in Helsinki, and to use this document as a screen for interfering in the internal affairs of the socialist countries, for anti-Communist and anti-Soviet demagogy in cold-war style.

In short, much persevering effort has still to be made to achieve truly lasting peace in Europe and to make détente irreversible. The Soviet Union will apply these efforts in close co-ordination with the fraternal socialist states, with all the peace-loving and realistic forces in Europe. Before us, comrades, is the great aim of making lasting peace the natural way of life for all European peoples.

Comrades, the turn for the better in our relations with the United States of America, the biggest power of the capitalist world, has, of course, been decisive in reducing the danger of another world war and in consolidating peace. This has beyond question contributed to the improvement of the international climate in general, and that of Europe in particular. Acting in complete accord with the guidelines set by the 24th Congress, we have devoted very great attention to the objective of improving relations with the United States.

As a result of the negotiations with U.S. President Nixon in Moscow and Washington, and later of the meetings with President Ford in Vladivostok and Helsinki, important and fundamental mutual understanding has been reached between the leaders of the Soviet Union and the United States on the necessity of developing peaceful, equal relations between the two countries. This is reflected in a whole system of Soviet-U.S. treaties, agreements, and other documents. Unquestionably the most important of these are the Basic Principles of Mutual Relations Between the Union of Soviet Socialist Republics and the United States of America, the Agreement on the Prevention of Nuclear War, and the series of strategic-arms-limitation treaties and agreements. What is the main significance of these documents? In all, they have laid a solid political and legal foundation for greater mutually beneficial co-operation between the USSR and USA in line with the principles of peaceful coexistence. To a certain extent they have lessened the danger of nuclear war. Precisely in this we see the main result of the development of Soviet-U.S. relations in the past five years.

There are good prospects for our relations with the United States in future as well—to the extent to which they will continue to develop on this jointly created realistic basis when, given the obvious difference in the class nature of the two states and in their ideologies, there is a firm intention to settle differences and disputes not by force, not by threats or saber-rattling, but by peaceful political means.

In recent years our relations with the United States have been developing in many areas. There is a frequent exchange of delegations, including parliamentary, and cultural exchanges have become more active. Many Soviet-U.S. agreements have been concluded, envisaging expansion of mutually beneficial co-operation in various economic, scientific, technical, and cultural areas. Most of them have already come into force and are being put into practice to the obvious benefit of both sides, and, more important still, of mutual understanding between the Soviet and U.S. peoples.

The essentially positive development of Soviet-U.S. relations in recent years is, however, complicated by a number of serious factors. Influential forces in the United States that have no interest either in improving relations with the Soviet Union or in international détente as a whole are trying to impair it. They portray the policy of the Soviet Union in a false light and refer to an imaginary "Soviet threat" to urge a new intensification of the arms race in the USA and in NATO. We may recall that there have also been attempts to interfere in our internal affairs in connection with the adoption by the USA of discriminatory measures in the field of trade. Naturally, we could not and will not suffer that sort of thing. That is not the kind of language one can use with the Soviet Union. By now, I think, this is clear to all.

It is no secret that some of the difficulties stem from those aspects of Washington's policy that jeopardize the freedom and independence of peoples and constitute gross interference in their internal affairs by siding with the forces of oppression and reaction. We have opposed and will continue to oppose such actions. At the same time I want to emphasize once more that the Soviet Union is firmly determined to follow the line of further improving Soviet-U.S. relations in strict accordance with the letter and spirit of the agreements reached and commitments taken, in the interests of both peoples and peace on earth.

Our relations with Canada are ever richer in content; we believe that their prospects are good. Ties with the Latin-American countries have expanded visibly. We support their wish to consolidate political and economic independence, and welcome their greater role in international affairs.

The development of our relations with Japan follows a generally positive direction. The Soviet Union trades extensively with that country. A number of mutually beneficial economic agreements have been concluded. Contacts between political and public personalities have become much more active, and our cultural ties are growing. However, in connection with questions relating to a peace settlement, certain quarters in Japan are trying—sometimes with direct incitement from without—to present groundless and unlawful claims to the USSR. This, of course, is no way to maintain good-neighbor relations. As we see it, good neighborliness and friendly co-operation should be the rule in Soviet-Japanese relations, and that is what we are working for. I would like to express the hope that Japan will not be induced to take the road onto which those eager to reap advantages from Soviet-Japanese differences would like to push her.

The improved international climate has created a favorable atmosphere for invigorating economic, scientific, technical, and cultural co-operation.

Soviet economic and scientific-technical ties with the capitalist countries have expanded considerably and changed in quality during the period under review. I will later deal with this at greater length.

The volume of our cultural exchanges with other countries has increased approximately fifty percent in the past five years.

In all this, comrades, we see a materialization of détente, an important area of our Party's general work to develop peaceful ties among peoples.

Efforts to end the arms race and to promote disarmament have been and remain—as the Peace Program requires—one of the main trends in the foreign-political activity of the Central Committee of the CPSU and the Soviet government. Today, this objective is more vital than ever. Mankind is tired of sitting upon mountains of arms, yet the arms race, spurred on by aggressive imperialist groups, is becoming more intensive.

The main motive for the arms race given by its advocates is the so-called Soviet threat. They invoke this motive when they want to drag through a larger military budget, reducing allocations for social needs, and when new types of deadly weapons are being developed, and when they try to justify NATO's military activity. In fact, of course, there is no Soviet threat either to the West or to the East. It is all a monstrous lie from beginning to end. The Soviet Union has not the slightest intention of attacking anyone. The Soviet Union does not need war. The Soviet Union does not increase its military budget, and, far from reducing, is steadily augmenting allocations for improving the people's well-being. Our country is consistently and staunchly fighting for peace, and making one concrete proposal after another aimed at arms reduction and disarmament.

Soviet Communists are proud of having undertaken the difficult but noble mission of standing in the front ranks of the fighters striving to deliver the peoples from the dangers ensuing from the continuing arms race. Our Party calls on all the peoples, all countries, to unite their efforts and end this perilous process. General and complete disarmament has been and remains our ultimate goal in this field. At the same time, the Soviet

Union is doing all it can to achieve progress along separate sections of the road leading to this goal.

An international convention on banning and destroying bacteriological weapons, based on a draft submitted by the Soviet Union and other socialist countries, was drawn up, signed, and has entered into force. In effect, it is the first real disarmament measure in the history of international relations. It envisages removal of a whole category of highly dangerous mass-annihilation weapons from the military arsenals of states.

The sphere of operation of the Treaty on the Non-Proliferation of Nuclear Weapons has expanded. Recently, other large states, including the FRG and Italy, have become party to it. But further effective measures to prevent the spread of nuclear weapons all over the planet are still a most important objective. The USSR is prepared to co-operate with other states in this matter.

Let me refer specifically to the current Soviet-U.S. negotiations on further strategic-arms limitation. We are conducting them in an effort to carry out the 1974 Vladivostok accord and to prevent the opening of a new channel for the arms race, which would nullify everything achieved so far. An agreement on this issue would obviously be of very great benefit both for the further development of Soviet-U.S. relations and for building greater mutual confidence and the consolidation of world peace.

Since we attach the utmost importance to the whole of this problem, we have persistently and repeatedly proposed to the United States that the two sides do not stop at just limiting existing types of strategic weapons. We thought it possible to go farther. Specifically, we suggested coming to terms on banning the development of new, still more destructive weapons systems, in particular, the new Trident submarines carrying ballistic missiles and the new strategic B-1 bombers in the United States, and similar systems in the USSR. Regrettably, these proposals were not accepted by the U.S. side.

But we have not withdrawn them. And need we say how beneficial their implementation would be for strengthening mutual confidence. Furthermore, both sides would be able to save considerable resources, and use them for productive purposes, for improving people's life.

Let me add one more thing. Of late, pronouncements have been proliferating in many countries against any of the powers setting up military bases in the region of the Indian Ocean. We are in sympathy with these pronouncements. The Soviet Union has never had, and has no intention now of building, military bases in the Indian Ocean. And we call on the United States to take the same stand.

Certainly, the time will come when the inevitable association of other nuclear powers with the process of strategic-arms limitation will arise on the agenda. And those who would refuse would assume a grave responsibility before the peoples.

On our country's initiative the UN General Assembly has in recent years adopted a number of important resolutions on questions of restraining the arms race and banning development and manufacture of new types of mass-annihilation weapons, of new systems of such weapons.

The task is to have these resolutions implemented. Frankly, this is not easy to achieve, because a number of major states are still obviously reluctant to end the arms race. The opponents of détente and disarmament still dispose of considerable resources. They are highly active, operating in different forms and from different angles. Though imperialism's possibilities for aggressive action are now considerably reduced, its nature has remained the same. This is why the peace-loving forces must be highly vigilant. Energetic action and unity of all the forces of peace and good will are essential.

Therefore, special importance is attached to the proposal supported by the vast majority of UN member countries to convene a World Disarmament Conference.

Political détente needs to be backed up by military détente. The Peace Program advanced a clear aim: to reduce armed forces and armaments in Central Europe. The Vienna negotiations on this issue have already been going on for more than two years. However, there has been no visible progress. For only one reason: the NATO countries refuse to give up trying to use the negotiations to secure unilateral military advantages. For some reason the West wants, even demands, concessions prejudicial to the security of the socialist countries. Yet we have not noticed any inclination on the part of the NATO bloc to make similar concessions to the other side.

Recently, the socialist states submitted new proposals in Vienna in an effort to get matters off the ground. For a start, we are prepared to accept a reduction of only Soviet and U.S. troops in the course of this year, while the strength of the armed forces of the other participants in the negotiations remains "frozen" and will not be subject to reduction until the second stage in 1977–1978. We have made perfectly concrete proposals concerning reduction by both sides of the number of tanks, nuclear-weapons-carrying planes, and missile launchers, along with a definite quantity of nuclear ammunition for these delivery vehicles.

Our proposals are based on the only realistic approach to preserving the existing relation of strength, in effect one of equilibrium, in the center of Europe. Their implementation will not prejudice the security of either side. And it is to be hoped that all this will evoke the right response from the Western countries and it will at last be possible to go from discussion to actual measures for reducing armed forces and armaments.

The 24th Congress set this objective: renunciation of the use and threat of force in settling disputed questions must become the rule in international relations. Later, this principle was reflected in a number of treaties concluded by the USSR with other countries. It is included in the Final Act of the European Conference. To make the danger of war recede still farther and to create favorable conditions for progress toward disarmament, we now offer to conclude a world treaty on the nonuse of force in international relations. Its participants, naturally including the nuclear powers, would undertake to refrain from using all types of weapons, including nuclear, in settling disputes that may arise between them. The Soviet Union is prepared to join other states in examining practical steps leading to the implementation of this proposal.

A great role and responsibility devolve on the mass public movement to consolidate peace. The past five years saw such milestones in the growth of this movement as the World Congress of Peace Forces in Moscow, the Brussels Assembly of Representatives of Public Opinion for European Security, and the World Congress of Women in Berlin. Our Party and the public in our country took an active part in all these events. In future, too, we will not spare strength in drawing the broad popular masses into the efforts to consolidate peace.

In its foreign policy, the Soviet Union intends to search patiently and consistently for more new ways of expanding peaceful, mutually advantageous co-operation between states with different social systems, and more new ways leading to disarmament. We shall continuously augment our efforts in the struggle for lasting peace.

Program of Further Struggle for Peace and International Co-operation, and for the Freedom and Independence of the Peoples

Comrades, assessing our country's international situation and world conditions, the Party's Central Committee considers that further struggle for peace and the freedom and independence of the peoples now requires first of all fulfillment of the following vital tasks:

• While steadily strengthening their unity and expanding their all-round co-operation in building the new society, the fraternal socialist states must augment their joint active contribution to the consolidation of peace.

112

• Work for the termination of the expanding arms race, which is endangering peace, and for transition to reducing the accumulated stockpiles of arms, to disarmament. For this purpose:

a) Do everything to complete the preparation of a new Soviet-U.S. agreement on limiting and reducing strategic armaments, and conclude international treaties on universal and complete termination of nuclear-weapons tests, on banning and destroying chemical weapons, on banning development of new types and systems of mass-annihilation weapons, and also banning modification of the natural environment for military or other hostile purposes.

b) Launch new efforts to activate negotiations on the reduction of armed forces and armaments in Central Europe. Following agreement on the first concrete steps in this direction, continue to promote military détente in the region in subsequent years.

c) Work for a switch from the present continuous growth of the military expenditure of many states to the practice of their systematic reduction.

d) Take all measures to assure the earliest possible convocation of a World Disarmament Conference.

• Concentrate the efforts of peace-loving states on eliminating the remaining seats of war, first and foremost on implementing a just and durable settlement in the Middle East. In connection with such a settlement the states concerned should examine the question of helping to end the arms race in the Middle East.

• Do everything to deepen international détente, to embody it in concrete forms of mutually beneficial co-operation between states. Work vigorously for the full implementation of the Final Act of the European Conference, and for greater peaceful co-operation in Europe. In accordance with the principles of peaceful coexistence continue consistently to develop relations of long-term mutually beneficial co-operation in various fields—political, economic, scientific, and cultural—with the United States of America, France, the FRG, Britain, Italy, Canada, and also Japan and other capitalist countries.

• Work for ensuring Asian security based on joint efforts by the states of that continent.

• Work for a world treaty on the nonuse of force in international relations.

• Consider as crucial the international task of completely eliminating all vestiges of the system of colonial oppression, infringement of the equality and independence of peoples, and all seats of colonialism and racialism.

• Work for eliminating discrimination and all artificial barriers in international trade, and all manifestations of inequality, *diktat,* and exploitation in international economic relations.

These, comrades, are the main tasks, the attainment of which, as we see it, is essential at present in the interests of peace and the security of peoples, and the progress of mankind. We consider these proposals in organic projection and development of the Peace Program advanced by our 24th Congress, a program of further struggle for peace and international co-operation and for the freedom and independence of the peoples. We shall direct our foreign-policy efforts toward achieving these tasks, and shall co-operate in this with other peace-loving states.

Permit me to express confidence that the lofty aims of our policy on the international scene will be received with understanding and win the wholehearted support of all the peace-loving, progressive forces, and all honest people on earth.

Speech at the Signing of Soviet-American Treaty on Underground Nuclear Explosions for Peaceful Purposes

May 28, 1976

The treaty was signed simultaneously in Moscow and Washington by Leonid Brezhnev and Gerald Ford, then President of the United States. The talks on its conclusion were conducted in accordance with the Soviet-American Treaty on the Limitation of Underground Nuclear Weapon Tests signed in Moscow on July 3, 1974, during a U.S.-USSR meeting. The new treaty established the procedure for conducting underground nuclear explosions and provided for co-operation between the two countries in peaceful uses of the atom.

Esteemed comrades,

Gentlemen,

A treaty on underground nuclear explosions for peaceful purposes between the USSR and the USA is being signed today in Moscow and Washington. For the American side it has been signed by President Ford.

The decision to draft such a treaty was made during top-level Soviet-American meetings. It has now been carried out. This is highly gratifying to us.

It may be said with confidence that a good deed has been done. The new treaty is designed to ensure that underground nuclear explosions, which is the subject of this treaty, are conducted for peaceful purposes and solely for such purposes. It provides the necessary guarantees for this, including provisions concerning verification. The treaty will also help to promote co-operation between the USSR and the USA in the peaceful use of atomic energy and this will be of benefit to other countries as well.

In the context of agreements reached earlier, this treaty represents yet another step in a series of measures aimed at containing the arms build-up and bringing about the general and complete cessation of nuclear-weapon tests.

The political significance of the treaty undoubtedly also lies in the fact that this is a practical step toward the positive development of relations between the Soviet Union and the United States of America.

While speaking about the success achieved—the conclusion of a treaty on peaceful nuclear explosions—one cannot but note that there remain major problems that need to be solved. Among them is the problem of completing the elaboration of a new long-term agreement between the USSR and the USA on the limitation of strategic arms. In this connection I would like to emphasize once again that, as before, the Soviet Union is doing all it can—all that depends on it—to achieve this.

In co-operation with other states we are ready to promote vigorously a broad range of undertakings that would help curtail the arms race and achieve disarmament. There is no objective more noble and humane than that of strengthening peace and international security and definitely removing the threat of war from relations among states.

Guided by this objective, the 25th Congress of our Party advanced a program of concrete actions, whose implementation would not only put an end to the dangerous arms build-up, which is still continuing, but also ensure a resolute turn toward the actual reduction of existing stockpiles of weapons, toward genuine disarmament. Governments and responsible statesmen must clearly realize that the urgent necessity to solve these questions is dictated by life itself.

From Speech at Kremlin Dinner for the

Prime Minister of India

June 8, 1976

The Prime Minister of India, Mrs. Indira Gandhi, visited the
Soviet Union from June 8 to June 13, 1976. The visit culminated in the signing of a declaration on further promoting
friendship and co-operation between the USSR and India.

Détente is now a tangible reality. There is no doubt that it has taken
root. The prerequisites do exist for détente to become a really irreversible
process. But at the same time we cannot ignore the fact that the opponents of détente have become noticeably more active of late. They seem
to have suddenly awakened on seeing that their ace had been trumped. In
their attempt to undermine détente they are casting aspersions on the
policy of the Soviet Union and the other socialist states. They resort to
accusations, which used to be trotted out in the "cold war" years, of "aggressive intentions," of seeking "hegemony," and so on.

Our answer is simple—we want no hegemony, we do not need it. It is
exactly those who so vigorously resist the consolidation of peace and the
deepening of détente that are driving for hegemony, that are interfering
in the affairs of other countries and peoples and trying to impose their
will on them. And it is well known who those are who reject our repeated
proposals to really reduce the arms race, who inflate military budgets and
accelerate the development of ever more destructive weapons. All this is
well known.

We are fully aware of these negative phenomena and are fully determined to oppose them. The development and extension of détente is a
demand of the times, a demand of all peoples, dictated by their vital
interest in a durable peace. And those who acquiesce in the campaign of
the opponents of détente or submit to their pressure for some expedient
reason are taking a grave responsibility upon themselves.

One's faithfulness to the cause of peace is now measured, to a greater
extent than ever, by concrete deeds, by day-to-day work for this great

goal. At the 25th Congress, our Party advanced a clear and realistic program of further struggle for peace and international co-operation, for freedom and independence of the peoples. We are pleased to say that it has already met with wide support from people throughout the world.

From Speech at Conference of European Communist and Workers' Parties in Berlin

June 29, 1976

This conference, held on June 29 and June 30 in Berlin, was attended by twenty-nine delegations from Communist and Workers' parties of Europe. The conference was an important contribution to peace in Europe, to security, co-operation, and social progress. It also revealed the determination of the parties whose delegates attended the conference to uphold democracy and socialism, taking into account the situations and national traditions of different countries and general laws of social development.

Many acute and explosive problems, which had troubled the continent since the Second World War, have finally been solved due to new conditions that have taken shape in Europe. The important treaties and agreements of recent years between the socialist states and France, the FRG, and other Western countries and the quadripartite agreement on West Berlin have changed the international situation in Europe for the better.

The principles of peaceful coexistence have become the leading trend in relations among states. This was most completely reflected in the successful European Conference, in which the USA and Canada participated. It is a tremendous political victory for the forces of peace.

The Conference's Final Act is a rich, multifaceted code for peaceful association and co-operation among states. We are striving to implement all its provisions. But what we value most highly is that this document is directed at achieving a lasting peace in Europe. That was the main goal of the European Conference—to help strengthen the peace and security of the European nations.

The success of international détente has inspired and strengthened the forces of peace and progress, and has heightened their prestige and influence among the people. It has shown that the positions of the realistically thinking representatives of the ruling circles in the bourgeois countries rest on solid ground. But it has also alerted and activated the forces of reaction and militarism, who would like to drag Europe and the entire world back to the "cold war" and the time of nuclear brinkmanship. It has alarmed those who wax fat on the production of weapons of death and destruction, who cannot envisage any other political career except that of launching "crusades" against the socialist countries, against Communists, and those who openly call for "preparing for a new war," as the Maoist leaders in China are doing in the hope of benefiting from the setting of countries and peoples against one another.

These different forces oppose détente in different ways. However, their main objective is to accelerate further the arms race, which is already of an unprecedented scope.

To do this, imperialism's aggressive forces and their henchmen have again resorted to the hackneyed myth about the notorious "Soviet threat" supposedly looming over the Western countries. Fantastic assertions grossly distorting the policy of the Soviet Union and the other socialist states constantly appear in the mass media and are quite often made by prominent officials.

Against all common sense, the socialist countries are held "responsible" for internal political events in other states and for civil wars, and wars of national liberation. Ordinary people are being intimidated by "hordes of Russian tanks," and are being told that the USSR and the other Warsaw Treaty countries are building up arms on a tremendous scale, preparing a "war against Western Europe."

But these fabrications collapse like a house of cards as soon as we look at facts, at the realities.

In Central Europe there is not much difference in the size of the armed forces of the Warsaw Treaty and the NATO countries. Their level has remained more or less equal, with certain differences in the types of forces each side has, for many years. And the Western powers know that as well as we do.

That is why the socialist countries propose that an equal reduction of armed forces and armaments on each side be agreed upon—say, starting with the USSR and the USA—not to change the correlation of forces, but to reduce the sides' military spending and lessen the risk of a clash. What could be more logical and fair? But no: the NATO countries are stubbornly trying to secure an unequal reduction, so that the correlation of forces would change in their favor and to the detriment of the socialist countries. Obviously, we cannot accept this, and our Western partners in the talks apparently realize it themselves. So their position can mean only one thing: slowing down the talks and impeding the reduction of armed forces and armaments in Central Europe.

It was the Soviet Union which proposed that the states taking part in the talks on the reduction of armed forces and armaments in Central Europe undertake an obligation not to increase the strength of their armed forces while the talks are in progress. But this proposal wasn't accepted by the West either. NATO continues to build up the numbers and the striking power of its combat units in Central Europe.

So who really wants to abate the threat of war in Europe and who is helping increase it?

The Soviet Union is the only great power which does not increase its military spending every year, and which is working for a generally agreed reduction in military budgets. At the same time, the United States's military budget is steadily growing, already exceeding $100 billion. And the West European NATO member countries more than doubled their military spending in the five years between 1971 and 1975.

Such is reality. It speaks for itself.

Let us recall some more vivid facts.

It was the Soviet Union which has made the important proposals that a world treaty be signed on the nonuse of force in international relations, and that a general ban on the development of new types and systems of mass-destruction weapons (and even more terrible weapons than nuclear weapons may be created) be imposed. These proposals were widely acclaimed throughout the world, but, unfortunately, we see no great desire on the part of the governments of the Western powers—to say nothing of China—to implement them.

At the Soviet-U.S. talks on the further limitation of strategic arms, the Soviet Union officially proposed that an agreement be reached on rejecting the development of new, even more destructive types of weapons, such as the U.S. missile-carrying Trident submarines and the B-1 strategic bombers, and similar systems in the Soviet Union. But the United States has rejected our proposals and started working on these new means of mass destruction.

It was the Soviet Union which proposed to the USA that an agreement be reached on the removal of Soviet and American warships and nuclear-missile-carrying submarines from the Mediterranean. But our proposal was rejected.

It was the Soviet Union which proposed the Treaty on the Complete and Universal Banning of Nuclear Weapon Tests. This proposal was broadly supported in the UN. However, the other nuclear powers refused to begin talks on this kind of agreement.

All these proposals still stand. Most of them, along with other concrete proposals, are included in the Program of Further Struggle for Peace and

International Co-operation, and for the Freedom and Independence of the Peoples, which was approved by the 25th CPSU Congress and which our Party and our state are working to implement.

I think, comrades, that what I have said is enough for a correct answer as to who is really trying to bridle the arms race and who is spurring it on.

Experience shows that winning a lasting peace is a complex question calling for great energy, perseverance, and consistency. Shortly after the October Revolution, V. I. Lenin, speaking about the tasks of the Soviet state in the struggle to end the First World War, stressed: "It is highly naïve to think that peace can be easily attained, and that the bourgeoisie will hand it to us on a platter as soon as we mention it." Lenin's words are as timely now as they were then. I assure you, comrades, that our Party will not slacken in its struggle for peace and the security of nations.

In this connection we still attach great importance to the improvement of Soviet-American relations and strict observance by both parties of the relevant treaties and agreements signed in recent years between the USSR and the USA as well as the conclusion of new agreements that would consolidate and further the cause started in 1972 and 1973.

The successful elaboration of a new agreement on strategic-arms limitation, which is being dragged out, would be of primary importance. As before, the USSR expresses its good will and its constructive approach to this question. It is all the more strange to hear responsible U.S. circles repeatedly call for a rapid arms build-up, using the dragged-out talks with the USSR as a pretext—the talks have been dragging for several months now. And it should be clearly stated that we are not at fault here.

Comrades, it is not that easy to defuse the powder keg or, to put it more precisely, the atomic magazine into which present-day Europe has been turned. But it is important to start really moving in this direction. Any concrete measures that will preserve and multiply the elements of trust that are growing in relations between the states of the East and the West are valuable in today's conditions.

The Soviet Union, true to the spirit and the letter of the Helsinki agreements, makes sure regularly to inform the participants in the all-European conference of military maneuvers in the border zones and invites observers from neighboring countries to attend them.

The socialist countries, as is known, have often proposed that the North Atlantic Treaty Organization and the Warsaw Treaty Organization be simultaneously dissolved, or, as a preliminary step, that their military organizations be abolished.

Naturally, we are far from equating these two organizations. The Warsaw Treaty is a purely defensive organization. As for NATO, that bloc was established as a weapon of aggression and suppression of the peoples' liberation struggle. And it still is the same today, despite all the whitewashing. But we in principle are against the division of the world into military blocs and are prepared to do everything possible so that the activities of both these groupings can be terminated simultaneously.

Comrades, the European peoples are heirs to and followers of noble traditions that cannot be separated from world culture. And so there is little need to point out that these great traditions place major responsibilities on contemporary European people.

And there is another thing: Europe had been the starting point of the most terrible wars in human history. Not less than a hundred million human lives lost—such is the grim record in Europe's history up to our time. It is also Europe's contribution to history, but it is a terrible contribution, a warning and a responsibility. It demands that we think of the past in the name of the future.

Europe has entered a fundamentally new era, totally different from everything that went before. If the Europeans should fail to understand this they would be heading for a catastrophe.

An ancient maxim says that "all who take the sword will perish by the sword." Whoever takes up the sword in contemporary Europe will not only perish himself; he cannot even imagine who else will perish in the flames—enemies, friends, allies, or simply neighbors, both near and far.

To the Soviet people the very thought of using nuclear weapons anywhere in Europe is monstrous. The European "house" has become crowded and is highly inflammable. There is no, nor will there be, fire brigade able to extinguish the flames if fire ever breaks out.

For Europe and its people, peace has become a truly vital need. That is why we Communists, who are partisans of the most humane, the most life-asserting world outlook, believe that it is now more important than ever to pave the road to military détente and to stop the arms race.

It is also exceptionally important to create, so to speak, the fabric of peaceful co-operation in Europe, the fabric that would strengthen relations among European peoples and states and stimulate their interest in preserving peace for many years to come. I am thinking of the different forms of mutually advantageous co-operation—in trade, production, and scientific and technological relations.

This task is quite feasible. Over recent years, in the course of strengthening détente, countries in both Eastern and Western Europe have gained much experience in this kind of co-operation. For example, the Soviet Union's trade with the European capitalist countries has more than trebled over the last five years. Co-operation in building large-scale projects on a mutually advantageous foundation is becoming more important.

I believe that the Communists of Europe think alike about the usefulness and the desirability of further developing such relations. They help build up the material foundations of a lasting peace. They are in working people's direct interests. It is enough to say that, according to data published in the West, the economic relations with the socialist countries are already providing work for hundreds of thousands, even millions, of people in Western Europe in this time of crisis.

However, there are quite a few obstacles on this road as well, which the capitalist countries have set up, often applying discriminatory measures against the socialist states.

Life is increasingly advancing the tasks of developing mutually advantageous, multilateral co-operation among European states, so that important problems directly bearing on their common interests can be solved jointly. As is known, we proposed all-European congresses and interstate conferences on co-operation to resolve issues such as environmental protection and the development of transport and power engineering. The Western states in words appear to be all "for," but in deeds they are evasive and aren't in any rush to take practical action. How can this be reconciled with the assurances of support for the Helsinki agreements?

As for the USSR, it will still continue to build up economic relations among European states in the name of a lasting peace and real benefit for European nations.

Comrades, in order to create an atmosphere of trust among states, so necessary for a lasting peace, peoples must get to know and understand each other better. This is the starting point from which we approach all cultural exchanges and human contacts.

And how do things stand in this area? We in the Soviet Union consider it important that our people know more about other peoples' past and present, know more about their culture so they can respect other countries' history and achievements.

That is why the Soviet state widely encourages cultural exchanges—consolidating them by intergovernmental agreements and organizing more every year. Today our country has cultural relations with 120 countries. In keeping with the Final Act of the Helsinki Conference, we have adopted additional measures that will lead to more exchanges of books, films, and works of art. As is known, the other socialist countries which attended the European Conference also take the same position on these issues.

As for the capitalist countries, we have heard more than enough splendid words about exchanges of cultural values, but there has been precious little when it comes to real action.

This shows in many diverse areas. Britain and France, for instance, publish books by Soviet authors in editions one-sixth or one-seventh the size of those by British and French authors published in the USSR. The number of Soviet films shown in Western countries is only a small fraction of the number of Western films shown in the Soviet Union, and that of TV programs is only one-third, and so on.

On the whole, people in socialist countries know much more about life in the West than the working people in the capitalist countries know about socialist reality. What are the reasons for this? The main reason lies in the fact that the ruling class in the bourgeois countries is not interested in having their countries' working people learn the truth about the socialist countries firsthand, about their social and cultural development, about the political and moral principles of citizens in a socialist society.

To weaken socialism's appeal, to denigrate it, bourgeois propaganda has come up with the myth of a "closed society." They claim that socialist countries shun communication with other peoples, that they avoid information exchanges and development of contacts between people.

Let us look at a few facts. Last year, 1975, alone, over 58 million guests from abroad visited the CMEA member states. In turn, some 35 million citizens of the socialist-community countries went abroad. This alone shows what all the talk about a "closed society" is really worth.

Or take contacts between mass organizations like trade unions. On more than one occasion U.S. authorities have denied visas to Soviet trade-union delegations invited by U.S. trade unions. There were even cases of representatives of Soviet trade unions not being permitted to attend international meetings in the United States.

The USSR last year received 980 trade-union and workers' delegations from abroad, while 750 Soviet delegations visited other countries.

No, the socialist countries are not a "closed society." We are open to everything that is truthful and honest, and we are ready to expand contacts in every way, using the favorable conditions détente offers. But our doors will always be closed to publications propagandizing war, violence, racism, and hatred. And even more so, they will be closed to the emissaries of foreign secret services and the emigree anti-Soviet organizations they have formed. When talking about "freedom" of contacts, certain people in the West are sometimes after free rein to engage in underhand play. We are not suffering from any "spy mania." But we will not give freedom for subversion against our system, against our society. Now that there has been so much scandal over the exposure of U.S. CIA activities, I think it will be clear to everyone that our stand on this matter is well grounded, to put it mildly.

We think that cultural exchanges and the information media should serve human ideals, the cause of peace, that they should promote international trust and friendship. But in certain European countries there are notorious subversive radio stations which have assumed such names as Liberty and Free Europe. Their existence contaminates the international atmosphere and is a direct challenge to the spirit and letter of the Helsinki agreements. The Soviet Union resolutely demands that the use of these means of "psychological war" be stopped.

From Interview on French Television

October 5, 1976

Leonid Brezhnev was interviewed in the Kremlin by Yves Mourousi, commentator for the French television network TF-1.

Here are some of the commentator's questions and Brezhnev's replies.

Mourousi: Your outstanding role in international affairs is widely known. Therefore, I would like to ask what are your opinions concerning some of the current problems.

There have been discussions on a fairly large scale in the Western countries lately concerning the value of a relaxation of international tension. It is even argued sometimes that détente benefits, first of all, the Soviet Union and other socialist countries. What is your opinion on this? What is now the Soviet Union's global approach, so to say, to international affairs?

It was over a year ago when you, Mr. General Secretary, President Valéry Giscard d'Estaing, and the leaders of other states signed the Final Act of the Helsinki Conference. Since I know how close the idea of this conference was to your heart, I would like to ask you how the Soviet Union assesses the progress in the implementation of the accords reached there, specifically those concerning a relaxation of tension.

Brezhnev: You say that the opinion is being voiced in the West that a relaxation of international tension benefits only the Soviet Union and other socialist countries. Such a viewpoint seems to us strange, to say the least.

Certainly we did not, nor do we now, make a secret of the fact that plans for the internal development of the Soviet Union rest on an expectation that there will be assured peaceful external conditions, and therefore détente is good for us. But does peace bode ill for other peoples? Is there really a people who can hope to gain something from unleashing a world war with the use of up-to-date means of mass destruction?

Let us take a closer look at what a relaxation of tension brings. This is the road from confrontation to co-operation, from threats and saber-rattling to a negotiated solution of disputed issues and, generally, to a reshaping of international relations on the sound foundation of peaceful co-existence, mutual respect, and mutual advantage.

All this creates conditions for fruitful contacts between states, the development of commercial and economic relations, and the expansion of scientific, technological, and cultural exchanges. We are aware that this, too, is sometimes referred to as a one-way street, supposedly benefiting the Soviet Union only. Thus it turns out that everything good, everything positive in international affairs benefits the Soviet Union alone. Thanks for a very flattering opinion, but, of course, the real situation is different.

Those who think that we need contacts and exchanges in the fields of economy, science, and technology more than anyone else are mistaken. Soviet imports from the capitalist countries account for less than one and a half percent of the country's gross social product. It is clear that this is not of decisive importance for the development of Soviet economy.

It is quite obvious that a relaxation of tension is needed by all countries which take place in normal international intercourse. It is therefore no exaggeration to say that the attitude toward détente is today a yardstick for evaluating the policy of any state and the true worth of any statesman.

I would like to emphasize that we assess international developments above all by the degree of progress achieved toward strengthening peace and eliminating the danger of a nuclear war. It is our opinion that definite positive results have been attained in this field in recent years.

Much has been done to make the necessity for peaceful coexistence of states with different social systems recognized. Clear-cut principles on which peaceful coexistence should rest have been worked out. A number of important interstate agreements to this effect, both on a bilateral and a multilateral basis, including the Final Act of the European Conference, have been signed. Constructive co-operation in economic, scientific, technological, and cultural fields is being established step by step.

But to ensure that these healthy trends become really irreversible, it is necessary to curb the arms race, to set a limit to it and then to scale it down. Otherwise, much of what has been achieved as a result of great efforts may one day be lost.

Some progress has been achieved in arms limitation in recent years. But it cannot be regarded as satisfactory.

We are surprised at the stand taken on this issue by the governments of some Western countries. Nobody seems to deny, at least in words, that arms reduction is important, but in fact spikes are being put in the wheels, so to say. Some circles in Western countries persistently spread allegations about a Soviet menace, speculating on the fear they themselves assiduously incite.

Yes, the Soviet Union has impressive armed forces. But we declare clearly and unequivocally: the Soviet Union has never threatened and is not threatening anyone and is ready any time to reduce our armed forces on a reciprocal basis.

We are forced to improve our defenses; I repeat, we are forced to do so, because we are faced with an unbridled arms race. Every now and then one hears statements to the effect that NATO's leading power "must be the strongest in the world" and that NATO as a whole must build up armaments so as to bring constant pressure to bear on the Soviet Union and other socialist countries. It is this that spurs on so vigorously the arms race in the world today.

If someone is really worried about the level of Soviet armed forces, then, it would seem, there would be all the more reason for the other side to get down in earnest to reducing armaments and advancing step by step toward a great goal—general disarmament. We are ready to take part in the working out of binding international agreements and we have made specific proposals to this effect at the United Nations, in particular, at the current General Assembly session, and at the Vienna talks. I will not repeat them here. I will only say that the struggle against the build-up of armaments has become extremely urgent. Therefore, it merits special attention from high-ranking leaders of states.

You have mentioned the Helsinki Conference in your questions.

On the whole, we assess positively what has been done over the period following the European Conference. New promising forms of co-operation emerge. The Soviet Union, guided by the principles worked out in Helsinki, has concluded a number of important agreements with countries that participated in the Conference. We can mention as an example the agreement with France on the prevention of an accidental or unsanctioned use of nuclear weapons, which was signed last July.

We have made it a practice to give prior notification of major military maneuvers and invite foreign observers to attend them. This is essential if confidence among states is to be built up.

Not everything, however, is running smoothly. Mention should be made of continuing attempts to distort the spirit and letter of the Final Act or to question its value altogether. This is done by those who advocate a return to the "cold war," to tension. Such forces exist in the USA, the FRG, and other countries. Therefore, the struggle to implement the provisions of the Final Act is at the same time a struggle against a return to the "cold war," against the intrigues of the adversaries of détente.

As regards the Soviet Union, we respect and observe the Helsinki agreements in all their aspects, I repeat, in all their aspects. The most important thing concerning these agreements includes everything that contributes to a strengthening of security and peace. But, naturally, we do not underestimate in the least the importance of co-operation in the fields of economy, science, and technology, culture and information, in promoting human contacts and implementing confidence-building measures.

The Soviet Union is for the pooling of efforts on an all-European basis to solve outstanding problems in the fields of energy, transport, and environmental protection. Our proposals to this effect are well known.

So facts show that the Soviet Union, displaying initiative and perseverance, together with other socialist countries, takes the lead in the great work of implementing everything that was agreed upon in Helsinki. We shall continue to act in this manner.

From Speech at Plenary Meeting of the Central Committee of the Communist Party of the Soviet Union

October 25, 1976

The Plenary Meeting, held on October 25 and 26, 1976, approved the drafts of the state five-year plan of national economic development for 1976–1980 and the national economic development plan and budget for 1977. In his speech at the meeting, Leonid Brezhnev reported on the work of the Politburo of the CPSU Central Committee to implement the socioeconomic program and the foreign-policy course elaborated by the 25th Congress of the Communist Party.

The foreign policy of our Party is first of all struggle for a lasting peace. We consider it to be one of our most important tasks to make full use, and not only in Europe, of the favorable possibilities created by the holding of the European Conference and by the document on peaceful coexistence and co-operation of states that was solemnly adopted at Helsinki. In full conformity with the program approved by the 25th Congress of the Party, we are continuing the work of developing equitable and mutually advantageous relations with capitalist states.

Every stage in this work has its own distinguishing features. Some five or ten years ago our task was to create a basis for normal relations of peaceful coexistence with France, the FRG, the United States of America, Canada, Italy, Britain, and other capitalist countries, to remove from our relations with these countries the main vestiges of the "cold war." When this had been accomplished in the main, we went further and began developing ever more extensive co-operation in the fields of politics, economics, science, technology, and culture.

Much that is positive has been done in this respect during recent months as well. For instance, agreements have been signed that fully accord with the spirit and letter of the Final Act adopted at Helsinki, including the ten-year agreement with Canada on promoting economic, industrial, scientific, and technological co-operation, similar agreements with Cyprus and Portugal, the Soviet-Portuguese agreement on cultural co-operation, the agreements with France on preventing accidental or unsanctioned use of nuclear weapons, on co-operation in the fields of energy, civil aviation, and aircraft manufacture, the agreement with Finland in the fields of public health and social security. As you see, things are moving forward. The whole world sees that the USSR is advancing along the road of peace and peaceful co-operation. And the world should know that we will continue to advance along this road!

It should be noted, however, that the development of our relations with a number of states has slowed down of late, and through no fault of ours. This was caused, to a considerable extent, by the complex political situation in some countries, in particular by the election campaigns in the United States and the Federal Republic of Germany.

Suffice it to say that things are practically at a standstill in such an important area of Soviet-American relations as the drafting of a new long-term agreement on the offensive-strategic-arms limitation, although the main content of this document was already agreed on at the top level in late 1974.

The American side, which had received our latest proposals on the unresolved questions already in March of this year, has not given its answer yet. We are given to understand that the reason for this lies in the complexities of the situation in an election year. We can only regret that an issue on which depend the strengthening of peace and security of the two great nations and the general improvement of the world situation for years ahead is approached in such a way.

But on the whole, our relations with the United States so far continue to develop in a positive direction. The Treaty on Underground Nuclear Explosions for Peaceful Purposes was signed recently. Mutually advantageous co-operation is taking place in many fields of science and technology. Cultural exchanges have acquired quite a wide scope. Economic relations are also somewhat expanding, despite the obstacles created by discriminatory trade legislation in the United States. Obviously, were it not for these obstacles, our economic relations would have acquired a totally different scope.

During the election campaign the rival candidates—President Ford and Mr. Carter—have repeatedly made statements on foreign-policy issues and on relations with the Soviet Union.

But these statements were mostly of a general and, not infrequently, contradictory nature. On the whole, both contenders appear to be in favor of a further normalization of the international situation and of developing good relations with the USSR. But one hears also their statements of a different type: calls for a further arms race, for the pursuance of a policy from "positions of strength," for the so-called tough line toward the Soviet Union, et cetera.

Nevertheless, whoever might be in office in Washington after the elections, the United States apparently will have to reckon with the actual alignment of forces in the world, which in recent years has prompted American ruling circles, after making a sober analysis of the existing situation, to seek ways of coming to an understanding with the world of socialism. In any case, one thing is absolutely clear: our policy toward the extensive development of relations with the United States, and lessening the threat of a new world war, remains unchanged. . . .

We would like to see peaceful co-operation of states not only take place on a bilateral basis, but also assume an ever wider, multilateral character and become, so to say, a part of the fabric of lasting peace. The Soviet Union's proposals to hold European congresses on problems pertaining to transport, energy, environmental protection were made with a view to accomplishing this aim in particular.

On the whole, the efforts to implement the Helsinki accords consist of scores and even hundreds of practical undertakings. Though not always conspicuous, they constitute Party and state work of exceptional importance. And we the Soviet people appreciate the efforts of those who work in the same direction. For the cause of peace, so close to the heart of every Soviet person, is our common cause.

The so-called confidence measures, the practice of giving advance notice to other countries about forthcoming major military exercises and inviting foreign observers to such exercises, approved on our initiative at the European Conference, have played a constructive role in creating a calmer atmosphere in Europe.

We also consistently implement those provisions of the Final Act adopted in Helsinki which deal with the extension of cultural and other ties and contacts among peoples, and the expansion of information exchanges. We proceed from the position that in the conditions of relaxation of tension the development of such ties and contacts is quite natural—of course provided that the principles of mutual respect for the sovereignty and noninterference in the internal affairs of the sides are strictly observed. But I'll have to say here, and some gentlemen may not like it, that we shall not allow anyone to violate such principles in conducting relations with the Soviet Union, to act against the interests of the Soviet people and our socialist system. . . .

Today there is no greater task in the struggle for lasting peace than to put an end to the arms race, unleashed by imperialist powers, and to go over to disarmament. The fact is that the aggressive circles of the capitalist world, in the face of their defeats in social battles, their loss of colonial possessions, the increasing number of countries rejecting capitalism, the successes of world socialism, and the growing influence of communist parties in bourgeois states, are feverishly intensifying military preparations. Military budgets are swelling, new types of armaments are being created, bases are being set up, military demonstrations are taking place. Acting from the "position of strength," imperialism seeks to preserve the possibility of dominating over other countries and nations, which is slipping away from it.

Striving to prop up their policy "ideologically," so to say, the imperialist inspirers of the arms race resort to any means, and do not even particularly care for elementary logic. When they require new credits for armaments, they frighten their parliamentarians and the public with "superior Soviet might," but when they want to show the electorate their concern for defense, they assure them of the "absolute military superiority of the West."

As to our defense, we spend on it exactly as much as is necessary for ensuring the Soviet Union's security, safeguarding, along with the fraternal countries, the gains of socialism, and discouraging potential aggressors from attempting to settle in their favor the historical contest between the two opposite social systems by force. To maintain the country's armed forces at a high level also in the future, to see to it that Soviet soldiers will always have the most up-to-date weaponry, the power of which the imperialists could not afford to ignore, is our duty to the people, and we shall fulfill this as our sacred duty!

At the same time we have no greater desire than to use the resources that now of necessity are being diverted from the national economy for raising the people's living standards, for constructive purposes. We are prepared, even starting tomorrow, to implement disarmament measures—be they large and radical or, for a start, only partial—but only on a truly fair and reciprocal basis. For our part we are ready!

Years ago Lenin spoke of disarmament as the "ideal of socialism." At that time there existed no real prerequisites for halting the development of militarism and for averting the threat of a world war. Today the situation has changed. The forces of socialism and peace exert such a strong influence that it has become possible to achieve progress in carrying out this task, which is so vital for all mankind, even if it is gradual and takes place only in individual sectors. Moreover, among the ruling quarters of capitalist states there is a gradually growing awareness that in the nuclear age to count on unleashing a new world holocaust is as futile as it is disastrous and criminal.

In recent years the joint efforts of the peace-loving forces, with the most active contribution of our country, have led to substantial results in the matter of lessening the threat of a new, nuclear war. Concrete, binding international treaties and agreements have been concluded on such matters as putting an end to many types of nuclear tests, on taking measures against proliferation of nuclear weapons, on their nondeployment in space, on sea and ocean floor, on carrying on strategic arms limitation by the Soviet Union and the United States, on prohibiting and eliminating bacteriological weapons. Those are not bad results at all. They disprove the arguments of the skeptics who proclaim the struggle for disarmament to be hopeless. But what has been achieved needs to be consolidated and further developed in order effectively to put an end to the new arms race.

You will remember, comrades, in what an urgent and principled way the question of disarmament was discussed at our 25th Party Congress. After the Congress, the Politburo has repeatedly discussed ways of providing a new impetus to the struggle for this most important goal. It has been decided, among other things, to advance a number of concrete proposals at the current session of the UN General Assembly.

The Soviet Union proposed to conclude a World Treaty on the Nonuse of Force in International Relations. A detailed description of this document was given at the session of the UN General Assembly. Here I only wish to stress that our proposals on the nonuse of force covers interstate relations without infringing the people's inalienable right to struggle for their social and national emancipation. We strictly distingush between these two spheres.

The USSR also submitted to the UN a comprehensive document—a memorandum proposing a broad and all-round program of disarmament measures, which are most topical at the moment.

In short, our country has again proposed to the world's nations a concrete program for disarmament. So that this program will be as realistic as possible, it contains essentially new elements. The positions of many states on a number of questions have been taken into account, of course, without prejudice to the interests of our security. To be flexible, we are prepared to start implementing either all the measures stipulated in the program, or, for a start, only some of them, progressing step by step.

Disarmament must become the common cause of all states without exception. Our proposals to convene a world disarmament conference or, at first, as a step in this direction, to call a special session of the UN General Assembly serve this purpose.

The Soviet Union's new proposals in the UN met with the understanding and support of dozens of states and broad circles of the peace-loving public. This pleases us and inspires us to new efforts in the name of lasting peace on earth!

I want to note specially that the Soviet Union continues to regard as a most important task a successful conclusion of the Vienna negotiations on reducing armed forces and armaments in Central Europe. We have made there some concrete proposals that would lead to a reduction of the military forces confronting each other in Europe, without harming the interests of any of the sides. We are prepared to discuss counterproposals based on the same principles. We are prepared to conduct jointly further constructive search (but really constructive and fair, and not aimed at getting unilateral advantages), to hold negotiations with our partners at any level, including the very highest.

Dear comrades, if we want to mention our main achievement in international affairs, we can say with a clear conscience: as a result of our efforts made in concert with the other socialist states, and with the support of all peace-loving and realistically minded forces, we have succeeded in lessening the threat of nuclear war, in making peace more reliable and stable.

We can all rejoice and take pride in such a result, comrades! The winner here is the whole of mankind!

From Speech at Soviet-Romanian
Friendship Rally in Bucharest

November 24, 1976

This speech was made by Leonid Brezhnev during his friendly visit to the Socialist Republic of Romania from November 22 to 24, 1976. The visit culminated in the adoption of a Soviet-Romanian statement on further promoting co-operation and fraternal friendship between the CPSU and the Romanian Communist Party, between the Soviet Union and Romania.

By combining our strength with a consistent and sincere love of peace and by appealing to the common sense and realism of politicians in the capitalist world we have brought about a situation in which international tension, mistrust, hostility, and intensive belligerent passions, typical of the "cold war" period, have given way to a much calmer and healthier atmosphere. A constructive dialogue has begun between socialist and capitalist states. Mutually advantageous co-operation between them, rather exceptional not so long ago, has now become a widespread and firmly established feature. In short, what Lenin, the leader of the world's first socialist state, advocated has become a reality, namely, in conditions of relaxation of tension, relations between states with different social systems have begun to develop on the principles of peaceful coexistence.

Comrades, this is a tremendous historic victory for mankind. Without any doubt, the decisive contribution to its attainment was made by the socialist countries, and they are continuing to make their contribution day after day.

Proceeding from the accords reached in Helsinki by thirty-five states of Europe and North America and sealed by the signatures of their leaders, including those of Comrade Ceausescu and myself, Romania, the Soviet Union, and other socialist countries of Europe are taking an active part in the development of peaceful relations between states. We are displaying a constant initiative in this matter. Scores of major political, economic, and other treaties and agreements, intensively developing economic, cultural, and scientific ties, contacts between mass organizations—all this is our asset, the asset of peace and good neighborly relations. Of course, the possibilities here are far from being exhausted. You obviously know about the Soviet Union's proposals for establishing all-European co-operation in such fields as transport, energy, and environmental protection. We will press insistently for their implementation. Mutually beneficial co-operation in many other fields is possible, of course, in conditions of peace. Europe is waiting for good, constructive initiatives.

Lasting peace, however, cannot be the privilege of Europe alone. Peace is indivisible, and today this truth is more correct than ever before. As long as the seats of war in the Middle East are not eliminated, as long as the Arabs are not given back their lands that were seized through aggression, as long as the Arab people of Palestine are denied the right to have a homeland, as long as the racialist regimes in Pretoria and Salisbury openly flout the rights of the indigenous population in the south of Africa and spill the blood of Africans, peace can nowhere be really secure.

To eliminate the centers of danger of war, to make the relaxation of tension universal—these are the truly pressing demands of our epoch. We are glad, dear friends, that in the struggle to accomplish these tasks the Soviet Union and Romania are marching together.

We also know, comrades, that peace cannot be secure until an end is put to the present arms race, to the inflating of military budgets, to the creation of ever more terrible means of mass destruction. Matters have already gone so far that were the weapons already stockpiled put to use, mankind could be totally destroyed. Where can we go to from this?

To continue or to end the arms race, to turn to disarmament or not—this is too serious a question to be left to be solved by the belligerent generals of the Pentagon and NATO and to the monopolies that batten on the manufacture of weapons. Responsible statesmen must act here, and the masses of people, whose destiny, after all, is at stake, must have their say.

Aware of all this, we in the USSR consider it to be our duty to do everything within our power to put the speediest end possible to the piling up of the means of destruction and to start the process of arms reduction. The Soviet Union's concrete proposals on the renunciation of the use of force in international relations, renunciation of the development of new weapons of mass destruction, reduction of military budgets, the complete end of nuclear-weapon tests, and on other relevant matters are known to the whole world. We are glad that in the struggle for these goals Romania, like other fraternal socialist states, goes along with us.

Our countries stand for the holding of a special session of the United Nations on disarmament and for the preparation of a world conference. We are working for progress at the Vienna talks on the mutual reduction of armed forces and armaments in Central Europe, which could lead to further steps in this respect already on an all-European scale. We would like to hope that after the change of administration in the USA the talks that we are conducting with the Americans to limit and then reduce strategic armaments will be continued and successfully concluded. A satisfactory solution of this problem—and we consider it quite possible, the more so since its main content has long been agreed on—would meet the interests not only of the Soviet and American peoples, but the interests of strengthening universal peace as well. This would be a good example to other countries.

Speech at Kremlin Dinner during the
Fourth Moscow Session of the U.S.–USSR
Trade and Economic Council

November 30, 1976

Esteemed American guests,

Comrades,

Allow me to welcome the participants in the meeting of the U.S.-USSR Trade and Economic Council—the prestigious forum of businessmen and representatives of the governments of the United States and the Soviet Union.

I am happy to see my good friends among the guests—the U.S. Secretary of the Treasury and Honorary Director of the Council, Mr. Simon, the American Co-Chairman of the Council, Mr. Kendall, and the Council President, Mr. Scott. All of them have made a considerable effort to advance economic co-operation between our two countries.

Esteemed members of the Council, we met here in the Kremlin two years ago. I remember that meeting and also the good conversation I had with prominent representatives of the American business world in Washington in 1973.

I would like to say that I consider such contacts important, above all, from the political point of view, because I well understand the great role that is being played—or can be played—by businessmen in establishing peaceful co-operation between states and between peoples. A similar viewpoint is expressed in the letter from President Ford, which was given me today.

In the general process of normalizing Soviet-American relations during the past few years, proper attention has also been given to questions of trade and economic relations. As you know, our countries have concluded several important intergovernment agreements on developing trade and economic, scientific, and technological co-operation. On the whole, a fairly good organizational foundation has been established, and mutually useful contacts in various fields between our countries have started to develop and multiply.

Whereas we noted that trade turnover between the USSR and the USA approached the $1 billion mark in 1974, it stood at $2 billion already in 1975, and will probably exceed $2.5 billion this year. We have concluded several important contracts with American companies, including contracts for supplying us with almost 1 billion rubles' worth of various equipment over the next few years.

Prospects for the future could be quite good if the Americans created normal conditions for them. On the whole, we expect that our trade with the industrialized capitalist countries will increase by more than thirty percent in the current five-year period, that is, from 1976 to 1980. According to the estimates of our organizations, the volume of our trade with the USA in industrial goods only, including raw materials, could reach approximately $10 billion, if not more. We would be ready to develop economic, technological, and industrial co-operation with you, including the conclusion of contracts on a compensation basis, in many industries: the automobile, oil and gas, chemical, pulp and paper, machine-tool building, electrical engineering, nonferrous metallurgy, shipbuilding, and other industries.

But naturally this will be possible only if a solution is found to the main question, that is, if the USA will put an end to discrimination against the Soviet Union in trade and extending credits. Promises that the U.S. administration gave as far back as 1972 have remained unfulfilled to this day. Of course, this is a serious obstacle to the development of trade between us and of economic relations in general.

Esteemed gentlemen, I ask you to take into consideration the fact that we are not at all raising the question of extending any privileges, any special benefits to the Soviet Union. All we want is that the USA should trade with us on the same legal basis as it trades with most other countries. This means that we want to receive the same treatment we extend to your country, that discrimination should not be allowed.

But if the present situation persists it does not bode well for Soviet-American trade. I will speak with absolute frankness with you businessmen. In spite of the general results, which look favorable so far, the volume of our economic contacts with the USA is virtually decreasing under present conditions. In many dealings we now naturally prefer partners who trade with us on a normal, equal basis. Discrimination also impedes the sale of our goods in the USA, increases the imbalance of trade, and diminishes our interest in the American market.

According to some estimates, the upshot in the last two years was that American companies lost orders from this country worth a total of $1.5 billion to $2 billion. You are the best judges of whether this is much or little, but I think such amounts are not to be found in the street.

We are living to a large extent on what might be called "old" capital. For example, almost all the equipment for the chemical complex, the KAMAZ, the iron-ore pellet plant, and a number of other projects has been supplied under contracts signed before the United States adopted its discriminatory trade legislation.

It therefore rests with the American side to rectify the abnormal situation. We are prepared to continue developing economic links in many areas and are prepared to trade with large and medium-sized firms, but only on the basis of full equality and mutual benefit. And of course we resolutely reject any attempts to link trade with political conditions and we will not tolerate any interference in our internal affairs. This must be made clear once and for all.

Those who believe that discrimination in economic relations could influence our policy or arrest our economic development are seriously mistaken. The Soviet Union has never allowed itself to become dependent in these matters on the benevolence of Western partners. We are successfully carrying out the great tasks of our Tenth Five-Year Plan, both in industry and in agriculture. And we will certainly fulfill them. The hard work and creative enthusiasm of millions of Soviet people are a guarantee of that. Our close co-operation with fraternal socialist countries is developing remarkably well. There is good progress also in the development of our economic links with many capitalist countries which honor in practice the principles of equality and the spirit of Helsinki in trade as well.

Given normal conditions for trade between the USSR and the USA we believe the prospects for its development are not bad at all. The volume of trade could well increase beyond the level envisaged earlier.

All this goes to show that in speaking about economic relations one cannot ignore the general state of political relations among states. In that respect our policy as regards our relations with the United States of America is perfectly clear and consistent. It is linked with the main principles of the peaceful foreign policy of our Party and our state. Our policy toward the United States is not based on considerations of expediency and looks not months but years and decades ahead. We want to see really stable peaceful relations take shape between the USSR and the USA in the interests of our peoples and universal peace, and not to the detriment of any third countries. The 25th Congress of the CPSU reiterated with all clarity our readiness to promote good, mutually beneficial relations with the USA.

This reminder is not irrelevant today because, of late, especially in connection with the recent election campaign, trends have emerged in the United States that, let us face it, run counter to the task of improving American-Soviet relations. Once again, as in the time of the "cold war," there are calls for pursuing "a tough line" with regard to the USSR and acting from a "position of strength." Some are persistently making the allegation that there exists a military threat stemming from the Soviet Union and that our country is interested in continuing the arms race. There are even attempts to stir up fears about Soviet "preparations for a first nuclear strike" against America. Who needs to utter this rubbish and to what purpose, I do not know. But it is a fact that there is such talk.

It would seem that the absurdity of these concoctions should be clear. This is at odds with the entire policy of the Soviet Union, which is aimed at decreasing and ultimately eliminating completely the threat of nuclear war, ending the arms race, and developing peaceful co-operation among states.

The whole world knows of the concrete and urgent proposals of the Soviet Union aimed at curbing the arms race and achieving disarmament. I may mention here such proposals as banning the development of new types and systems of mass-destruction weapons, complete and universal halting of nuclear-weapons tests, and the conclusion of a world treaty on the renunciation of the use of force in international relations. To back up our proposals with deeds we recently again cut our military budget.

As regards the Soviet-American dialogue, we have proposed to the United States that our two countries abandon work to develop new generations of nuclear-powered submarines such as your Trident and new heavy bombers like your B-1 and corresponding types of Soviet submarines and bombers. We have proposed the withdrawal by both the USA and the USSR of nuclear-armed ships from the Mediterranean. All these proposals remain standing.

The latest evidence of the peaceful nature of our policy is the recent proposal of the Soviet Union and its Warsaw Treaty allies addressed to all the participants in last year's conference in Helsinki, including the United States, that they sign a treaty pledging not to be the first to use nuclear weapons one against the other. We are awaiting a reply to this proposal and hope it will be a positive one.

The talk about alleged sinister plans of the Soviet Union with regard to the United States is pure invention. And malicious invention at that. For it provides a cover for unbridled inflation of military budgets and further arms build-up. And that is a dangerous thing. It is not to be ruled out that by raising a hue and cry about imagined Soviet intentions some quarters in the United States are actually nurturing plans of "a first strike" without considering the consequences. As for the Soviet

Union, I must reiterate emphatically that it has been and remains a convinced opponent of any such adventurist concepts and of nuclear war in general. We honor the agreement with the USA on the prevention of nuclear war and proceed from the assumption that the American side will honor its commitments under the agreement.

We set great store by what has been done by our two countries jointly to lessen the threat of nuclear war. We are prepared to go further along this road in co-operation with the new U.S. administration if it is prepared to act in the same spirit. The Soviet Union thinks that there is a need to intensify efforts to bring about the conclusion of a new agreement on limiting strategic offensive weapons on the basis of the accord reached in Vladivostok long ago. We believe it is high time to put an end to the "freezing" of this important question imposed by Washington almost a year ago. The Soviet Union is prepared to discuss new possible steps to prevent effectively the proliferation of nuclear weapons on our planet and other measures aimed at reducing the threat of nuclear war.

Esteemed guests,

While economic links depend on the political atmosphere, their development in turn helps create a healthier and more stable political climate. Businessmen can do a great deal in this direction not only for their firms but also for their nation as a whole, for peace and the prosperity of mankind. With this in mind, I extend my sincere wishes for new successes to the U.S.-USSR Trade and Economic Council, whose constructive activity we in the USSR value highly.

Replies to Questions by Joseph
Kingsbury-Smith, Hearst Corporation

December 29, 1976

Question: What message would you like to convey to the American people for the New Year?

Answer: For the Soviet people the coming year will be a jubilee year. It will be the year of the sixtieth anniversary of the Soviet state, which was born under the star of Lenin's famous Decree on Peace. Of course, in the coming year we would like to see new major steps taken to maintain and strengthen peace, to further enhance peaceful coexistence as the only reasonable and the only acceptable norm in relations between states.

History has proved that our two countries, when they act reasonably and take into account their responsible positions in the modern world, can make an important contribution to the cause of peace and the development of mutually advantageous co-operation.

I am glad to avail myself of this opportunity to convey to the women and men of America cordial New Year greetings on behalf of all the peoples of the Soviet Union and on my own behalf.

Question: What do you consider to be the most important measures of co-operation the USSR and the USA could take in 1977 to serve the cause of world peace and to strengthen Soviet-American relations?

Answer: I believe that our countries could do a lot in this respect. I shall only mention what is most important: we are in favor of the earliest possible completion of the work on a Soviet-American strategic arms limitation agreement on the basis of the understanding reached in Vladivostok in 1974. On our part, there has never been, nor will there be, any obstacle to this agreement, which is a matter of concern to all mankind. A Soviet-American agreement would undoubtedly represent at this time a very important step toward effectively ending the arms race. The solution of this task is most directly connected with the main goal of our time—to prevent a nuclear war. Conversely, delay of the agreement, while the development of even more horrible types and systems of weapons continues, is fraught with new threats to peace, international stability and security. Judging by recent statements of President-elect

Carter, the U.S. side is also aware of the urgency of this matter. Let us hope that this promises early success.

I must say that we in the Soviet Union are baffled by the position of certain circles in the West, both in the United States and in other NATO countries. They behave as if nothing has happened in recent years, as if nothing has changed and the world continues to be in a state of "cold war." They instigate one noisy campaign after another about an allegedly increasing "military threat" from the USSR, demand more and more military appropriations, and are intensifying the arms race.

We believe that things should not continue in this way. Having achieved the relaxation of political tension, we have also made it possible to deal seriously with cardinal issues of arms limitation and disarmament. I would like to reaffirm most definitely: the Soviet Union does not threaten anyone and has no intention of attacking anyone. It makes no sense to be frightened by mythical threats; it is better to discuss in a businesslike and constructive manner the problems and opportunities that exist here. The continuation of the arms race cannot be justified by assertions that arms limitation allegedly carries a risk to national security.

Today a far greater risk to universal security lies in inaction, in letting the unrestrained arms race go on.

We would like very much to see the year 1977 become a real turning point in ending the arms race. It would then surely find a worthy place in history.

Question: Would you welcome the opportunity to confer early in the new year with the new American President at a mutually convenient location?

Answer: Experience, including that of Soviet-American relations, has shown the usefulness and fruitfulness of summit meetings when each participant strikes for a constructive, businesslike dialogue. That is why we are for the continuation of this practice. The timing of the next Soviet-American meeting will naturally be determined by mutual agreement and will depend on progress on appropriate issues.

In conclusion I would like to repeat what has been said at the 25th Congress of the Communist Party of the Soviet Union: our country is firmly determined to follow the line of further improving Soviet-American relations, which is in the interests of both the American and Soviet peoples, as well as in the interests of universal peace.

From Speech upon Presenting the Gold Star Medal to the Hero City of Tula

January 18, 1977

The honored title of Hero City was awarded to the city of Tula for the courage and staunchness shown by its defenders during the Great Patriotic War (1941–1945). At the award's presentation ceremony, Leonid Brezhnev made a speech in which he recalled the heroic defense of Tula and dwelt upon some domestic and major international problems.

Everywhere our great nation is absorbed in peaceful creative work; it is engaged in an undertaking of tremendous scope and historical importance. And the Soviet people do not want the threat of war to weigh down on them like a heavy burden. The 25th Party Congress instructed the Central Committee unswervingly to intensify efforts to ensure a lasting peace. And that is what we are doing, perseveringly and, I would say, consistently.

Soviet people fervently support the Party's foreign policy. They know that this policy is designed to safeguard their country against war and that it accords with the interests of all nations, that it opens vast vistas for promoting friendship and co-operation between nations and advances the cause of social progress on our planet. At many meetings and rallies, in thousands upon thousands of letters to the Central Committee of the CPSU, to newspapers, radio, and television, they highly praise the Central Committee, its Politburo, and the Soviet government for their unremitting struggle for peace.

No other country has ever offered the world such a sweeping, clear-cut, and realistic program for lessening and then fully eliminating the danger of another war as the Soviet Union.

This program includes such a global measure as the conclusion of a world treaty on the nonuse of force in international relations. It encompasses all the key problems relating to the arms drive and maps out effective measures to curb it, to achieve disarmament. This program is aimed at preventing the appearance of new types and new systems of weapons of mass destruction, and at putting a total ban on nuclear tests. The Soviet Union has proposed to the United States that they refrain, on the basis of reciprocity, from creating new types of submarines and strategic bombers.

All of our peaceful initiatives accord with the common political line of the fraternal socialist countries in the international arena. We are working together to promote these initiatives. The proposals advanced by the Soviet Union and its friends are supported by dozens of countries at the United Nations, by the popular masses on all continents.

Fresh convincing proof of the peaceful nature of the defensive alliance of the socialist states—Bulgaria, Hungary, the German Democratic Republic, Poland, Romania, the Soviet Union, and Czechoslovakia—is the important proposals they set forth at a recent meeting of the Political Consultative Committee of the Warsaw Treaty Organization. They call on all the participants in the European Conference to pledge not to be the first to use nuclear weapons against one another and not to take actions that could lead to an increase in membership of the Warsaw Treaty Organization and NATO.

We believe that the noble ideas of peace upheld by the Leninist party and the Soviet state will ultimately be translated into reality.

But this can be achieved only through struggle, precisely through struggle, comrades, because our constructive proposals often come up against mute opposition and at times open resistance.

When, for example, the members of the Warsaw Treaty Organization raised the question of not being the first to use nuclear weapons, NATO's reply amounted to the following: no, that won't do, for we want to retain the ability to threaten the Soviet Union with nuclear weapons. We hope, however, that those who have the final say in matters of national policy will exercise realism with respect to our proposal.

Here is another example. At the talks on the reduction of armed forces and armaments in Central Europe we are told in effect: you should reduce more and we shall reduce less. This position certainly will not facilitate the progress of the talks.

Behind all that one feels the pressure exerted by the more aggressive forces of imperialism, the military and the military-industrial quarters and politicians bogged down in the mire of anti-Sovietism, the "hawks," as they are called in the West. It is precisely on their orders that intelligence agencies, military staffs, and all sorts of institutes draw up bulky reports and treatises that interpret in a most arbitrary way the policy of the Soviet Union and its measures to strengthen its defense capability. And all that misinformation is, as if by command, circulated far and wide by news

them. The purpose he
started by the Europea.
nake such attempts care
They are concerned with
on us, to have us live ac-
cialist democracy, with
s is a lost cause.

and states with a differ-
important results. This
common interest in mak-
ation should be carried
, as you know, have al-
articular on several eco-

develop further bilateral
ain, and other European
ll continue to build our
of peaceful coexistence.
ve and augment Lenin's

orous measures to elimi-
bloodshed in Lebanon,
ain with what dangers a
Middle East conflict is

ment that would not im-
ple. Israel, of course, has
ecure existence. But the
estine.

blem lies—and we have
va Peace Conference on
tes appear to favor a re-
this imparts still greater
men of the Geneva Con-
Given the will, they can
t in seeking mutually ac-

tional issues.
try has entered the new
ward this goal—that the

agencies, the press, radio, and television. Frankly, we are tired of that blather. In the West, too, when serious politicians are asked whether they feel concerned over this alleged Soviet threat, their reply is an emphatic "No."

Of course we are improving our defenses. We cannot do otherwise. We have never yielded, and shall never yield, in matters of our own security or the security of our allies.

However, the allegations that the Soviet Union is going beyond what it actually needs for its national defense, that it is trying to attain superiority in weapons in order to deal "the first blow," are absurd and totally unfounded. Not so long ago, at a meeting I had with a group of leading U.S. businessmen, I said, and today I want to repeat it, that the Soviet Union has always been and remains strongly opposed to such concepts.

Our efforts are directed precisely at averting the first strike and the second strike, indeed at averting nuclear war in general. Our approach on these questions can be formulated as follows: the defense potential of the Soviet Union must be at a level that would deter anyone from attempting to disrupt our peaceful life. Not superiority in weapons, but a course aimed at reducing armaments, at easing the military confrontation—such is our policy.

On behalf of the Party and the entire people, I hereby declare that our country will never embark on the road of aggression, will never raise the sword against other nations.

It is not we, but certain forces in the West, who are stepping up the arms race, particularly the nuclear-arms race. It is not we, but those forces, who are swelling military budgets by throwing money—hundreds of billions—into the bottomless pit of military preparations. It is those forces that represent an aggressive line in international politics today under the false pretext of a "Soviet menace."

Unless this line is duly rebuffed, the threat of war will grow anew. This line is dangerous to the peoples both in the East and in the West. The Soviet Union will do all it can to counter it and expose the danger it presents.

From the experience of recent years we know that the policy of capitalist states can sometimes be determined by other forces—forces which realize the danger of playing with fire and which are capable of reckoning with the realities of the present-day world. We hope that notwithstanding all the hesitations and an inclination toward phrasemongering, which is often dictated by the domestic situation, reasonableness and a sober approach to the problems of world politics will prevail in those states.

Indeed, it is precisely such an approach that made possible a change in

the relations between the USSR and France,
known treaties between the USSR and the Fe
the quadripartite agreement on West Berlin,
between the Soviet Union and the United State
tries, and the convening of the Conference on
in Europe. In other words, détente was set in m

What is détente, or a relaxation of tensions
vest in this term? Détente means, first and f
war" and going over to normal, stable relation
willingness to settle differences and disputes n
and saber-rattling, but by peaceful means, at a
trust among nations and the willingness to ta
interests into consideration.

Practice has shown that the international atm
changed within a short time. Contacts between
economic, cultural, and other fields have been
important thing, comrades, is that the danger
been reduced. People are giving a sigh of relie
hopeful about the future. This is détente; these a

What can the "cold war" generals offer in
taxes and greater military expenditure? A furtl
social needs? Building up stockpiles of weapon
whipping up of war hysteria and of fear of the
accepted by the peoples. Definitely not.

A relaxation of international tension, as we all
at the price of tremendous efforts. And it is not e
cal capital of détente that has been accumulated
obstacles will make us retreat. There is no tas
than making peace lasting and inviolable.

Statesmen who are aware of their responsit
people, of their responsibility for the destinies of
mind the desire of the peoples for peace. As for
not fail to do its duty in this.

We are prepared to co-operate with the nev
United States in order to take a new major step
relations between our countries.

First of all, it is necessary, we are convinced, to
future the drafting of an agreement on limiting str
we had agreed upon in Vladivostok back in late 1
Washington now express regret over the fact that

ments from the Final Act and launch polemics o
is obvious: it is to obstruct the positive processes
Conference. Judging by everything, those who
little about ensuring a lasting peace in Europe.
something else. They would like to put pressure
cording to rules that are incompatible with s
socialist law and order. I would like to say that th

In Helsinki, states with a socialist social syster
ent social system worked together and achievec
was serious, businesslike co-operation based on
ing the conference a success. Now this co-ope
forward. We are ready to work toward this anc
ready made a number of concrete proposals, in
nomic problems.

We regard it as a big and important task to
relations with France, the FRG, Italy, Great Bri
and non-European states. We have built and w
relations with them on the basis of the principle
This is a Leninist principle, and we shall prese
legacy, all of it, which we hold sacred.

We are for the implementation of the most vi
nate the seat of war in the Middle East. The
stopped with such difficulty, has shown once a
further delay in reaching a settlement of the
fraught.

The Middle East needs a lasting and just settl
pinge on the vital rights of any state and any peo
the right to independence as a state and to a
same right belongs also to the Arab people of Pal

The path to a solution of the Middle East pr
said this on many occasions—through the Gen
the Middle East. At present all the interested st
sumption of the work of the Conference. And
importance to co-operation between the cochai
ference—the Soviet Union and the United States
do much to help the sides involved in the confli
ceptable solutions.

Such is our stand on a number of major intern
Such are the intentions with which our cou
year, 1977. The Soviet Union will do all it can t

results of the work this year would be better than those of the previous one in strengthening peace and security of the peoples, in promoting peaceful co-operation among states. We will make our constructive contribution, and we would be justified in expecting all those to whom we address ourselves to do the same.

From Speech at the 16th Congress
of Trade Unions of the USSR

March 21, 1977

In the USSR, 113,500,000 people in the cities and country-side are trade-union members. In this speech Leonid Brezhnev dwelt upon the role of trade unions in developed socialist society and their tasks in the world today. He also discussed some international problems.

In our foreign policy we and our socialist allies firmly adhere to the Leninist course of peace. Developing and deepening co-operation with countries which have freed themselves from the colonial yoke, and co-operating, where this is possible, with realistically minded circles in bourgeois states, the countries of socialism come forward with concrete initiatives directed at improving the world's political climate. Precisely such proposals were made by the members of the Warsaw Treaty Organization at the November meeting of their Political Consultative Committee. The consistent struggle by the socialist community for peace and security for all nations is widely welcomed among the European and world public.

But there still exist in the world of capitalism influential political circles interested in disrupting the constructive international dialogue. The reactionary forces of the old world will not reconcile themselves to the growth and consolidation of the new.

For instance, they do not want to reconcile themselves to the free, independent policy and progressive development of African and Asian states that have freed themselves from colonial oppression. The latest instances of this are the interference of NATO countries in the internal military conflict in Zaïre and the new campaign of slander against the People's Republic of Angola. It is also shown by the dastardly assassinations a few days ago of two prominent leaders of the national-liberation struggle—the President of the People's Republic of the Congo, Marien Ngouabi, and the Chairman of the Progressive Socialist Party of Lebanon, Kamal Joumblatt. The Soviet people wrathfully condemn these murders.

With no less persistence, "operations" are conducted against the world of socialism. Attempts are being made to weaken the socialist community, and various means are employed in an effort to undermine the unity of its members. Attempts are also made to weaken the socialist system.

Our opponents would like to find forces of some sort opposed to socialism inside our countries. Since there are no such forces, because in socialist society there are no oppressed or exploited classes or oppressed or exploited nationalities, some sort of substitute has been invented and an ostensible "internal opposition" in socialist countries is being fabricated by means of false publicity. That is the reason for the organized clamor about the so-called dissidents and why a world-wide hullabaloo is being raised about "violations of human rights" in socialist countries.

What can be said about this? In our country it is not forbidden "to think differently" from the majority, to criticize different aspects of public life. We regard the comrades who come out with well-founded criticism, who strive for improvement, as well-intentioned critics, and we are grateful to them. Those who criticize wrongly we regard as people who are mistaken.

It is a different matter when a few individuals, who have estranged themselves from our society, actively oppose the socialist system, embark on the road of anti-Soviet activity, violate the laws, and, finding no support inside the country, turn for support abroad, to imperialist subversive centers—those engaged in propaganda and intelligence. Our people demand that such so-called public figures be treated as opponents of socialism, as persons acting against their own Motherland, as accomplices, if not agents, of imperialism. Naturally, we take and will continue to take measures against them under Soviet law.

And in this matter let no one take offense: to protect the rights, freedoms, and security of the 260 million Soviet people from the activities of such renegades is not only our right, but also our sacred duty. It is our duty to the people who, sixty years ago, under the guidance of the Party of Lenin embarked on the road of building socialism and communism, to the people who, defending their socialist Motherland, their right to live the way they want, sacrificed 20 million lives in the great war against the fascist aggressors—precisely for the freedom and rights of the peoples—and who will never depart from that road!

As for the Soviet Union, we do not interfere in the internal affairs of other countries, although, of course, we have our own, quite definite opinion about the order reigning in the world of imperialism, and we make no secret of this opinion. In full accordance with the decisions of the 25th CPSU Congress, we strive to build our relations with capitalist countries on the basis of long-term mutually advantageous co-operation in various spheres in the interests of strengthening universal peace.

I will say a few words about the present situation in this regard.

First of all, about Soviet-American relations, to the positive development of which we have always attached and continue to attach great importance. I would say that here the situation at present is determined by three basic factors. The first is the sound foundation in the form of the important treaties and agreements on co-operation in various fields concluded in 1972–1974. The second is a state of certain stagnation. The American side at first explained it by the election campaign in the United States; but the first two months the new Washington administration has been in power do not seem to show a striving to overcome this stagnation. And, finally, the third factor—the existence of important objective possibilities for further developing equal and mutually advantageous co-operation in various spheres for the good of both countries and of universal peace.

In this connection, I will mention several concrete and, we believe, quite attainable tasks. First, the completion of the drafting and the signing of a new agreement on the limitation of strategic offensive arms, which was already agreed upon in the main in 1974, and further advance on this basis to mutual arms reduction with strict observance of the principle of equality and equal security of both sides. Then there are possible joint initiatives of the USSR and the United States in the field of banning and liquidating the most dangerous lethal types of chemical weapons, and other measures restraining the arms race and strengthening the security of nations. There is also the extensive development of mutually advantageous trade and economic ties on the basis of a removal of discriminatory barriers created by the United States, and entry into force of agreements on these questions signed a long time ago. Lastly, these tasks include concerted actions by our countries to achieve a just and lasting peace settlement in the Middle East.

We are for actively utilizing all these possibilities. But there are also circumstances obstructing further improvement and development of Soviet-American relations. One of them is the whipping up of a slanderous campaign about the mythical "military threat" posed by the USSR. I have already spoken on this matter recently. Another circumstance is the outright attempts by U.S. official bodies to interfere in the internal affairs of the Soviet Union.

Meanwhile, Washington's pretensions to teach others how to live are, I am sure, unacceptable to any sovereign state, not to mention the fact that neither the situation in the United States itself nor U.S. actions and policies in the world at large justify such pretensions.

I repeat: we will not tolerate interference in our internal affairs by anyone, no matter what the pretext. Any normal development of relations on such a basis is, of course, unthinkable.

The Soviet Union has always firmly upheld and will continue to uphold its sovereign rights, its honor, and its interests. At the same time, a constructive, realistic approach by the other side will always meet with understanding on our part and readiness to reach agreement.

The U.S. Secretary of State, Mr. Cyrus Vance, is coming shortly to Moscow for negotiations. We shall see what he brings with him. Everybody, of course, realizes the importance of how Soviet-American relations develop further. We would like them to be good-neighborly relations. But this requires a certain level of mutual understanding and at least a minimum of mutual respect.

Of course, we are confident that the interests of the people of two countries and the interests of universal peace will prevail, and that relations between the USSR and the United States will eventually be resolved satisfactorily. The point is *when* will this be achieved and how much time will be lost in which many useful things could have been accomplished?

Speaking of our relations with West European countries, we must say that they are developing, on the whole, quite well. At one time the USSR and France were, so to say, the trail blazers of détente, and their relations were described as "preferential" ones. To a certain extent, this is still so: we are maintaining lively ties in the economic and cultural fields. We also co-operate in some foreign-policy matters. The fact that the leaders of France, the FRG, Italy, and Great Britain support the policy of relaxation of tension, the policy of peaceful coexistence, is appreciated in the Soviet Union. In relations between the USSR and FRG, we believe, much can still be done and should be done. We have already covered some ground and should follow this through. As is known, I will be visiting France and the FRG this year. We hope that the forthcoming talks will give fresh impetus to the development of relations with these countries.

The recent restoration of the USSR's relations with Spain was a notable event in Europe's political life. Lately we have developed adequate co-operation with that country, mostly in economic matters. Now, it can be expected that our relations will be further developed. We are following the process of democratization of political life in Spain with interest, and wish the Spanish people further success along this road.

Comrades,

Twenty months have passed since the day when the heads of state and government of thirty-five countries affixed their signatures to the Final Act of the European Conference on Security and Co-operation. During this period peace in Europe has strengthened, while economic, cultural, and other ties and contacts among countries have become noticeably broader and richer. We in the Soviet Union welcome this. We want détente to continue. We will promote this in every way, because it is in the interests of the peoples.

In the countries which took part in the Helsinki Conference preparations have now started for the Belgrade meeting, the first full meeting of their representatives since Helsinki. We, for our part, want a constructive, businesslike discussion there by sovereign partners. The Helsinki Conference, as is known, was called the Conference on Security and Co-operation in Europe. We consider, therefore, that concern for peace and security in Europe, for developing co-operation between the nations of Europe, should be the main content of the Belgrade meeting. In our view, the main task of the meeting in the Yugoslav capital should be not simply to sum up what has already been done, but to reach agreement on some concrete recommendations and proposals on questions of further co-operation.

The Middle East is another area that continues to attract attention. A noticeable increase in diplomatic activity has been observed there in recent weeks. Judging by everything, the resumption of the Geneva Conference is gradually becoming an increasingly more realistic possibility. Such a course of events, naturally, can only be welcomed.

But the conference in Geneva, of course, is not an end in itself. A fruitful and just outcome of its work is the most important thing. It goes without saying that the drawing up of peace terms in full detail is primarily a matter for the opposing sides themselves. But the Soviet Union, as a cochairman of the Geneva Conference and a state situated in close proximity to the area in question, has views of its own concerning the main principles that should be observed in a future peace settlement and the direction it should take.

We consider, in particular, that the final document, or documents, on peace in the Middle East should be based on the principle that the acquisition of territory by means of war is impermissible, and on the right of all states in the area to independent existence and security. It goes without saying that the inalienable rights of the Arab people of Palestine must be ensured, including their right to self-determination and establishment of their own state.

We consider there is no question but that the documents on peace must provide for the withdrawal of Israeli troops from all Arab territories occupied in 1967. Such a withdrawal could be carried out not all at once, but in stages, in the course of, say, several months, within strictly defined time limits. The appropriate border lines between Israel and its Arab neighbors involved in the conflict should be clearly defined. These borders should be declared finally to be established and inviolable.

We proceed from the premise that as soon as the withdrawal of the Israeli troops has been completed, the state of war between the Arab states involved in the conflict and Israel will be at an end, and relations of peace will be established. Furthermore, the sides will undertake mutual obligations to respect each other's sovereignty, territorial integrity, inviolability, and political independence, and to resolve their international disputes by peaceful means.

Demilitarized zones, which afford no unilateral advantage to either side, could be created on both sides of the established borders—with the consent of the respective states, of course. Either a United Nations emergency force or United Nations observers could be stationed within these zones for some stipulated period of time.

Evidently, the final documents of the Conference should also contain a provision for the free passage of ships of all countries, including Israel (after the ending of the state of war), through the Strait of Tiran and the Gulf of Aqaba, as well as a statement by Egypt concerning the passage of ships through the Suez Canal, which is entirely under Egyptian sovereignty.

In our opinion observance of the terms of the peace settlement could be guaranteed, should the negotiating parties so desire, by the United Nations Security Council or, perhaps, by individual powers, for instance, the Soviet Union, the United States, France, and Britain. The guarantor states could have their observers in the United Nations contingents stationed in the respective zones.

Comrades, these are very briefly our tentative ideas on the possible foundations of a just peace in the Middle East. We are not forcing them on anyone, but we felt it would be useful to let them be known, because we, naturally, are prepared to hear the views of others.

We have already said that as far as a peace settlement in the Middle

East is concerned, the relevant states could explore the possibility of facilitating an early stop to the arms race in that area. In general, the problem of international trade in arms seems to warrant an exchange of views.

Now a few words on the problem of limiting arms and attaining disarmament, which was defined by the 25th Congress as the central problem of ensuring peace and the security of nations.

I have already touched upon the Soviet-American strategic arms limitation talks. Banning all nuclear-weapon tests is an extremely important, pressing issue. Its settlement would exert a beneficial influence on our planet's life both in a direct, biological, and in a moral-political sense. It is no less important, also, that such a settlement should limit the possibilities of qualitatively perfecting nuclear arms and developing new types of such weapons.

For a long time the opponents of a complete ban on nuclear-weapon tests had cited the difficulties involved in settling the question of control. We are still convinced, and our view is supported by specialists, that national means of detection are quite sufficient to exercise control. And yet, to remove the obstacles from the road to agreement, the Soviet Union has taken a serious step to meet the Western powers halfway. Our draft treaty on the complete and general prohibition of nuclear-weapon tests now includes a provision for on-the-spot inspection, on a voluntary basis, should doubts arise about any country's failure to honor the treaty commitments. This is a reasonable compromise, which takes into account the positions of all sides.

Naturally, a complete stop to nuclear-weapon tests can be effected only when all nuclear powers accede to the treaty. Only then will the treaty truly serve its purpose.

We are closely following the reaction in various countries to the proposal by the Warsaw Treaty countries to the effect that all the participants in the European Conference should undertake not to be the first to use nuclear weapons against each other. We would like Western statesmen, and first of all members of NATO, to give serious thought to the meaning of this important proposal and abandon the formal, mechanical approach, which is to reject a proposal as dangerous only because it comes from the other side.

It is high time to realize that a policy based on the nuclear threat and on the readiness to use nuclear weapons is becoming increasingly dangerous for mankind. From the first day of the advent of nuclear weapons the Soviet Union has come out for their prohibition and destruction. Such was its stand when the United States had a monopoly on nuclear weapons, and such is it now when the nuclear potentials of the USSR and the United States have been generally acknowledged as equal.

When disarmament questions are discussed one often hears talk about the possibility and usefulness of introducing the practice of reciprocal example, that is, of a state taking constructive action in the hope that others will respond in the same spirit. Perhaps such a method could also be used. But it will be effective only if there is mutual good will and mutual trust.

I will cite one concrete example. Talks on the reduction of armed forces and armaments in Central Europe began four years ago. *On reduction.* What could be more logical and natural, it would seem, than for the participants in the talks to refrain at least from increasing their armed forces in this area while the talks are in progress. Precisely this step has been proposed several times by the USSR and its allies. For a number of years now we have refrained from increasing the size of our armed forces in Central Europe. How have NATO countries reacted to this example set by us? They have continued to build up their armed forces in this region.

What are we to do now? Maybe the Soviet Union should follow the example of the Western powers? But this is a negative example and, frankly speaking, we would not like to follow it.

Today we declare once again: we are prepared to refrain from increasing the numerical strength of our troops in Central Europe till agreement on the reduction of armed forces and armaments in that area is reached, provided, of course, that the NATO forces there will not grow either. Accept this proposal, esteemed partners in the talks, accept it as the first real step on the road to reducing armed forces! To be sure, nobody stands to lose from this, while the cause of peace, and the cause of the security of nations will only gain.

Comrades,

The Soviet people have weathered many trials. They have gone through the flames of war, experienced the agony of loss and the joy of victory. The happy life that the Soviet people have created for themselves by their own hands is a well-deserved reward. A well-deserved reward also are the thirty-two peaceful years which we have already had since the end of the war. This, I believe, is the longest period of peace in the entire centuries-long history of our country. At the same time wars and armed conflicts have flared up in the world more than a hundred times during the period since 1945 alone.

The Soviet people appreciate the peace-oriented policy of their Party. They are prepared to do, and are doing, everything that is necessary to make peace stable, lasting, and reliable. And I can say, comrades, that for me, just as for every one of us Communists to whom the Party and the people have entrusted the country's foreign-policy matters, there is no greater duty and no greater happiness than to work in the name of this noble, humane aim.

From Speech at Kremlin Dinner
for Fidel Castro Ruz

April 5, 1977

This speech was given during the friendship-promoting visit to the USSR made by Fidel Castro Ruz, First Secretary of the Communist Party of Cuba, Chairman of the State Council and the Council of Ministers, April 4 to 8, 1977.

Comrade Fidel, you have just visited a number of African countries. It was with much comradely interest that we followed this visit. It clearly showed that the policy pursued by socialist Cuba had broad international recognition. This policy, which has nothing in common whatever with any interference in the internal affairs of other states, is imbued with a noble striving to strengthen peace, and to help the peoples who have thrown off the hateful yoke of colonialism to uphold their gains and consolidate the independence of their countries.

The achievements of the Cuban revolution are a source of inspiration for many states which have freed themselves from the chains of colonialism. In the not so distant past Cuba itself experienced imperialist oppression and the sway of foreign exploiters. The revolution put an end to that. It ensured genuine independence for the country, freed the people from exploitation forever, ensured their right to work, threw the doors of the schools and higher educational establishments wide open to young workers and peasants, upheld the dignity of women, and gave every working man and woman confidence in the future. This is priceless capital, both political and moral.

The emergent countries regard the Soviet Union, Cuba, and other fraternal socialist states as friends who can be counted on. . . .

The enemies of Cuba, the enemies of socialism are spreading the most absurd concoctions about the aims and intentions of socialist countries with regard to the emergent states. But no slander can refute facts.

And the facts show that the socialist countries are always on the side of peoples who are confronted by imperialist aggression, *diktat,* and violence; that the socialist countries are developing equitable relations with the young states and are assisting their economic growth as much as they can; and, finally, that the policy of the socialist countries acts as a restraint on the forces of imperialism, the forces of the past which are trying to preserve the obsolete orders and to sow the seeds of enmity and conflict among the emergent states.

Sometimes our adversaries, and adversaries of the most varied kinds at that, present matters in such a way as to suggest that Asia, Africa, and Latin America are simply an arena for rivalry between socialist and capitalist countries, and in the first place between the Soviet Union and the United States. All this is totally false. The peoples of these continents have long ceased to be passive objects of history. Actively and with all their strength, they are struggling for their rights and searching for their road to progress.

And it can be regarded as something quite natural when these peoples, who have undergone immense suffering and humiliation in the course of imperialist domination, renounce the capitalist roads and choose a socialist orientation. Behind that choice stands the will of the masses, against which the bullets of hired assassins, acts of subversion, blackmail, and slanderous propaganda are helpless.

We welcome the progressive role played by the emergent countries, including the role of the nonalignment movement, in international politics, since this strengthens the preconditions for establishing a lasting peace.

It is our policy and our aim to secure the solution of one of the most important problems of our times—the problem of curbing and ending the arms race, and especially the nuclear-arms race.

Objectively speaking, there appears to be a good basis, especially as regards Soviet-U.S. relations, for taking practical steps in that direction. Of course, this basis should be strengthened and expanded. But, as recent contacts and talks have shown, instead of moving forward, our partners are departing from their constructive approach and are keeping so far to a one-sided position.

A reasonable agreement is possible, but it is necessary that not only we, but the other side, too, should fully realize its responsibility in curbing the arms race, and should search for mutually acceptable solutions not in words but by deeds.

From Speech at Kremlin Dinner for
President of Finland Urho Kekkonen

May 17, 1977

From May 17 to 24, 1977, Urho Kekkonen was in the Soviet Union on an official visit. The talks that were held during the visit resulted in the signing of a long-term program of development and deepening trade, economic, industrial, scientific, and technical co-operation to cover the period up to 1990.

As for the international situation as a whole, the main direction of the effort to consolidate détente and achieve a lasting peace still consists in the task of restraining the arms race and of moving on to a real reduction of armaments. Progress in talks between the USSR and the USA on these problems can certainly have considerable significance in this respect.

We are continuing the talks with the aim of concluding a new, a second, agreement on limiting strategic offensive arms. The guidelines for such an agreement were determined by the well-known 1974 Vladivostok accord. Successful completion of this great work would be of fundamental significance from the point of view of the general climate of Soviet-U.S. relations and would undoubtedly serve to stimulate new and still more far-reaching international actions to curb the arms race.

We are confident that this would definitely help to solve such important problems as the banning of all kinds of nuclear-weapon tests, the banning of new types and systems of weapons of mass destruction, and the limitation of the development and testing of a number of other kinds of arms.

I feel that attempts should also be made to discuss in detail such questions as the abolition of foreign military bases in the Indian Ocean and the withdrawal of ships carrying nuclear weapons from the Mediterranean. These questions should be settled on a mutually acceptable basis for the benefit of peace and the security of peoples.

In short, one can see that there are good prospects here. We feel that these prospects are completely realistic if all the participants in the talks show a sincere desire to strengthen peace and a true readiness to seek solutions that do not damage the interests of some states and do not give unilateral advantages to others. This is precisely the direction in which the Soviet Union will act.

The struggle to strengthen peace is not a policy of the moment for the Soviet Union. It is our principled course. When we set forth proposals aimed at strengthening détente in contemporary conditions, we also think constantly about its future and work to ensure its long-range prospects for many years and even decades ahead.

It is necessary to combine efforts so that the indicator of the world's political barometer should not constantly waver but should always point to "clear." This places a great responsibility on all who initiated the process of détente, who safeguarded its first moves, and who are introducing this policy into the broad arena of international life today.

From Address for French and
Soviet Television

May 29, 1977

In October 1976, Leonid Brezhnev appeared on a program
telecast to France in connection with Soviet Union Week on
French television. He made a similar appearance to conclude
France Week on Soviet television.

The importance of strengthening trust between countries in our time
is clear to everyone. Trust is exceedingly important when it concerns
such a delicate sphere of relationships as that of safeguarding the security
of every nation and of all nations. The crucial task here is to prevent the
further spiraling of the arms race.

Some people may say that much has already been said on this subject.
But truth is not a coin that wears out through frequent handling. What
is more, a spiral is not simply a repetition of what has already taken
place. Not only is the planet already oversaturated with means of mass
destruction, but there is a real and annually growing danger of new kinds
and new systems of weapons being created, weapons that will be many
times more destructive than the old ones. You might say, what else and
what more could there be? That's just it: the time has come to stop!

I am certain that not a single statesman or public figure and not one
thoughtful individual can evade his share of responsibility in the struggle
against the danger of war. For it is a matter of responsibility for the very
future of mankind.

Frankly speaking, our concern about the continued arms race, including the strategic-arms race, has grown because of the line taken on these
questions by the new American administration. That line is patently
geared to obtaining unilateral advantages for the USA. Naturally, such
a line is hardly conducive to the preparation and conclusion of a new
long-term agreement on the limitation of strategic arms between the
USSR and the USA, the drafting of which has been delayed long enough
as it is.

True, the meeting between the USSR Foreign Minister and the U.S.

Secretary of State in Geneva several days ago did show signs—compared to the Moscow talks in March—of some rapprochement between the sides' stands on some of the issues that had not been agreed upon earlier. But, frankly speaking, the fact is that no serious advance has so far been made owing to the unconstructive line of the USA. Clearly much effort will still be needed here. The most important thing is that the American administration should take a fully realistic stand and proceed from the principle of equality and equal security.

As for the Soviet Union, I have said this recently and shall repeat it again: we shall spare no efforts in the struggle not only for curbing the arms race—as regards both quantity and quality—but also for disarmament on mutually acceptable and equitable conditions. If it is impossible to move at one time the whole pile of related problems that have accumulated in the postwar years, we are prepared to take partial measures. "Partial" is only a modest name for them, but the realization of each of them would, to a certain degree, ward off the threat of war and ease the burden of the arms race, which weighs heavily on the shoulders of the working masses.

What measures do I have in mind?

I shall start with the problem of nuclear nonproliferation. The spread of nuclear weapons from country to country will not strengthen the security of any nation and will not in any way help to maintain the relative balance that has been established to date. It will, however, increase the danger of nuclear conflict, even if accidentally started, and then no "nuclear umbrellas" will afford protection from the lethal storm. That is why further efforts are required for achieving an effective and universal solution to this problem.

Further, we propose concluding an agreement banning the development of new kinds and systems of weapons of mass destruction. Everybody would only benefit by this.

Together with our Warsaw Treaty allies we suggested that the countries which participated in the Helsinki Conference should agree to pledge not to be the first to use nuclear weapons against one another. Negotiations on this issue and its solution would be important not only in themselves. I am confident this would also open new opportunities for the reduction of conventional arms in Europe, especially in places where their concentration is great.

I shall not enumerate everything we have proposed in the last few years with a view to reducing the threat of war. Our proposals on this issue are well known. We advance them because the policy of building up military might is coming into ever sharper and crying contradiction to the interests of international security. And our initiatives have only one purpose: to ensure security through curbing the arms race and through disarmament.

Of course, the positive solutions I speak of require the joint efforts of many states and peoples. And there is a wide field of activity here for each of them. There is no doubt that such a power as France could make a substantial contribution to this undertaking. We took note of what President Valéry Giscard d'Estaing said in his interview to French television on October 12, 1976, about France being dedicated to the idea of general, total, and effective disarmament. This is an important statement.

I have on more than one occasion spoken of the favorable influence exerted by détente on the entire world climate. I see no reason to change this estimate in any way. Nevertheless, it would be correct to say that détente has sowed a measure of complacency here and there.

I shall say again and again: the cause of peace and détente should be the concern of each and every one. What has been achieved in the consolidation of peace is not the limit, but, rather, the starting point for new actions. We are ready for them, and we hope that France will also move in the same direction.

In connection with the Belgrade meeting, which will be held soon, all the states that participated in the all-European conference have an opportunity once again to demonstrate their good will in practice. We would like the meeting to be, as it was conceived, the continuation and development of the Helsinki spirit and another link in the continuing process of détente. Can this be achieved? It can, if the meeting is prepared and held as an undertaking of co-operation and not of discord. Anyone who might try to orient it in a different direction would be assuming a great responsibility.

The strengthening of peace is one of the most important guarantees of the greatest human right—the right to life. But we understand life not simply as existence, but as existence worthy of a human being. Of course, different social strata and different political forces have different social ideals. Sixty years ago our people firmly and irrevocably decided on their road—the road to socialism and communism.

There are many indices, including figures, facts, and comparisons, by which to judge the results achieved on this road. It would take too long to speak of all this, so allow me to choose one yardstick—the place of man in society. Having taken it, we can say: every Soviet man is now confident that he will never be unemployed, that he will receive the necessary education, that all his abilities and talents will find application, that he will not be abandoned in case of illness, that he will have security in old age, and that he need not be anxious about the future of his children. I think that this is not so little. But that is not all that we have achieved and still less is it all that we are striving for.

The realization of the Tenth Five-Year Plan of national economic development of the Soviet Union, the guidelines of which were laid down by the 25th Party Congress, will create even more favorable social and economic conditions for the working people in our country. The new constitution of the Soviet Union, which will be adopted after a nation-wide discussion, will provide the political and legal base for the continued perfection of democracy in a developed socialist society. The new Fundamental Law of the Soviet state is to affirm the Leninist principles of the USSR's foreign policy—our consistent peace-loving policy. Appropriate clauses in the constitution will be in harmony with the new favorable tendencies developing in international relations.

From Replies to Shoryn Hata,
Editor in Chief of *Asahi Shimbun*

June 6, 1977

Besides the subjects dealt with in the questions and answers
of this interview, Leonid Brezhnev touched upon some problems of the Soviet Union's socioeconomic development after
the October Revolution and on Soviet-Japanese relations.

Question: I would like to ask this question on behalf of the only people
in the world who have fallen victim to nuclear weapons. What are the
prospects for nuclear disarmament and the strategic arms limitation
talks?

Answer: The Soviet Union has not forgotten the tragedy of Hiroshima
and Nagasaki, when the world first learned the meaning of nuclear
weapons. We share the feelings of the Japanese people about the unnecessary victims of the first atomic bombings.

The power of these weapons has now increased many times over, and
everyone agrees that the nuclear-arms race endangers peace and security
on our planet. It might seem that all states should exert efforts to halt
the further spread of nuclear weapons, ban their testing, and eventually
end the nuclear-arms race and abolish nuclear weaponry altogether. This
is what the Soviet Union is working for. Our country has always called
for a complete prohibition of nuclear weapons. It has been calling for
this since the time they first emerged. As is known, the UN General
Assembly, in 1972, adopted a Soviet-sponsored resolution prohibiting the
use of force in international relations and simultaneously banning for all
time the use of nuclear weapons. It is also a well-known fact that the
United Nations is currently studying the Soviet-proposed draft of a
world treaty banning the use of force in international relations, which
commits states to refrain from using any types of weapons, including
nuclear weapons. Unfortunately, little progress has been made so far
because of the negative position taken by a number of states. I can tell
you definitely that the Soviet Union is prepared at any time to sit at the

negotiating fable with all other nuclear powers to work out together practical ways of resolving the nuclear-disarmament problem.

For several years the Soviet Union and the United States have been conducting negotiations on strategic-arms limitations. We believe that substantial results have been achieved. The negotiations are still in progress. They are based on the well-known Vladivostok agreements. We are seeking an early and productive completion of the talks. This will be possible, of course, provided our partners give up seeking unilateral advantage. We will not accept an agreement that could impair the security of the Soviet Union or our allies.

Q: Pondering the situation in Asia, one comes to realize that the Soviet policy in Asia has a great role to play. What is your opinion about relations with the People's Republic of China, prospects for the development of the situation on the Korean peninsula, and the policy pursued by Southeast Asian nations, including Vietnam?

A: Historically, economically, and geographically, our country was and remains inseparably bound with the Asian continent. It is only natural therefore that we earnestly seek to consolidate peace in that area. We believe that having become a dominant trend of world development, détente should not bypass the Asian continent, where more than half of the world's population lives.

The historic victory of the Vietnamese people and the establishment of a large peace-loving state, the Socialist Republic of Vietnam, the settlement of the conflict in Southeast Asia, and the withdrawal of American troops from Indochina—all these events created, in our opinion, more favorable conditions for ensuring a lasting peace and security in Asia through the joint efforts of all states on the continent. This is just the development of events in Asia that the Soviet Union favors.

As regards Soviet-Chinese relations, our position is well known. We want to normalize interstate relations with China. The re-establishment of really good-neighborly relations between our two countries would be of great importance for the USSR and the PRC and would also improve the international situation as a whole.

It is through the fault of the other side that there is no sign yet of any improvement in Soviet-Chinese relations. Unfortunately, the new Chinese leadership is following the old, worn-out road, so to speak. It is common knowledge that a campaign of denunciation of the policy of détente continues and everything is being done to thwart any measures in the field of disarmament. Or take the thesis about struggle against "hegemony." Some people may fail to see anything dangerous in it. But isn't this thesis being used as a cover to sow strife between states or, at least, to prevent improvements in relations between them? What is the purpose of all this? Are there not any hidden motives running counter to the interests of peace and co-operation? We have a fairly definite view about this anyway, and Japan knows what this view is.

As regards the situation on the Korean peninsula, we support the proposal of the Democratic People's Republic of Korea for a withdrawal of all foreign troops from South Korea and for creating favorable conditions for the country's unification on a peaceful and democratic basis without any interference from the outside. We are not alone in holding this view. Judging by the UN General Assembly resolution urging the creation of favorable conditions for the turning of the armistice in Korea into lasting peace and the speeding up of a peaceful reunification of Korea, most UN member countries share it.

Message to the Conference of Writers
of Europe, the U.S., and Canada

June 8, 1977

This Conference was held in Sofia, Bulgaria, from June 7 to 9, 1977, under the title "The Writer and Peace: The Spirit of Helsinki and the Duty of Masters of Cultures." It was attended by writers from the countries that signed the Final Act of the Helsinki Conference.

I cordially greet the participants in the conference of writers of European countries, the United States, and Canada.

You have assembled in Sofia, the capital of the People's Republic of Bulgaria, nearly two years after the conclusion in another European capital, Helsinki, of the Conference on Security and Co-operation in Europe. It was a momentous event in the life not only of our own continent. It became at once an expression and a symbol of the deep shifts that are taking place in international relations. The Final Act signed there has helped, and continues to help, make grow stronger the wholesome shoots of lasting peace, the equal co-operation and reliable security of peoples, and the peaceful co-operation of states with different social systems.

However, in Europe as well as on other continents there still are those who would like to trample these shoots into the mud, to hurl mankind back to the "cold war" times and to prevent a radical improvement of the international atmosphere.

And here your voice, the voice of writers, who are called upon to be the conscience of their time, is particularly valuable. That is why your forum "The Writer and Peace: The Spirit of Helsinki and the Duty of Masters of Cultures" is an event that has been met in Europe and beyond it with great interest and justified hope.

It is gratifying to see those whose authority in society is so high, whose words are capable of touching the hearts, souls, and minds of millions, join in active struggle against the arms race, against all enemies of détente, security, and social progress.

For sixty years now, ever since Lenin's famous decree, the Soviet Union has been doing everything to uphold peace and secure the limiting and ending of the arms race and the development of the peaceful good-neighborly co-operation of all peoples. You may rest assured that any initiative aimed at strengthening détente, filling it with material content, and promoting the exchange of genuine cultural values will meet with energetic and sincere support on our part.

I wholeheartedly wish the conference participants success in their work and great creative achievements in the name of mankind's present and future.

From Replies to Questions by *Le Monde*

June 15, 1977

This interview was given by Leonid Brezhnev before his
official visit to France. In it he touched upon the development of Soviet-French relations since the top-level meeting
in Rambouillet in December 1974 and upon a number of
international issues.

Question: Many events have taken place in the world during this time.
The arms race is continuing. Africa is being shaken by stormy movements. Do you expect a stabilization of international relations or do you
believe that détente is being threatened?

Answer: First of all I would like to emphasize that in the past three
years the process of détente, the development of all forms of equitable
co-operation in the interests of all states and peoples, and the establishment of the principles of peaceful coexistence in international relations
have become a reality, and it is to an increasing extent determining the
course and nature of world developments.

Moreover, the atmosphere of détente is gradually becoming part of
the everyday life of people; it is becoming an everyday fact.

One needs only to look at how economic, cultural, sports, and other
ties have grown between dozens of countries and how international
tourism has expanded in order to realize the progress achieved in the
development of peaceful co-operation as compared to the period of the
so-called cold war and sharp confrontation.

But nevertheless we have never thought that everything has already
been done and that one can calmly reap the fruits of détente. We are
only at the beginning of a restructuring of international relations, which
all of us will have to carry out together. I say "all of us" because détente
should be universal and all-embracing. In our time, when technology, including military technology, is developing so rapidly, when the intercon-
nection of various areas of the world is becoming ever closer, any local
conflict can easily develop into a global one.

You mentioned the arms race. Unfortunately, it is continuing and
even mounting. The latest NATO recommendations aimed at increasing

the military spending of the members of that organization, the continuously swelling military budget of the United States, and that country's constant efforts to create more and more new types of weapons—all this shows that the ground is being prepared for a new spiral of the arms race. We are deeply convinced that the task of limiting armaments is central for preserving peace and further developing détente. If this diabolical race is not stopped, we will all once again find ourselves on the brink of the unpredictable, as in the years of the "cold war."

That is why our country is working so persistently and steadfastly for the adoption of effective measures for ending the arms race and ultimately achieving disarmament. No other country in the world has come forward with so many initiatives in this respect and advanced so many proposals as the Soviet Union. I declare with all responsibility that we are ready to support any proposal that would really lead to the termination of the arms race, but we definitely will not support proposals that contain only words about arms reduction and in reality are nothing but attempts to upset the balance of strength and to secure one-sided military advantages and thereby jeopardize the security of other countries.

We are realists and therefore, of course, we are clearly aware of the difficulties involved in solving these problems. However, it is precisely as realists that we declare that important prerequisites now exist in the world for making détente stable and irreversible, for concentrating the efforts of states on achieving a breakthrough on the question of disarmament.

Much depends here, of course, on public opinion. We know that in all countries, including France, broad sections of the public are deeply concerned about the question of disarmament. They have for a long time insisted that declarations in favor of disarmament be backed up by practical action, that a breakthrough on the matter of disarmament become a reality of world politics. We in the Soviet Union have deep respect for the views of these sections. They represent the aspirations of the peoples of the world and should be respected everywhere.

You mentioned Africa, and in a way that implied that the "stormy movements" there impeded détente and created instability in international relations. But that is not the case at all.

The peoples of the African continent are carrying on a resolute struggle for their freedom and independence, for the right to choose their road of development without outside interference. They are waging a struggle against the shameful phenomena of racialism and apartheid. This is a just struggle, and our country has always supported and will support such a struggle.

177

Instability in Africa is caused by something else. It is caused by external forces that are trying to prevent the African peoples from choosing the road they consider the most suitable for themselves. They are encouraging and inciting strife and provoking disputes over problems inherited by African peoples from colonial times. It is this policy that runs counter to the demands of détente and principles of peaceful coexistence, and may lead to the emergence of new centers of international tension. It is in this that we see the cause of instability in Africa.

The Soviet Union is resolutely against interference in the internal affairs of African countries. We do not seek any advantages or privileges for ourselves in Africa. Our policy on that continent, too, is directed at building peaceful, friendly relations with all peoples, at helping them to advance successfully along their chosen road of independence and progress.

Question: The view is becoming increasingly widespread in the West that the way out of the economic and moral crisis experienced by our societies lies in the search for a new world economic order, that is, in changing relations between the industrially developed and the developing countries. Do you share this view? To what extent could the Soviet Union take part in the search for, and in guaranteeing the stability of, this new order?

Answer: First, a clarification. You are evidently talking about the crisis that is gripping the capitalist countries. Neither the Soviet Union nor the other socialist countries are experiencing a crisis. True, to a certain extent we indirectly feel the consequences of the economic upheavals experienced by the capitalist world: for instance, in the course of our foreign-trade operations we have to take into account the process of inflation. But that is a different question altogether.

The restructuring of international economic relations on a democratic basis and the elimination from such relations of discrimination, *diktat,* and inequality are important demands of the present epoch, and the Soviet Union is consistently working for this. We have made concrete suggestions on this matter, including proposals submitted to the United Nations. Our country forms its economic ties with the countries of Africa, Asia, and Latin America, as with all other countries, on the basis of strict observance of equality, mutual advantage, and noninterference in internal affairs. We are giving all possible aid to many newly free states in overcoming the economic backwardness inherited from the past.

We are convinced that the development of international economic relations on the just principles of equality and mutual advantage and the ruling out of discrimination would accord with the interests of every nation and with the interests of strengthening peace and international security, although this will not save capitalism from crises.

I will emphasize another point: the Soviet Union, like the other socialist countries, naturally is not responsible either for the consequences of colonialism or for the harmful influence that the remaining inequality in economic relations has on the developing countries.

Question: Are you satisfied with what has been done to implement the Helsinki accords?

Answer: I think no one doubts today that the Helsinki accords could exert a great, positive impact on relations between states, on the situation in Europe and beyond. More than that, the Final Act signed in Helsinki has already become an important political reality in international life and is being actively implemented. Much has been accomplished, though, naturally, the extent of progress made is not the same in all fields. The Final Act—and all participants in the all-European conference agree with this—is a broad program of action to be carried out by the participating states for strengthening peace in Europe, a program projected for a long period ahead. I especially want to emphasize that this program could be more successfully implemented in the future if fewer attempts were made to poison the atmosphere of relations between states.

Question: Both parts of Europe are now in a state of peaceful co-existence on the military and political planes. There is co-operation in the economic sphere and antagonism in the ideological sphere. How long do you think such a situation can last?

Answer: Indeed, substantial progress has been made in Europe in recent years in developing equal, mutually advantageous co-operation based on the principles of peaceful coexistence. Good headway has been made toward turning Europe into a continent of lasting peace and security. This aim, we believe, is attainable. But even then, we are convinced, the ideological struggle, that is, the struggle of ideas, will not cease. And there is no contradiction here. Since there exist or, to be more exact, co-exist states with different social systems, the differences in views, ideas, and ideologies inherent in these systems remain and cannot be removed by any agreements. But in our time it would be senseless and dangerous to try to ensure the victory of particular ideas, of a particular ideology, by means of force, by the use of weapons. The ideological struggle should not grow into a "psychological war." It should not be used as a means of interference in the internal affairs of states and nations, nor should it lead to political and military confrontation.

Otherwise this ideological dispute may develop into a catastrophe in which millions of people, and with them their ideas and concepts, so to speak, will perish.

The conflict between the two social systems and between their ideologies can be settled only by life itself, by historical experience, by the test of practice. We Communists, of course, are deeply convinced of the advantages of the socialist system. We hold that socialist, communist concepts better meet the vital aspirations and interests of society and of every person individually and the interests of universal peace and social progress.

Question: How do you view the evolution of the Middle East situation? Do you think Israel may agree to the idea of a Palestinian state?

Answer: Our position on the Middle East is determined by our desire to see a dangerous center of tension eliminated, justice restored, and a lasting peace in the area ensured.

The task of achieving a Middle East peace settlement is acquiring ever greater urgency. In view of this, I think the fact that the Soviet Union and the USA, cochairmen of the Geneva Middle East Peace Conference, have agreed to work for the reconvening of the conference in the autumn of 1977 should be assessed positively.

Of course, a Middle East settlement involves not only the participants in the Geneva Conference, but all those who are interested in ending the conflict. We have always attached and still attach great importance to co-operation with France in this matter. We believe that France, in view of its international prestige and influence, can effectively facilitate a Middle East settlement and participate in its guarantees.

As to the second part of your question, it should be addressed to the Israeli government.

From Speech at Elysée Palace Dinner

June 21, 1977

From June 20 to 22, 1977, Leonid Brezhnev was in France on an official visit. It was his first trip to the West after the Helsinki Conference and his first visit to a foreign country in his new capacity as head of state. Considered in the course of the talks that were held were a number of key questions pertaining to further development of Soviet-French relations and a wide range of international problems.

Europe has not known war for a third of a century now. People are looking to the future with growing hope. This does not represent a gift from heaven, but is the result of deliberate efforts and purposeful actions by statesmen, political figures, and broad sections of people who are demanding lasting peace.

Peace in Europe, however, and still more in the world at large, is far from being as firm as one would wish it to be. It is threatened with many dangers, overt and covert. And the main danger is the uninterrupted and mounting arms race. The arms race is being instigated by the poisonous propaganda of militant opponents of détente, whose aim is to sow distrust and hostility between peoples and between states.

Even though I risk being accused of repeating myself, still I shall say once again: There is no more urgent problem, no more important task, than that of ending the arms race and introducing real disarmament measures. How much will all the fine words and declarations of loyalty to peace and all that has been achieved so far in the field of détente and peaceful co-operation among nations be worth if some day a spark flares up in a sensitive place and sets on fire all the stocks of the means of destruction capable of devastating the earth and of killing whole nations?

The prospect of the further proliferation of nuclear weapons in the world, as well as the creation of new, perhaps even more terrible and even more destructive types and systems of weapons of mass annihilation, constitutes a particularly grave danger under present conditions. The Soviet Union clearly sees the danger threatening mankind. Our country has been doing and will do everything in its power to prevent the development of such a dangerous situation. We would also like France to act vigorously in this direction.

It is important that all countries of the world take part in the examination and settlement of such a vital problem as disarmament and reducing the threat of a nuclear war. We believe that in order to ensure progress toward this objective all forums must be used—the United Nations and special international conferences, bilateral talks and broad public movements.

In short, in these matters, too, which literally affect the fate of the whole human race, we count on the understanding and support of the French Republic.

The basic document Principles of Co-operation Between the Union of Soviet Socialist Republics and France, signed in 1971, says: "The two sides shall give every assistance in the solution of the problem of general and complete disarmament, and first of all, nuclear disarmament." I think that it is our joint duty to act in such a way that this principle, like all the others in this document, is translated into practical deeds to the greatest degree possible by both our states.

The road to general and complete disarmament may still be long, but it is necessary to ensure a continuous advance toward this goal, so that there will be no halting on the way, so that every year and month will bring new practical steps in some field related to curbing the arms race, reducing the arsenals of states, and lessening the danger of nuclear war.

This means that the leaders of states must also devote constant and unremitting attention to these questions. It is clear, therefore, that such questions hold no small place in our exchanges of views these days with President Giscard d'Estaing and other French leaders. And I would like to express satisfaction over the fact that we are, it seems to me, increasingly finding a common language on these issues.

From Speech at Kremlin Reception for
Heads of Diplomatic Missions in Moscow

July 8, 1977

At the reception the heads of the diplomatic missions ac-
credited in Moscow congratulated Leonid Brezhnev on his
election as Chairman of the Presidium of the USSR Supreme
Soviet.

I believe that today at this meeting there is no need to discuss the
basic principles and directions of Soviet foreign policy. You cannot fail
to know them. I have no doubt that you thoroughly study and analyze
every move made by the Soviet Union in its bilateral relations with other
countries, and closely follow our actions in the international sphere,
whether in matters of world or of regional politics.

At the same time, you explain to us the policies of your states. This,
too, is an important function of an ambassador, and we appreciate it.

Being aware of the range of your responsibilities and concerns, I
should like to emphasize one point. It is only through profound knowledge of the policy of the state in which you work, only through carefully
weighed and unbiased assessment of concrete proposals or actions by
the Soviet Union, that it is possible to arrive at objective conclusions and
find the right path toward the truth.

And who can have a more subtle and accurate perception of the
political pulse of the country of their residence than ambassadors and
their embassies? Who but they, through their contacts and their information, can help to dissipate the misunderstandings and misconceptions
that sometimes arise between capitals? Who but they can see to it every
day that the intentions of both sides are understood correctly, that the
imaginary is not taken for the real and vice versa?

In a word, a lot depends on you, ambassadors, in creating an atmosphere of friendship and good will, of greater or lesser confidence in the
relations between your countries and the Soviet Union. Of course, in dis-
charging your important mission in the Soviet Union you will always meet

with assistance from the Presidium of the USSR Supreme Soviet and the Soviet government.

Today's international life is very dynamic. The opportunities to strengthen peace are growing, and growing constantly. At the same time the dangers threatening peace are growing as well. Evidently, one of the primary objectives of a farsighted policy and sensible diplomacy is to do everything to expand the range of opportunities and reduce the size of dangers. As I see it, the role of ambassadors and embassies in achieving this objective, too, is a big one.

I will tell you in passing that we exercise a similar approach to the work of Soviet ambassadors in foreign countries. So we do not apply any "excessively high" criteria in your case.

I take this opportunity to ask you to convey the following to your heads of state and leaders of your countries:

There is no country, or people in the world, in fact, with which the Soviet Union would not like to have good relations.

There is no outstanding international problem to the solution of which the Soviet Union would not be willing to contribute.

There is no center of war danger, the removal of which, by peaceful means, the Soviet Union would not be interested in.

There is no type of armaments and, most of all, weapons of mass destruction which the Soviet Union would not be willing to limit or prohibit on a reciprocal basis, in agreement with other states, and then to remove from the arsenals.

The Soviet Union will always be an active participant in any negotiations or any international action aimed at developing peaceful co-operation and strengthening the security of peoples.

It is our belief, our firm belief, that realism in politics and the desire for détente and progress will ultimately triumph, and mankind will be able to enter the twenty-first century in conditions of peace, stable as never before. And we will do everything in our power to see this come true.

From Speech at Kremlin Dinner for

Yugoslav President Josip Broz Tito

August 16, 1977

From August 16 to 19, 1977, Josip Broz Tito, President of Yugoslavia and Chairman of the League of Yugoslav Communists, was in the USSR at the invitation of the CPSU Central Committee and the Presidium of the USSR Supreme Soviet.

Our foreign policy is well known. It is a policy of peace and international co-operation. The 25th CPSU Congress described it quite distinctly. I myself and other comrades, members of the Politburo, have frequently spoken about it at various forums and meetings. I would like to stress one thing now: when a good initiative appears somewhere we are always ready to respond to it.

We are all familiar with the latest statements by U.S. President Carter. He speaks, in particular, about the desirability of developing Soviet-American relations for the sake of a stronger world peace. Compared with previous moves by the U.S. administration, these are positive-sounding statements. Well, if there is a desire to translate them into practical deeds we shall willingly search for mutually acceptable solutions.

From Speech at Kremlin Dinner for the
Prime Minister of India

October 21, 1977

From October 21 to 26, 1977, the Prime Minister of India, Morarji Desai, was in the USSR on an official, friendship-promoting visit. There was an exchange of opinions on a wide range of questions pertaining to Soviet-Indian relations and outstanding international problems.

Developments on the continent of Asia are of immediate interest for both our countries. Our Indian friends, we believe, are well acquainted with the Soviet Union's point of view. We are convinced that one of the most reliable means of achieving détente and security in Asia consists in joint efforts by the Asian states in a form they consider acceptable to themselves.

An agreement on curtailing military activities in the Indian Ocean would be in the interests of the peoples of Asia, and of the world at large. We are prepared to co-operate with India on questions concerning the Indian Ocean.

The greatest danger now threatening the peace and security of peoples is undoubtedly the continuing arms race. The basic task today is to halt it, to prevent the world from sliding down toward a nuclear catastrophe as if by inertia, by virtue of the terrible logic of building up military arsenals.

Of no small importance in this connection are the Soviet-U.S. strategic arms limitation talks. A definite change for the better has taken place recently in the course of these talks. We would like to bring these negotiations to a successful conclusion without unnecessary delays. Given a realistic and businesslike approach on the U.S. side, this is quite attainable.

As for Europe, the task of supplementing political détente with military détente assumes a special urgency. What can be done toward this end? As we see it, the following could be done:

To have the participants in the European Security Conference conclude a treaty undertaking not to be the first to use nuclear weapons against one another. The draft of such a treaty has already been proposed by the Warsaw Treaty countries. It is clear that provided all the parties to such a treaty observe it, this will rule out nuclear war in Europe, and also between European countries and the United States and Canada.

To agree, at least, not to enlarge the military-political groupings and alliances confronting each other in Europe, by admitting new members.

Consistently to translate into life such measures as have already been stipulated in the Final Act of Helsinki—notification of major military exercises, invitation of observers to some of the exercises, and exchanges of military delegations. The experience of two years indicates that these measures do to a certain extent promote greater trust and military détente. Bearing this in mind, we believe that it will perhaps be worthwhile to agree not to hold exercises above a certain level, that, say, of 50,000 to 60,000 men, since massive troop maneuvers cause apprehension and look rather like military demonstrations.

Should the countries of the southern Mediterranean wish that the military confidence-building measures envisaged by the Final Act also cover that area, which is adjacent to Europe, we would regard this with sympathy.

Such is the program of action that we are putting forward with the aim of achieving military détente in Europe.

It goes without saying that if other states have their own constructive proposals as regards this matter, we shall consider them seriously and with close attention.

All these problems could be discussed in detail in the near future—parallel with the current Vienna negotiations—through special joint consultations by all the states that took part in the Conference on Security and Co-operation in Europe.

We have always considered peace to be indivisible. And today this is perhaps truer than ever before. A military conflagration in one area can spread in a matter of hours to other continents, eventually engulfing the whole planet. On the other hand, real progress in strengthening peace and good-neighborliness in one part of the world can improve the entire international climate. We are confident, therefore, that peace-loving India duly appreciates the efforts toward strengthening peace in Europe.

From Report to Joint Meeting of the CPSU Central Committee and USSR and RSFSR Supreme Soviets on the Sixtieth Anniversary of the Great October Socialist Revolution

November 2, 1977

Soviet power was established under the sign of Lenin's Decree on Peace, and, ever since, our country's entire foreign policy has been one of peace. Objective historical conditions have dictated its concrete expression as the peaceful coexistence of states with different social systems.

In our day the principles of peaceful coexistence have by and large taken firm root in international affairs as the only realistic and reasonable principles. This is a result of the changed correlation of forces in the world—above all, of the growth of the strength and international authority of the Soviet Union and the entire socialist community. It is also a result of the successes of the international working-class movement and the forces of national liberation. And, finally, it is a result of the acceptance of the new realities by a certain section of the ruling circles in the capitalist world.

At the same time, it is a result of the tremendous work done in recent years by the Soviet Union and other countries of the socialist community to reshape international relations in the direction of peace.

The changes for the better in the world, which have become especially appreciable in the 1970s, we refer to as international détente. These changes are tangible and specific. They consist in the recognition and enactment in international documents of a form of code of rules for honest and fair relations between countries, which erects a legal and moral-political barrier against those given to military gambles. They consist in the achievement of the first agreements—modest though they may be for the moment—for blocking some of the channels of the arms race. They consist of a whole system of agreements covering many areas of peaceful co-operation between states having different social systems.

The changes for the better are most conspicuous in Europe, where good-neighborly relations, mutual understanding, and the nations' mutual interest in, and respect for, one another are gaining in strength. We prize this achievement, and consider it to be our duty to safeguard and consolidate it in every way. We therefore attach great importance to co-operation with such countries as France, the Federal Republic of Germany, Britain, and Italy—with all the European states, big and small, of a different social system.

It is natural, too, that we attach great importance to relations with the United States. There is much that divides our countries—from the socioeconomic system to ideology. Not everyone in the United States likes our way of doing things, and we, too, could say a great deal about the way things are in America. But if differences are accentuated, and if attempts are made to lecture one another, the result will only be a build-up of distrust and hostility, useless to both countries and dangerous to the world as a whole. At the very inception of the Soviet state Lenin made it clear to the American leaders of the time that "whether they like it or not, Soviet Russia is a great power" and "America has nothing to gain from the Wilsonian policy of piously refusing to deal with us on the grounds that our government is distasteful to them." This was true half a century ago. It is all the more true today.

Life itself demands that considerations of a long-term character, prompted by a concern for peace, be decisive in Soviet-American relations. This is the course we follow, and this is what we expect in return. There is no lack of will on our part to continue developing relations with the USA on the basis of equality and mutual respect.

International relations are now at a crossroads, as it were, which could lead either to a growth of trust and co-operation or to a growth of mutual fears, suspicion, and arms stockpiles, a crossroads leading, ultimately, either to lasting peace or, at best, to balancing on the brink of war. Détente offers the opportunity of choosing the road of peace. To miss this opportunity would be a crime. The most important, the most pressing task now is to halt the arms race, which has engulfed the world.

Regrettably, the arms build-up continues and is acquiring ever more dangerous forms. New modifications and types of weapons of mass destruction are being developed, and it is well known on whose initiative this is being done. But every new type represents an equation having several unknown quantities in terms of political as well as military-technical or strategic consequences. Rushing from one type of arms to another—apparently with the naïve hope of retaining a monopoly on them—only accelerates the arms race, heightens mutual distrust, and hampers disarmament measures.

In this connection I would like to reiterate, most forcefully, something I said earlier. The Soviet Union is effectively ensuring its defense capability, but it does not, and will not, seek military superiority over the other side. We do not seek to upset the approximate equilibrium of military strength existing at present, say, between East and West in Central Europe, or between the USSR and the USA. But in return we insist that no one else should seek to upset it in his favor.

Needless to say, maintaining the existing equilibrium is not an end in itself. We are in favor of starting a downward turn in the curve of the arms race and gradually scaling down the level of military confrontation. We want to reduce substantially and then eliminate the threat of nuclear war, the most formidable danger facing humanity. That is the objective of the well-known proposals made by the Soviet Union and other socialist countries.

Today we are proposing a radical step: that agreement be reached on a simultaneous halt in the production of nuclear weapons by all states. This would apply to all such weapons—whether atomic, hydrogen, or neutron bombs or projectiles. At the same time, the nuclear powers could undertake to make a start on the gradual reduction of existing stockpiles of such weapons, and move toward their complete, total destruction. The energy of the atom for peaceful purposes exclusively—this is the appeal of the Soviet state, in the year of its sixtieth anniversary, to the governments and peoples of the world.

There is another important task that has a direct bearing on the problem of reducing the danger of nuclear war, namely, that of seeing through to the end the work of banning nuclear-weapon tests, so that such tests are banned entirely—underground as well as in the atmosphere, in outer space, and under water. We want to achieve progress in the negotiations on this matter and bring them to a successful conclusion. Therefore, we state that we are prepared to reach agreement on a moratorium covering nuclear explosions for peaceful purposes, together with a ban on all nuclear-weapon tests for a definite period. We trust that this important initiative on the part of the USSR will be favorably received by our partners at the negotiations and that the road will thus be cleared for concluding a treaty long awaited by the peoples.

The Soviet Union is confidently pursuing a policy of peace. We actively and persistently call for the contest between socialism and capitalism to be decided not on the field of battle, not on munitions conveyors, but in the sphere of peaceful work. We want the frontiers dividing the two worlds to be crossed not by flight paths of missiles with nuclear warheads, but by threads of broad and diversified co-operation for the good of all mankind. By steadfastly pursuing this policy, we are giving practical expression to one of the main rallying cries of the October Revolution and carrying out one of Lenin's most important behests: Peace to the peoples!

If it should prove possible to solve the main problem—that of preventing another world war and establishing durable peace—new bright vistas would open before the inhabitants of our planet. There would then exist the preconditions for solving many other vitally important problems confronting mankind today.

What are these problems?

One such problem, for example, is that of providing enormous numbers of people with food, raw materials, and sources of energy. For according to the estimates we have, by the end of the century the population of the Earth will have increased from 4 to 6 billion people. Another problem is that of ending the legacy of economic backwardness bequeathed by colonialism in Asian, African, and Latin-American countries. This is necessary for normality in the future development of relations between states and generally for the progress of humanity as a whole. Finally, there is the problem of protecting man from the many dangers with which further uncontrolled technological development threatens him, in other words, the conservation of nature.

These are very real and serious problems. With every decade they will become more acute, unless a rational collective solution is found for them through systematic international co-operation.

Our world today is socially heterogeneous—it is made up of states with different social systems. This is an objective fact. By its internal development and by its approach to international relations the socialist part of the world is setting a good example of how the major problems facing mankind can best be solved. But, needless to say, it cannot solve them for the whole of humanity. What is needed is purposeful effort by the people of every country, broad and constructive co-operation by all countries, all peoples. The Soviet Union is wholehearted in its desire for such co-operation. In this—if one looks deeper—lies the essence of the foreign-policy course that we refer to as the policy of peaceful coexistence.

From Speech at Kremlin Reception for
Heads of Diplomatic Missions in Moscow

November 3, 1977

At the reception the heads of diplomatic missions congratulated Leonid Brezhnev and all Soviet people on the Sixtieth
Anniversary of the Great October Socialist Revolution.

You were probably present yesterday and today at the celebration
meetings in the Kremlin. They were devoted to the main results of the
six decades of struggle and labor by the Soviet people, and to our present
concerns and future plans. You have heard the high assessment given
our policy by the fraternal socialist countries, young independent states,
and all those who set peace, freedom, and progress as their goal.

In addressing you, I would like particularly to stress the continuity of
our policy from Lenin's time to this day. It has been and remains the
policy of peace and peaceful coexistence, of friendship among peoples,
and of international solidarity.

We proceed from the belief that our relations with other states—big,
medium, and small—can and must be relations of fruitful co-operation
and joint efforts aimed at achieving peace, détente, and disarmament.
And in most instances this is the case. Now we would like to hope that
good relations will continue to develop between us and all the countries
you represent here.

I repeat once again: peace, a peaceful future for the peoples, and
progress—this is the road along which the Soviet Union has traveled
and will steadfastly continue to travel.

Message to Visitors to the Soviet

National Exhibition in Los Angeles

November 12, 1977

The Soviet National Exhibition, which opened in the United States on November 12, 1977, was dedicated to the Sixtieth Anniversary of the Great October Socialist Revolution.

I heartily greet visitors to the USSR exhibition in Los Angeles and take this opportunity to extend my best wishes to all the citizens of the United States of America.

I hope the exhibition will give Americans a graphic idea of the life of our country, of what our people have achieved since the Great October Socialist Revolution, the sixtieth anniversary of which we have just celebrated.

Sixty years is a historically short space of time, but the changes that have taken place in the Soviet Union during this period are truly tremendous. From a backward country it has become a highly developed industrial state; from a country where unemployment, the suppression of national minorities, and the inequality of women were widespread it has become a country of genuine political, social, and national equality, a country where not a single person has been unemployed for more than forty-five years now; from a country where three-quarters of the population were illiterate it has become a country where three-quarters of all adults have a higher or secondary education, a country where more books are read than anywhere else in the world, where the number of visitors to theaters, concerts, museums, and exhibitions is greater than in any other state.

As I see it, even this brief enumeration of what has been accomplished in our country within a mere six decades makes clear why Soviet people take such pride in their revolution, cherish so greatly their achievements, and with such unanimity support the further strengthening of socialism, and communism. All this was displayed vividly during the recent nationwide discussion of the draft of the new constitution in which more than

140 million people—practically the whole of the country's adult population—took part.

This constitution has now been adopted. It embodies in law everything our people have achieved in the post-October years. For instance, it formulates explicitly the political freedoms and social and economic rights of citizens, and concrete guarantees of these rights, which include the right to work and to learn a trade or profession, the right to rest and leisure, the right to housing, free education, free medical assistance, maintenance in old age, and other rights. The motto of our society is: "The free development of each is the condition of the free development of all."

The new constitution also reflects the Soviet Union's striving for peace and co-operation with other countries and it gives legal force to the peaceable principles of the foreign policy of the Soviet state enunciated by its great founder, Vladimir Ilyich Lenin.

The preservation of world peace depends in large measure on the state of relations between the Soviet Union and the United States of America. A great deal has been done of late to remove the mutual distrust and estrangement of the "cold war" period. A number of Soviet-American summit meetings and the conclusion of important bilateral agreements have helped develop co-operation and improve mutual understanding between our countries and peoples. This has become one of the decisive elements in the relaxation of world tension.

We are prepared to proceed further along this path. Naturally, this is possible only given observance of the principles of equality, mutual account of the parties' interests, and noninterference in each other's internal affairs.

Four years ago I was on a visit to the United States and had the opportunity of visiting California. Meetings with American citizens convinced me that the possibilities for mutually advantageous co-operation between our countries are very great and that the people of the United States are sincerely striving for better mutual understanding, for friendship with the peoples of the Soviet Union. This is what all the Soviet people also desire.

I hope that the Soviet national exhibition will provide better acquaintance with the life of our country and will mark an important new step in improving mutual understanding between the peoples of the USSR and the USA.

Replies to Questions by
a *Pravda* Correspondent

December 24, 1977

Question: Now that the year 1977 is ending, what do you think is most characteristic of the international position of our country and its efforts for peace and détente?

Answer: A short time ago, during the jubilee celebrations, I had occasion to dwell in detail on various aspects of the Soviet Union's international position. So I shall touch upon only a few points.

First of all, the celebration of the sixtieth anniversary of the Great October Socialist Revolution and the adoption of the new constitution of the USSR became a vivid demonstration of the Soviet Union's high prestige in the international arena, its growing influence on the development of world events. The world could see once again that the state brought into being by the October Revolution has been pursuing in the international arena, consistently, on a principled basis, and with great success, a policy of peace and friendship among nations, an honest and just policy. In short, the kind of policy that should be pursued by a socialist country, the homeland of Lenin.

The new foreign-policy initiatives we advanced during the jubilee days met with a broad and, on the whole, favorable response. Some of them have already been put on a practical basis: they are being discussed at various forums, including the United Nations Organization and the Belgrade meeting.

The Soviet Union will continue to direct its efforts toward the complete removal of the threat of nuclear war, toward stabilizing the changes for the better in international relations, deepening détente, and broadening peaceful co-operation among states.

In this connection I would like to express the hope that my forthcoming visit to the Federal Republic of Germany, which is to take place shortly, and the talks with Federal Chancellor Schmidt will serve not only the further development of Soviet–West German co-operation in a number of fields, but also the broader interests of détente and of peace in Europe.

Just the other day the UN General Assembly adopted a very important and extremely timely document—a declaration specially devoted to the need for deepening and strengthening the relaxation of international tension. All UN member states voted for this declaration with the exception of China and Albania. This is a good mirror of world opinion. It correctly reflects the will of the peoples to reduce tension and safeguard peace. And how many other concrete and, I emphasize, really feasible proposals have been made by the Soviet Union, in particular in the field of disarmament! All this offers convincing proof of the dynamism and effectiveness of the foreign policy of the Communist Party and the Soviet state.

Question: What is your opinion of the state of affairs as regards disarmament?

Answer: Such an important area of work in the foreign-policy sphere as disarmament is always in the field of vision of the CPSU Central Committee and its Politburo. An important place in this respect is occupied, for understandable reasons, by the Soviet-American strategic offensive arms limitation talks. There is no lack of willingness on our part to bring these talks to a successful conclusion. In our opinion there exist opportunities, and very good ones, for this. To judge by some statements, the American side also expresses some optimism. We would wish this optimism to be backed by practical deeds. I think that a new agreement would be a good and important thing both for the USSR and the USA, and for world peace.

The present disarmament talks cover a broad spectrum of issues—from termination of all nuclear tests and prohibition of chemical means of warfare to consolidation of relaxation of military tension in Europe and curtailing of military activities in the zone of the Indian Ocean. The initiative in raising these questions belongs, to a considerable extent, if not overwhelmingly, to the Soviet Union. The main thing now is to move on from talks on disarmament to real steps that would mean the beginning of disarmament. This and this alone will really accord with the aspirations of the peoples who want lasting peace and who resolutely condemn actions aimed at increasing the threat of a new world war and condemn the arms race.

And such actions do occur. How else could one assess, for example, the persistent stepping up of the arms race in the NATO military bloc? This is an extremely dangerous tendency for mankind. It is becoming even more dangerous with the appearance of ever more barbarous means of warfare.

Take, for instance, the neutron bomb. This inhuman weapon, especially dangerous because it is presented as a "tactical," almost "innocent" one, is now being persistently foisted upon the world. In this way an attempt is being made to erase the distinction between conventional and nuclear arms, to make transition to a nuclear war outwardly unnoticeable, as it were, to the peoples. This is a downright fraud, a deception of the peoples.

The neutron bomb is being insistently recommended for deployment in Western Europe. Well, this may be an easy and simple matter for those who live far from Europe. But the Europeans, who live, figuratively speaking, under one roof, are presumably of a different opinion. They will hardly care to have an additional dangerous load placed on this common roof of theirs, which is sagging as it is under the enormous weight of weaponry.

The Soviet Union is strongly opposed to the development of the neutron bomb. We understand and wholly support the millions of people throughout the world who are protesting against it. But if such a bomb were developed in the West—developed against us, a fact nobody even tries to conceal—it should be clearly understood there that the USSR will not remain a passive onlooker. We will be confronted with the need to answer this challenge in order to ensure the security of the Soviet people, their allies and friends. In the final analysis, all this would raise the arms race to an even more dangerous level. . . .

We do not want this to happen and that is why we propose reaching agreement on the mutual renunciation of the production of the neutron bomb, so as to save the world from the advent of this new mass-annihilation weapon. This is our sincere desire, this is our proposal to the Western powers.

Question: What could you say about the present developments in the Middle East?

Answer: Middle East affairs are an acute problem. Of late, changes, unfortunately of a negative character, moreover, have taken place in it. And they have taken place at the very time when it seemed that things were moving in a positive direction, toward the convocation of the Geneva Peace Conference, and when much had already been accomplished to this end, including what was done through the joint efforts of the USSR and the United States as cochairmen of the Conference. Today, however, the situation has been sharply aggravated. The convocation of the Geneva Conference and the reaching of an over-all settlement in the Middle East have become more difficult.

The course of recent events in the Middle East is well known. I would like to stress here only the following. The Soviet Union has been and remains a consistent advocate of an over-all settlement in this region of the world, with the participation of all the sides concerned, including, of course, the Palestine Liberation Organization. A settlement that would envisage the withdrawal of Israeli troops from all the Arab territories occupied in 1967; realization of the inalienable rights of the Palestine Arab people, including their right to self-determination, to the creation of their own state; guaranteeing of the right to an independent existence and security of all the states directly involved in the conflict, both the Arab countries, neighbors of Israel, and the state of Israel; ending of the state of war between the Arab states concerned and Israel. Only if these fundamental provisions are implemented will peace in the Middle East really be durable and not turn into a precarious armistice.

We by no means consider that the road of unilateral concessions to Israel and separate negotiations with it, such as the notorious talks between the Egyptian and Israeli leaders, leads to this goal. On the contrary, it leads away from it, creating a deep split in the Arab world. This line has the purpose of thwarting a genuine settlement, and primarily of undermining the Geneva Conference even before it opens.

The lavish praising of the imaginary "advantages" of the so-called direct talks, that is, of Israel's negotiations with each of the countries subjected to its attack, is actually nothing but an attempt to deprive the Arabs of the strength that lies in their unity and in the support given to their just cause by friendly states.

This is why the USSR stands for the convocation of the Geneva Conference, moreover in conditions that would rule out the possibility of its turning into a screen covering up separate deals to the detriment of the interests of the Arabs and the cause of a just and lasting peace. This is our stand. It is fully supported by the Soviet people and approved by the peace-loving forces of the whole world.

From "A Historic Stage on the

Road to Communism"

1977

This article, published in *World Marxist Review,* No. 12, the theoretical and informational magazine of the Communist and Workers' parties, was written in connection with the adoption of a new constitution of the USSR. It summed up the results of the work of the CPSU and the Soviet people following the victory of the October Revolution and outlined prospects for the country's further development. The excerpts given here deal with the international significance of the new constitution.

Yet another aspect of the international importance of the new Soviet constitution is that in both spirit and letter it serves the cause of peace, the security of the peoples, the strengthening of the anti-imperialist solidarity of all progressive forces.

All the aims and thoughts of our people revolve around peaceful, creative endeavor. In the USSR and other socialist countries, as distinct from the imperialist states, there are no classes or social groups that have any interest in the arms race, in military preparations. By including in the new constitution a special chapter enacting the peaceful character of the foreign policy of the Soviet Union, our people have once again stressed their determination to follow the Leninist course of peace, the course of ridding humanity of the horrors of war, of the material hardships and mortal dangers implicit in the arms race. This chapter contains clauses corresponding to the fundamental obligations that the Soviet Union has undertaken as a participant in vital international agreements, including the Final Act of the Helsinki Conference. Indisputably this imparts additional weight to the efforts that are being made in the world for a further normalization of the international situation, for the development of détente.

The Soviet Union is a component of the world system of socialism. A profound and consistent international solidarity unites our Party, the whole people, with the progressive liberation forces of the world, with the international Communist movement. It is natural therefore that the constitution should clearly reflect the class character of the Soviet state's foreign policy, its social ideals and political sympathies, its traditional support of the peoples' struggle for national liberation and social progress. It also reflects the positions that have been worked out by the CPSU on a collective basis with the other Communist parties and that have been recorded in their joint documents, for example, at the Berlin Conference of Communist and Workers' Parties of Europe.

In short, our constitution elevates to the rank of a state law of the USSR that which constitutes the very essence of the foreign policy of the socialist state—its concern for peace, for the creation of international conditions consonant with the struggle for national freedom and social progress, for socialism and communism.

From Speech Aboard Cruiser

Admiral Senyavin in Vladivostok

April 7, 1978

During his tour of several cities in Siberia and the Far East, Leonid Brezhnev visited industrial enterprises and construction projects. He also paid a visit to military units of the Far East and the Pacific Fleet and took part in naval exercises aboard the cruiser *Admiral Senyavin*.

In considering the plans worked out by the Party for the further development of our country and the problems of economic growth, we cannot, of course, ignore the way the international situation unfolds.

The present state of affairs in the world is characterized by a turn toward a relaxation of international tension. The consistent implementation by our Party of a Leninist foreign policy and the purposeful efforts of the Soviet Union, the fraternal socialist states, and all the peace forces and peoples have played a tremendous role in achieving the impressive successes on this road.

These successes did not come easy; they were achieved by intense struggle. And the struggle over the question of the further destiny of détente is still going on, at times becoming even more acute and persistent.

Comrades,

For all the significance of this or that problem, there is no more important task at present than that of achieving real disarmament; this is a task that concerns the destiny of every person on earth. The main problem now is to stop the arms race, to ensure progress toward reducing and eventually removing the threat of a thermonuclear disaster. It is here, in this direction, that the basic question—the question of how the world situation will develop further—will be decided; and it is here that the most bitter struggle is unfolding.

It is no secret that both to the west and to the east of our frontiers there are forces that are interested in the arms race, in working up an atmosphere of fear and hostility. They sow doubts as to the possibility of taking

---

practical steps to limit armaments and achieve disarmament, and hamper efforts to reach agreement in this field.

The activities of these forces have an adverse effect on the position of the USA and of some other countries that are partners of the Soviet Union in the talks on curbing and stopping the arms race.

As is known, a Soviet-U.S. summit meeting took place in the Far East, in Vladivostok, in November 1974. It led to an accord on the conclusion between the USSR and the USA of a long-term agreement on the limitation of strategic offensive arms. Having assessed all aspects of the matter, the two sides concluded that it would be possible to complete the drafting of the agreement in the following year, 1975.

However, almost three and a half years have passed since that time and an agreement has not yet been signed. I have already had occasion to mention the reasons for this. The experience of the talks and our earlier agreements in this sphere show that given proper awareness of the great importance of the problem and a real desire to reach agreement on the basis of equality and equal security the sides can together resolve what would seem to be the most complex of problems. And the documents that are being prepared now have already been thrashed out and have been largely agreed upon.

And if the final completion of this work is, nevertheless, being delayed, this is, evidently, due to political reasons. The point is that the United States government is both indecisive and inconsistent; it constantly looks back over its shoulder at those circles that have been against this agreement from the very start and that are now doing everything they can to thwart it and thus to free their hands for carrying on an uncontrolled missile nuclear-arms race. That is apparently why the U.S. side has repeatedly attempted during the talks to amend in its favor or to call into question what was agreed upon earlier, and, instead of conducting a businesslike discussion, has tried to raise all kinds of questions behind which is concealed only one thing—the absence of a readiness to look for practical solutions. Moreover, it has shown a tendency to link in some way progress at the talks and the future of the agreement in general with other political problems in the hope of bringing pressure to bear on the Soviet Union.

Such a policy line on the part of the United States manifested itself soon after the Vladivostok meeting. As a result of this, work on the agreement was practically stalled and even set back in several aspects.

Great efforts were required to put the talks back on the track of the Vladivostok accord. But this has finally been done. Principled solutions of some remaining questions have been found and the range of questions still to be worked upon has, on the whole, been considerably narrowed. This has been achieved largely owing to the Soviet Union's patient and constructive stand.

It is understandable, however, that the remaining questions cannot be solved without the United States taking steps and meeting us halfway. But, frankly, we have not seen such steps of late. One gets the impression that some people in the United States are inclined to interpret our readiness to conclude an agreement as an opportunity for the USA to gain unilateral advantages. This is the only way to explain the continued attempts at the talks to erode somehow the understanding reached, for instance, on limitations on Cruise missiles or to impose unjustified limitations on Soviet missiles while leaving for the United States full freedom of action for modernizing and creating new types of practically all components of strategic arms.

We resolutely reject any attempts to impose unacceptable terms of agreement on us. We have said and we say now that the Soviet Union stands for the earliest achievement of an agreement, but only the kind of agreement that would be strictly in keeping with the principle of equality and equal security and that would really embody this basic principle. We do not demand that the agreement give us any advantages at the expense of the other side, but we expect the other side to take a similar approach. There can be no other solution.

Further delay and all kinds of maneuvers around the talks can only lead to missing the very opportunity to conclude an agreement and, hence, an opportunity to move on later to more far-reaching steps to limit and reduce strategic arms. It is our firm conviction that such a prospect cannot benefit anyone.

We would like to hope, therefore, that proper conclusions will be drawn in Washington and that a course will be finally taken there toward a fruitful completion of the talks.

There are a whole number of other disarmament questions which are now being discussed and whose solution is long overdue. Our constructive proposals on this matter are well known. Also well known is the broad series of concrete measures our country has proposed for consolidating the relaxation of military tension in Europe. We intend to work persistently for the implementation of all these measures.

Statements in favor of disarmament have been made lately in the West, the USA included. But the peoples of the world judge not by words but by deeds. The question of neutron weapons provides a good example of this. This is a new type of mass-destruction weapons. Any talk about such weapons being "defensive" in character does not correspond to reality.

These are nuclear offensive weapons, weapons designed chiefly to destroy people. This weapon increases the risks of a nuclear war.

Faced with a mass protest movement against the plans to develop and deploy these weapons in Europe, the USA and some other NATO countries are trying to mislead the peoples by pretending that they are ready to hold talks with the Soviet Union on this question while in fact they are trying to make it the subject of bargaining and tying this weapon to unrelated issues. Concealed behind all this is only a desire to evade considering the clear-cut and concrete Soviet proposal for mutual commitment not to manufacture neutron weapons. Such maneuvering, of course, does not testify to any serious intention to achieve disarmament. Nor does it facilitate progress toward this goal.

It is high time some leaders of the West ponder in earnest their responsibility to their own peoples, to all peoples for the destiny of the world, and show in deed a readiness to take effective steps toward curbing the arms race.

The Soviet Union, for its part, will continue its efforts to achieve a steady advance along the road of military détente and the transition to real disarmament. Such is our firm policy and we shall continue to implement it unswervingly.

Comrades,

We do not threaten anyone. The talk about the so-called Soviet menace is an invention of the opponents of the relaxation of international tension and nothing more. We are improving our defenses for the sole purpose of upholding the gains of the Great October Revolution, of safeguarding the peaceful work of the Soviet people, of our friends and allies. It is this noble aim that the Soviet Army and Navy serve.

From Speech at the 18th Congress of

the Komsomol (Young Communist League)

April 25, 1978

The 18th Congress of the Leninist Young Communist League, the highest forum of the league, which has nearly 38 million members, was held in Moscow during the last week of April 1978.

Comrades, your fathers spent their youth in soldier's uniform at the front in the Great Patriotic War. This was truly, as the poet said, "a battle not for glory but for life upon the Earth." Many years have passed since then. Today more than half the population of our country knows about the war, its hardships and suffering, only from the stories of their elders, from books and films. But in different conditions the fight for life on Earth continues today, too. To secure lasting and stable peace—this is the aim of our foreign policy and of its fundamental principles, such as peaceful coexistence and détente.

Today détente is not just a theory or a slogan, or wishful thinking. It has to its credit quite a few good, perfectly specific and tangible deeds. In Europe it has laid the groundwork for relations between states and embraced various fields in their life. For all the ups and downs in Soviet-American relations, these, too, have a new appearance, more favorable to peace. The policy of détente has been recognized and is supported by the peoples as the only sensible policy in our troubled times.

The most essential and urgent task today is to secure a further easing of the war danger and to check the arms build-up. All peoples are aware of this and most of the governments of the world recognize it. This is also borne out by the fact that, for the first time in history, a session of the UN General Assembly specially devoted to arms limitation and disarmament will open in a few weeks' time. We wish it success and we shall actively promote this.

We are in favor of general and complete disarmament. It is not our fault that the talks on this problem, now nearly twenty years old, are deadlocked. And yet agreements on arms limitation in certain fields have been concluded during this period. And talks are continuing on a number of questions.

The central goal of our struggle for peace in the present circumstances is to reduce the menace of another world war and of the mass extermination of people with nuclear weapons. For this purpose the Soviet Union has taken several major steps. One of these is the negotiations with the United States on the limitation of strategic offensive arms.

As you know, Moscow has just been visited by the U.S. Secretary of State, Cyrus Vance, who came on President Carter's instructions. There was a thorough exchange of opinions. As a result, some progress was made in working out an agreement on strategic-arms limitation. By no means have all problems yet been resolved. We cannot accept at all certain positions of the American side. I believe, however, that through mutual efforts based on sensible and realistic compromise we can complete the drafting of an agreement that will justly take into account the security interests of both powers. This will enable us substantially to bridle the arms race and will therefore also help to strengthen peace.

For several years now the Soviet Union has been pressing for an agreement on the general and complete banning of nuclear-weapons tests. We are negotiating with the United States and Britain on banning tests in all media, that is to say, including underground tests. And we are gratified to note that definite progress has been made of late in these talks. We would like to hope that the work will be completed and an appropriate treaty will be signed in the near future. This will be a notable achievement in the struggle for peace and international security.

Along with other peace forces in the world, the Soviet Union is taking active steps to prevent the development of the neutron weapon, which is a new and particularly inhuman weapon of mass annihilation. Our stand on this issue is absolutely clear and radical: that the countries concerned should, before it is too late, conclude an agreement reciprocally renouncing the manufacture of this weapon. And may mankind be delivered from it once and for all.

Unfortunately, the United States, which is poised to develop the neutron bomb, has not yet agreed to our proposal. But President Carter has recently declared that he has postponed a final decision on starting the manufacture of the neutron weapon. This, of course, does not settle the matter and is at best a half-measure. However, I can say that we have taken the President's statement into account and that we, too, will not start production of neutron weapons so long as the United States does not do so. Further developments will depend on Washington.

In line with its fundamental policy aimed at reducing the nuclear-war danger, the Soviet Union has also decided to subscribe in due form to the international treaty banning nuclear weapons in Latin America. Thereby, we, like the other nuclear powers, will take a pledge not to help any Latin-American state gain access to nuclear weapons, and not to use such weapons against the states party to the treaty. . . .

So, as you see, comrades, the work for peace is continuing and our country is making ever new efforts to this end.

We intend that my forthcoming visit to the Federal Republic of Germany should also not only help determine the prospects for further broad and mutually advantageous co-operation between our two countries —which is important in itself—but also contribute to consolidating détente and universal peace, especially in Europe.

Of late the opponents of détente and disarmament in the NATO countries—all those generals who dabble in politics and all those bellicose politicians—have been raising a propaganda howl and spreading lies about an allegedly threatening military superiority of the Warsaw Treaty states over the NATO bloc in Europe, about alleged Soviet aggressive intentions in Europe, and the like. All this is nonsense, needless to say. Not harmless, but malicious, nonsense, however, because it serves to justify and camouflage actions that are truly dangerous and potentially aggressive: precipitating another round in the arms race, building up military forces and contaminating the international atmosphere with poisonous fumes of fear, suspicion, and hostility.

More than any other country, does the Soviet Union, which suffered the greatest ravages in the Second World War, want peace in Europe never to be violated again and Europe to be a continent of lasting peace and peaceful co-operation. And, perhaps, no other state has done more for this than our country.

For some years, at the talks in Vienna, we have been working for a considerable reduction of the armed forces of the West and East in Europe—without prejudice to the security of any side—but we have so far encountered only attempts by the West to change the balance of forces in its own favor. A few days ago in Vienna, it is true, the Western countries submitted slightly refurbished proposals. These take note of the standpoint of the socialist states in some respects, although the general impression of a one-sided approach clearly remains. Well, we intend to continue our work. We are prepared to do everything in our power to find mutually acceptable solutions and to relieve military tension in a region of the world where it is especially great and dangerous.

Everybody should know that, far from harboring any aggressive designs and building up any "strike forces" in Europe for action against the West, the Soviet Union has always done and will continue to do everything it can to relieve tensions and to facilitate agreement. Unlike the NATO countries, we have not for a long time increased our armed forces in Central Europe, and we do not intend—I wish to stress this most emphatically—we do not intend to increase them by a single soldier, by a single tank.

And we call on the Western states to follow this good example.

Trying to distort the meaning and goals of Soviet foreign policy, imperialist propaganda maintains that there is a contradiction between our country's policy of détente and peaceful coexistence and our relations with countries that have thrown off the colonial yoke. The Soviet Union and other socialist countries are being falsely accused of interfering in the affairs of young states. Our opponents go so far as to accuse us of an "expansionist policy" and "stoking up tension." All this, of course, is sheer fabrication with no basis in fact.

We want friendly co-operation with those countries on a basis of complete equality. We support their independence and their advance along the road of peace and social progress. The Soviet Union invariably advocates strict respect for the sovereignty of those—and all other—states, for non-interference in their internal affairs, and for the inviolability of their frontiers.

It is the imperialist powers which are continuously interfering—openly or under slight camouflage—in the affairs of independent, newly free states. They are interfering in order to obstruct their progressive development. They infringe on their sovereignty in order to secure the selfish interests of their own monopolies or the plans of their own military strategists.

As a rule, such interference leads to violence and encroachments on the rights of the peoples. This occurs either in the home life of the countries concerned, as, say, in the case of Chile, or in the form of undisguised foreign aggression, as in the case of the brazen conduct of the Israeli rulers.

The facts show that the peoples of the young states are able to defend their independence and vital interests more successfully the more solid their unity and solidarity and the more solid their friendship with the countries of the socialist world, on whose support they may rely in their just struggle.

One does not have to look far for examples of this, too. It was thanks to the solidarity of progressive forces that attempts by the imperialists and their puppets to overthrow the people's government in Angola and to dismember revolutionary Ethiopia were foiled.

Peace, noninterference in internal affairs, respect for independence and territorial integrity, equality and mutually beneficial co-operation—all these are the indispensable and the most important elements of détente and lasting peace. Such is our policy in Europe, and it is the same in Africa, Asia, Latin America, and everywhere else in the world. And if anyone thinks that the Soviet Union can be diverted from this course by means of slander and threats, then he is deeply mistaken.

Comrades, analyzing the world situation, we have arrived at the firm conviction that it is high time to give thought to putting a *complete stop to any further quantitative and qualitative growth in the armaments and armed forces of states with a large military potential,* and thereby to create conditions for their subsequent reduction. Specifically, we are calling for discussion of a program of the following measures, to be put into effect within a definite time limit:

• to stop manufacturing nuclear weapons of all types;

• to stop manufacturing and to ban all other types of mass-destruction weapons;

• to stop developing new types of highly destructive conventional arms;

• to renounce the expansion of the armies and the increase of the conventional armaments of the permanent members of the UN Security Council and countries associated with them under military agreements.

It is certainly not simple to agree on such matters. We could probably tackle one particular angle first—say, the stopping of nuclear-arms manufacture, as we have already proposed. The main thing is that the problem as a whole is made easier to solve by the fact that these steps would not upset the balance of forces now existing between states. Nobody would be the loser.

We must not, nor have we the right to, forget that the nuclear peril is still hanging over the world and arousing the alarm of nations for their future. Joint efforts by all the nuclear powers are obviously needed to remove this peril. And each of them can and must do its bit. For its part, the Soviet Union declares unambiguously: we are against the use of nuclear weapons; only extraordinary circumstances, an act of aggression against our country or its allies by another nuclear power, could compel us to resort to this extreme means of self-defense. The Soviet Union is doing and will continue to do everything to prevent an atomic war, so that the nations will not fall victim to atomic strikes—neither a first strike nor subsequent ones. This is our firm line, and we will act accordingly.

To preserve this Earth of ours and to hand it over to the rising generation with all its wealth and beauty unblemished by a nuclear holocaust —this, as we see it, is the goal to which the thoughts of humanity should be directed. The Soviet Union is doing everything in its power to maintain and consolidate peace. We trust that your future, dear young friends, will be the happiness of free labor on a peaceful planet.

From Interview Given to *Vorwärts*

May 4, 1978

Leonid Brezhnev gave this interview to the weekly newspaper of the Social Democratic Party of West Germany on
the eve of his official visit to that country.

Question: What opportunities do you see for taking concrete steps
toward further détente in Europe?

Answer: Further détente in Europe largely depends on how matters
will proceed in resolving urgent questions of détente in the military field.
It can even be said that we have reached the point where the process of
political détente should merge with the process of military détente. That
is why the most important thing now is to take practical steps to re-
strain the arms race, to curb this race.

As everyone knows, the Soviet Union has set forth a whole program of
measures for military détente. They include the pledge not to be the first
to use nuclear weapons, nonexpansion of existing military groupings, and
limitation of the number of troops taking part in maneuvers.

Naturally, the political aspect of the matter must also not be forgotten
for a single moment. The climate in Europe favoring military détente is
being shaped on the basis of a comprehensive development of relations
among states, a strengthening of trust among their leaders, respect for
treaties that have been concluded, and consistent fulfillment of the agreements reached at the conference in Helsinki.

Many people in the West favor our suggestions for holding all-European congresses on co-operation on environmental protection, transport,
and energy. It would seem that it is possible to get down to business, but
unfortunately even here our Western partners are slow to respond and
inconsistent.

And there is another point. We also do not want West Berlin to remain
a blank spot on the map of European détente. We have often come up
against attempts to circumvent the quadripartite agreement. There have
been actions that show a real unwillingness to accept the fact that the city
is not a part of the FRG. This all contradicts the spirit of détente and

complicates the international situation. We cannot appraise this matter in any other way.

Thus, there are many factors determining the destiny of détente. One would like to hope that only those that facilitate its consolidation come into play.

Question: There are apprehensions—and not only in the FRG—that the Soviet Union is building up its military strength qualitatively and quantitatively, systematically and consistently, to an extent surpassing defense requirements. Don't you also believe that détente calls for agreements in the military fields as well—on the basis of parity?

Answer: To begin with, let me point out one main thing: the apprehensions you allude to are totally groundless.

A Soviet military threat with regard to Europe or to any other part of the globe does not exist and cannot exist.

Let us first look at the purely factual aspect of the question.

With regard to Europe: In the press of Western countries and in the comments of certain Western political and military leaders, one frequently comes across the allegation that the Soviet Union and other Warsaw Treaty member countries have attained "military superiority" on the European continent over the NATO countries and continue to build up their armed forces there.

This, to put it mildly, is a tendentious and misleading allegation.

Let me start by saying that for a number of years now the Soviet Union has not been building up and increasing its armed forces in Central Europe, that is, in that area about which talks are now proceeding in Vienna. Furthermore, in these talks we and our allies keep proposing to the Western side that the two sides commit themselves directly not to increase their armed forces and arms in Central Europe for the entire period in which the Vienna talks are under way. Regrettably, the Western countries have not so far accepted our proposal, while the practical steps they have taken are in the opposite direction.

As regards "superiority," at those same talks in Vienna, the sides have exchanged official statistics clearly showing that no "superiority" or "disproportion" exists at all. The West and the Warsaw Treaty countries have an approximately equal number of troops in Central Europe, a little over 980,000 men on each side.

Naturally, this parity is not full equality. Each side has its own structure of armed forces. We, let us say, are superior in land-force missiles, whereas the NATO bloc is superior in air-force missiles with nuclear warheads, and so on.

Furthermore, Western military and political leaders frequently claim that the West has what is in their opinion a qualitative superiority in arms. One may well ask: Where, then, is the logic in the assertions of those same circles concerning the imaginary "threat from the East"?

By and large, in Europe, where the main forces of the two military-political groupings confront each other at close range, a military equilibrium undeniably does exist. The question is whether it is necessary to maintain this equilibrium at such a high level as at present, whether this level can be lowered without upsetting the balance in anyone's favor. We in the Soviet Union are firmly convinced that it can and should be lowered.

As regards the global correlations of forces between the biggest participating powers in these two military-political groupings, that is, the Soviet Union and the United States, here, as is officially acknowledged by both sides, a rough parity, that is, a balance of strategic forces, has taken shape and is maintained. It is precisely this parity that lies at the basis of the Soviet-U.S. agreement on strategic offensive arms limitation, concluded in 1972, and also at the basis of the agreement now being drawn up.

I can add that the over-all numerical strength of Soviet armed forces also does not spell any "military threat" to the West at all, though it is enough, if necessary, to deliver a retaliatory blow at the aggressor, no matter where he may be, in the West or in the East. Incidentally, this is well understood and admitted by unbiased observers, including those of the U.S. press.

And now about our Navy. First of all, I will recall a simple fact, namely that the Soviet Union has more than 40,000 kilometers of sea borders. With the NATO countries having strong offensive means on the high seas, we are obliged to think about corresponding defense in this sphere, too. We have built an ocean-going fleet of our own which can carry out the tasks of such defense. The potential of this fleet does not exceed that of the fleet of the Western countries, but, from the standpoint of structure, it is of a purely defensive nature. For instance, it is not accidental that we do not have and are not building strike aircraft carriers.

Another favorite subject of those who like to talk about a "Soviet military threat" is the civil-defense measures taken in the USSR. It may seem incredible, but it is a fact that even these measures, which are aimed at ensuring the safety of the peaceful population in the event of war, are interpreted by the experts in anti-Soviet slander as a sign of "aggressiveness": the USSR, you see, is getting ready for the "first strike," hoping to take cover in shelters from a retaliatory one.

One must truly have a pathologically distorted imagination to turn everything upside down in this way! Can any normal person really believe such concoctions?

We do not want war and we are not preparing for a war, but the Soviet people know from their own bitter experience what immense losses among the population can be caused by an aggressor's actions. We have heard too often talk by the other side about its readiness to deliver "strong, destructive, pre-emptive strikes" and so on, not to take any measures for defense. Only shameless slanderers can regard this as preparation for an attack against anyone you wish.

Alien to us is the callous quantitative approach to the prospects of a nuclear war, an approach that is popular in some other countries, where a certain percentage of losses among the civilian population is declared "acceptable." We are not heartened at all by the predictions, which can be heard in the West, that "only ten percent" of the planet's population will perish in a world nuclear war and that this, you see, will not be so dreadful; it will not be the end of the world. We do not wish anyone, not a single person, to fall among those "ten percent."

As for the Soviet Union, I repeat, it is not thinking of "making a first strike." On the contrary, everyone knows very well our official proposal to all the participants in the all-European conference, including the United States, that an agreement be concluded on not being the first to use nuclear weapons against each other. It is also common knowledge that the NATO countries reject this proposal, making it rather transparently clear that they are reluctant to give up their plans of delivering the first strike against our country. Who then is threatening whom?

Such is the factual aspect of the matter.

Now let us look at its political aspect.

The Soviet Union is indeed a powerful state; it is powerful in a political, economic, and military sense. But the Soviet Union is a peaceful state. Its peaceableness stems from the very nature of our society, where the supreme goal, proclaimed by the laws and decisions of the highest political bodies, is to work for the steady growth of the material well-being and cultural standards of the people. There is not a single task that we intend to acomplish by military means. There is not a single state to which we would lay territorial or any other claims, fraught with the danger of a military clash. Furthermore, the Soviet people, including the Soviet leaders, know very well and remember from their own experience what war is like in our times. Those inhabitants of the Federal Republic of Germany who belong to the older generation also have an idea of what war is like, and possibly they would understand much better than, say, the inhabitants of the United States, the Soviet people's fervent desire to live in peace.

The main "argument" in the discussion in the West about the notorious "Soviet military threat" consists in ascribing to the Soviet Union some kind of sinister intentions arising from its military potential. Talk about the number of hours it will take the Soviet Army to reach the English Channel is an example of this kind of word juggling.

But the Soviet Union has no intention of attacking any state, in either the west, east, north, or south. The Soviet Union is not at all getting ready to "conquer" Western Europe. And our General Staff is not working on the timetable of any "plan to reach the English Channel." The framework of Soviet military development is determined by the country's defense needs. And in assessing the defense needs of the USSR, it is also necessary to remember the geographic position of our country. The real Soviet intentions are clearly outlined in official Party and state documents. They can also be judged by the whole moral and political atmosphere in which the Soviet people live and are educated. Propaganda of militarization, calls for preparations for war, and the whipping up of distrust and animosity toward other nations are all alien to this atmosphere.

The history of the Soviet state provides many examples of its peaceableness. It clearly shows the real causes and sources of military danger. It shows why we have to devote serious attention to questions of national defense. When, in the early days following the October Revolution, our state urged all the belligerent powers to conclude a peace treaty, the Western countries responded with joint hostile intervention. When, from the high international tribune, the USSR came out in the thirties for ensuring European collective security, the response was the Munich agreement and the Hitler aggression that followed it. When, after the defeat of the aggressor, the Soviet Union began rebuilding its war-ravaged economy, the West launched a "cold war" against us and began blackmailing us with atomic weapons, evidently in the belief that the USSR, weakened by the war, would bow to *diktat* from outside. And when in our times the Soviet Union advances concrete, realistic, and far-reaching proposals for curbing the arms race and for disarmament, neutron weapons are brandished in response.

By the way, anyone who is familiar with postwar history will recall that the arms race developed according to the "action-counteraction" pattern: when the West issued a challenge, the Soviet Union had to accept the challenge. This was the case throughout, from the first atomic bomb down to our times. And the start of each new round in the arms race was invariably accompanied by a fresh outcry of "Soviet threat."

There is one more thing I would like the esteemed readers of your paper to recall. It was not we, but the United States, who set up dozens of military bases, with bombers and submarines with nuclear and other long-range weapons, bases that stretched out in an ominous chain along the borders of the USSR and our allies in the south, north, west, and east. I would like to suggest to those who today are sowing groundless fears and hysteria in connection with the Soviet Union's understandable defense undertakings, and also to those who believe these sowers of panic, at least for a short time to put themselves mentally in the place of the Soviet people. After all, our country has been encircled by these bases for several decades. It would be interesting to know what these nervous gentlemen would say in such a situation.

Soviet people, however, have strong nerves. They have never panicked and will never panic; they take the necessary steps to defend the country against a rising danger and work persistently and consistently for a lasting peace, for a lowering of the level of military confrontation, first of all, in Europe.

Frankly, it seems to me that those who today are fanning the artificial campaign in the West about a "Soviet military threat" are really thinking of something else. They do not want to reconcile themselves to the rough equilibrium that has taken shape in the balance of military forces of the sides, and want to achieve superiority. This is dangerous, because such an approach will prompt a fresh unbridled race in arms production and is fraught with the danger of military gambles. But these people must, at last, realize one thing, namely: to any military challenge, the Soviet Union has always found, and, you can be sure of it, will find in the future, the proper reply.

As for the Soviet Union, it considers that approximate equilibrium and parity are enough for defense needs. We do not set ourselves the goal of gaining military superiority. We also know that this very concept loses its meaning with the present enormous stockpiles of nuclear weapons and systems for their delivery.

The Soviet Union is firmly opposed to an "equilibrium of fear." We stand for equilibrium of trust. That is why we have so persistently proposed that détente be deepened and the level of international co-operation be raised and its content enriched, and that there be a persevering search for an effective way, first, of ending the arms race and, later, of achieving disarmament.

We are ready at any moment to sign an agreement in Vienna on a reduction of the armed forces and arms of the sides in Central Europe by five, ten, twenty, and, if you like, by fifty percent. But let us do this honestly, so as not to upset the existing correlation of forces, and so that there will be no gain for one side and no loss for the other. Let us carry out such steps as are realistic and acceptable to both sides right now, and not try to use the talks for gaining unilateral military advantages.

This is my answer to your question.

From Speech at Prague Meeting

May 31, 1978

This speech was made during the official friendship-promoting visit to Czechoslovakia by a Communist Party and Soviet
government delegation headed by Leonid Brezhnev.

Much has been done in recent years to improve the international situation, particularly in Europe. The residents in the same house of Europe,
so to speak, now do not only greet each other, but also speak to each
other in peaceful terms, and have learned to co-operate quite well in many
matters. This was clearly in evidence during my recent visit to the Federal
Republic of Germany. We have, in our opinion, worked out an extensive
program for raising the level and quality of our mutual relations. This
program, meeting, naturally, the interests of both countries, is no less concerned with consolidating détente on the European continent.

A durable peace in Europe is, beyond all doubt, one of the major preconditions for preventing another world war. The Helsinki Conference,
held three years ago, created all opportunities for the development of good
relations on the European continent. A solid political foundation, it would
seem, has thus been laid for détente. But some political quarters have
since come to the fore in an obvious attempt to wreck the process of
détente, both in Europe and elsewhere, and to return to a "chilly" war,
if not a "cold" one.

The same attempt is, of course, behind such acts as the savage intervention by NATO countries in Zaïre, a cynical operation which the men
behind it have been trying to cover up by launching a noisy propaganda
campaign about an alleged "Soviet" or "Cuban" involvement in the affair.

Another fact is that many important initiatives of the socialist countries,
undoubtedly meeting the interests of the European peoples and, indeed,
those outside of Europe, have not received the attention they deserve, although everybody would quite obviously stand to gain from them.

There is no question that the ground for peaceful co-operation of states
has been badly damaged because of the continuing arms race. To put an
end to it and take practical steps toward disarmament—this is the great
task today, not only for governments and not only for those wielding

power. It is a task for all political parties and political trends, for trade unions and other social organizations, and for the mass media. Nobody has the right to stand aloof from it. One cannot expect that the present course of events will be reversed, that is, from the arms build-up to disarmament, without vigorous efforts on the part of the international community and of the broadest possible spectrum of political forces.

It is our fervent wish to bury the ax of war so deep under the ground that no sinister forces could ever dig it out again. This is the purpose behind our proposals for merging political détente with military détente and for conducting all-encompassing negotiations on disarmament, including nuclear disarmament.

We approach the talks on curbing the arms race in all seriousness and in good faith. We are against fruitless verbal exchanges and against such talks coming to resemble that "disarmament conference," if one may say so, that was held up to ridicule by Jaroslav Hašek. You may recall that his heroes, stupefied after endless night-long sessions and banquets, began to urge everybody to arm himself, as if out of good intentions.

A special disarmament session of the UN General Assembly has been meeting in New York for the past few days. Its participants are discussing the disarmament problem in its entirety for the first time in UN history.

The Soviet Union and the fraternal socialist countries have set forth at the session proposals and initiatives which have been thoroughly considered and which are designed to lead to constructive efforts and practical results.

Our position on disarmament issues is, to put it briefly, as follows. There is no type of arms that the USSR would not be prepared to limit and ban on a reciprocal basis agreed upon with other states. The important thing is that all this should be done without damage to anybody's security and on terms of complete reciprocity of states in possession of the armaments in question. It is important that the desire to stop the arms race should be sincere, and not ostentatious.

Unfortunately, the position of our major partners in the negotiations is full of contradictions. Here is a good case in point.

A top-level NATO Council session is now under way in Washington. Some of its participants stopped over in New York, on their way to or from the NATO meeting, to utter some high-sounding words about disarmament at the special UN session. Meanwhile, at the NATO Council session, the participants, in the same breath, as it were, are discussing further plans for military preparations for many years ahead. So, where are the Western powers talking business and where are they bandying words?

219

It is high time to realize that the arms race can do no one any good. It must be stopped, and an honest effort must be made to achieve disarmament.

The socialist countries have done much work to get things started on the way to disarmament. And however great the obstacles may be, we shall move on, together with all supporters of the policy of peace and good-neighborly relations, in search of a dependable and complete solution to this urgent problem.

From Speech upon Presenting the Order
of Lenin and the Gold Star Medal to
the Hero City of Minsk

June 25, 1978

The capital of Soviet Byelorussia, Minsk, was awarded the honored title of Hero City for its outstanding service to the country, for the valor and heroism shown by its citizens in the struggle against the Nazi invaders, the important role it played in organizing a mass guerrilla movement during the Great Patriotic War, and in celebration of the thirtieth anniversary of Byelorussia's liberation from Nazi occupation.

Here, on Byelorussian soil, over which the bells of Khatyn ring like a tragic warning, one especially feels how important is the persistent struggle for peace the Soviet Union is waging, a struggle to prevent the outbreak of a new world war.

The UN General Assembly's special session on disarmament is drawing to an end in New York. It has reaffirmed the profound interest of all mankind in terminating the arms race. The overwhelming majority of UN members have spoken out in favor of disarmament.

The Soviet Union and other socialist countries have submitted to the session a broad, bold, and at the same time realistic program for a complete termination of the arms race. Their proposals have been the main subject of businesslike discussion at the Assembly.

The session has also shown that the leaders of several major NATO countries, and above all the USA, clearly do not wish to display a constructive approach to the implementation of disarmament tasks. How else is one to appraise the holding of the NATO Council session in Washington which adopted a new long-term armament program at a time when the special session of the UN General Assembly in New York was discussing a diametrically opposite problem—how to curb the arms race and achieve disarmament? Is this not disregard for the vital concerns and expectations of peace-loving peoples? It appears that in Washington the NATO countries were laying down a "real policy" while in New York they participated in the discussions only to distract attention, so as not to draw just criticism and censure.

The Peking rulers are coming forward in support of this position. It seems that their representative was confused as to the rostrum from which he was speaking. With his bellicose speech he should have spoken not in the United Nations, but at the NATO bloc's session.

By the way, this line taken by Peking is well appreciated in Washington. Of late, attempts have been made in the USA—at a high level and in a rather cynical form—to play the "Chinese card" against the USSR. This is a shortsighted and dangerous policy! Its authors may bitterly regret it.

The General Assembly session is completing its work. The ideas and proposals put forward at the session will undoubtedly live on and exert their influence. The struggle for the implementation of practical steps to curb the arms race and bring about disarmament continues and must be intensified.

One of the main trends of development in this sphere is the Vienna talks on limiting armed forces and armaments in Central Europe. I have spoken on many occasions about this problem and, to tell the truth, it was with a heavy heart that I did it. Actually, the fifteenth round of the talks has begun; the talks have been going on for almost five years now, but no practical results are yet in sight. But this question is not a trivial one; it matters much for Europe and for the international situation as a whole.

Having carefully considered the situation, the socialist countries have taken an important new step aimed at breaking, at long last, the impasse the negotiations have reached. Our countries have submitted in Vienna new wide-ranging and concrete proposals, taking the entire experience of these talks into account.

What are the most important points in these proposals?

First, these are absolutely clear-cut, precise proposals. They put down concrete figures of Soviet and U.S. troops that would be withdrawn in the first stage. And these figures are fairly large. The USSR, for its part, is prepared to withdraw a total of three divisions, with relevant military equipment, including about a thousand tanks, in the course of a year.

Second, a reduction of the armed forces of the NATO and Warsaw Treaty countries is to be carried out in such a way as to preserve their balance or, as one says, their parity. As a result of the reduction of the forces of all countries, an equal ceiling would be established for each of the groupings in Central Europe.

By the way, the very idea of such a ceiling is in line with what was proposed by the Western countries. But, of course, we firmly believe that none of the participants in the talks has the right, hiding behind others' backs, to try to evade a reduction or, all the more so, build up his armaments at the expense of reductions made by others.

The socialist countries are suggesting to their partners a reasonable and workable compromise. By submitting their proposal they have in fact gone farther than their half of the road. We say to the NATO countries: Let us get down to business at last. The basis for agreement, undoubtedly, already exists. Everything now depends on the political will of the West.

The achievement of an agreement in Vienna would make it possible in future to move on to the discussion of other specific issues of European military détente that are of interest to the sides.

The improvement of the political climate in Europe is one of the most important peace achievements of the last decade. This could particularly be felt during our recent visit to the Federal Republic of Germany.

There is hardly any other country in Europe, along the way of establishing relations, with which there would be so many obstacles—objective and subjective—and where each step would be so difficult. However, relations between the USSR and the FRG today, without shutting one's eyes to the negative aspects, have become one of the main elements of stability in Europe, of détente on the Continent.

A long road in the development of relations has been traveled by the Soviet Union and France; our ties are developing in a positive direction in all spheres with Italy, Sweden, and Austria, and, of course, with our neighbor, friendly Finland.

The visit to the Soviet Union by the Turkish Prime Minister, Mr. Ecevit, has been a practical contribution to the advancement of peaceful co-operation between countries participating in the all-European conference. The talks with Mr. Ecevit and the signing of a political document on the principles of good-neighborliness and friendly co-operation between the USSR and Turkey mark an important stage in the development of our relations along the road charted long ago by Lenin and Ataturk.

In general I agree with the words of West German Chancellor Schmidt, who declared recently from the rostrum of the General Assembly that there is much more mutual trust in Europe now than there was in past decades.

But this common gain of the peace-loving states of Europe must be constantly buttressed, strengthened, and extended. This is especially important today when international tensions are once again being aggravated. It is Europe that can show in practice how nations should coexist, co-operate, and work together.

The struggle for a lasting peace is not only a matter for governments, but also for peoples. Back in the middle of the last century Karl Marx appealed to the working class to master the secrets of international politics and fight vigorously for peace among nations. This idea lives on in the consciousness and actions of the broad working masses and their political vanguard.

The vital interests of the working people of all countries demand that all the achievements of the last few years in the world arena not be cast aside and that efforts be made to advance toward a genuinely lasting peace for all nations. By the combined efforts of all peace-loving forces this aim can be achieved, and we believe it will be achieved.

Appendix I

Basic Principles of Relations Between
the Union of Soviet Socialist Republics
and the United States of America

The Union of Soviet Socialist Republics and the United States of America,

Guided by their obligations under the Charter of the United Nations and by a desire to strengthen peaceful relations with each other and to place these relations on the firmest possible basis,

Aware of the need to make every effort to remove the threat of war and to create conditions which promote the reduction of tensions in the world and the strengthening of universal security and international co-operation,

Believing that the improvement of Soviet-US relations and their mutually advantageous development in such areas as economics, science and culture, will meet these objectives and contribute to better mutual understanding and business-like cooperation, without in any way prejudicing the interests of third countries,

Conscious that these objectives reflect the interests of the peoples of both countries,

Have agreed as follows:

First. They will proceed from the common determination that in the nuclear age there is no alternative to conducting their mutual relations on the basis of peaceful coexistence. Differences in ideology and in the social systems of the USSR and the USA are not obstacles to the bilateral development of normal relations based on the principles of sovereignty, equality, non-interference in internal affairs and mutual advantage.

Second. The USSR and the USA attach major importance to preventing the development of situations capable of causing a dangerous exacerbation of their relations. Therefore, they will do their utmost to avoid military confrontations and to prevent the outbreak of nuclear war. They will always exercise restraint in their mutual relations, and

---

will be prepared to negotiate and settle differences by peaceful means. Discussions and negotiations on outstanding issues will be conducted in a spirit of reciprocity, mutual accommodation and mutual benefit.

Both sides recognize that efforts to obtain unilateral advantage at the expense of the other, directly or indirectly, are inconsistent with these objectives. The prerequisites for maintaining and strengthening peaceful relations between the USSR and the USA are the recognition of the security interests of the Parties based on the principle of equality and the renunciation of the use or threat of force.

Third. The USSR and the USA have a special responsibility, as do other countries which are permanent members of the United Nations Security Council, to do everything in their power so that conflicts or situations will not arise which would serve to increase international tensions. Accordingly, they will seek to promote conditions in which all countries will live in peace and security and will not be subject to outside interference in their internal affairs.

Fourth. The USSR and the USA intend to widen the juridical basis of their mutual relations and to exert the necessary efforts so that bilateral agreements which they have concluded and multilateral treaties and agreements to which they are jointly parties are faithfully implemented.

Fifth. The USSR and the USA reaffirm their readiness to continue the practice of exchanging views on problems of mutual interest and, when necessary, to conduct such exchanges at the highest level, including meetings between leaders of the two countries.

The two governments welcome and will facilitate an increase in productive contacts between representatives of the legislative bodies of the two countries.

Sixth. The Parties will continue their efforts to limit armaments on a bilateral as well as on a multilateral basis. They will continue to make special efforts to limit strategic armaments. Whenever possible, they will conclude concrete agreements aimed at achieving these purposes.

The USSR and the USA regard as the ultimate objective of their efforts the achievement of general and complete disarmament and the establishment of an effective system of international security in accordance with the purposes and principles of the United Nations.

Seventh. The USSR and the USA regard commercial and economic ties as an important and necessary element in the strengthening of their bilateral relations and thus will actively promote the growth of such ties. They will facilitate cooperation between the relevant organizations and enterprises of the two countries and the conclusion of appropriate agreements and contracts, including long-term ones.

The two countries will contribute to the improvement of maritime and air communications between them.

Eighth. The two sides consider it timely and useful to develop mutual contacts and cooperation in the fields of science and technology. Where suitable, the USSR and the USA will conclude appropriate agreements dealing with concrete cooperation in these fields.

Ninth. The two sides reaffirm their intention to deepen cultural ties with one another and to encourage fuller familiarization with each other's cultural values. They will promote improved conditions for cultural exchanges and tourism.

Tenth. The USSR and the USA will seek to ensure that their ties and cooperation in all the above-mentioned fields and in any others in their mutual interest are built on a firm and long-term basis. To give a permanent character to these efforts, they will establish in all fields where this is feasible joint commissions or other joint bodies.

Eleventh. The USSR and the USA make no claim for themselves and would not recognize the claims of anyone else to any special rights or advantages in world affairs. They recognize the sovereign equality of all states.

The development of Soviet-US relations is not directed against third countries and their interests.

Twelfth. The basic principles set forth in this document do not affect any obligations with respect to other countries earlier assumed by the USSR and the USA.

MOSCOW, *May 29, 1972*

For the Union of Soviet
Socialist Republics

LEONID I. BREZHNEV

General Secretary of the
Central Committee,
CPSU

For the United States
of America

RICHARD NIXON

President of the
United States
of America

Appendix II

Agreement Between the Union of Soviet Socialist Republics and the United States of America on the Prevention of Nuclear War

The Union of Soviet Socialist Republics and the United States of America, hereinafter referred to as the Parties,

Guided by the objectives of strengthening world peace and international security,

Conscious that nuclear war would have devastating consequences for mankind,

Proceeding from the desire to bring about conditions in which the danger of an outbreak of nuclear war anywhere in the world would be reduced and ultimately eliminated,

Proceeding from their obligations under the Charter of the United Nations regarding the maintenance of peace, refraining from the threat or use of force, and the avoidance of war, and in conformity with the agreements to which either Party has subscribed,

Proceeding from the Basic Principles of Relations Between the Union of Soviet Socialist Republics and the United States of America signed in Moscow on May 29, 1972,

Reaffirming that the development of relations between the Union of Soviet Socialist Republics and the United States of America is not directed against other countries and their interests,

Have agreed as follows:

ARTICLE I

The Soviet Union and the United States agree that an objective of their policies is to remove the danger of nuclear war and of the use of nuclear weapons.

Accordingly, the Parties agree that they will act in such a manner as to prevent the development of situations capable of causing a dangerous exacerbation of their relations, as to avoid military confrontations, and as to exclude the outbreak of nuclear war between them and between either of the Parties and other countries.

ARTICLE II

The Parties agree, in accordance with Article I and to realize the objective stated in that Article, to proceed from the premise that each Party will refrain from the threat or use of force against the other Party, against the allies of the other Party and against other countries, in circumstances which may endanger international peace and security. The Parties agree that they will be guided by these considerations in the formulation of their foreign policies and in their actions in the field of international relations.

ARTICLE III

The Parties undertake to develop their relations with each other and with other countries in a way consistent with the purposes of this Agreement.

ARTICLE IV

If at any time relations between the Parties or between either Party and other countries appear to involve the risk of a nuclear conflict, or if relations between countries not parties to this Agreement appear to involve the risk of nuclear war between the Union of Soviet Socialist Republics and the United States of America or between either Party and other countries, the Soviet Union and the United States, acting in accordance with the provisions of this Agreement, shall immediately enter into urgent consultations with each other and make every effort to avert this risk.

ARTICLE V

Each Party shall be free to inform the Security Council of the United Nations, the Secretary General of the United Nations and the Governments of allied or other countries of the progress and outcome of consultations initiated in accordance with Article IV of this Agreement.

ARTICLE VI

Nothing in this Agreement shall affect or impair:

(a) the inherent right of individual or collective self-defense as envisaged by Article 51 of the Charter of the United Nations,

(b) the provisions of the Charter of the United Nations, including those relating to the maintenance or restoration of international peace and security, and

---

(c) the obligations undertaken by either Party towards its allies or other countries in treaties, agreements, and other appropriate documents.

ARTICLE VII

This Agreement shall be of unlimited duration.

ARTICLE VIII

This Agreement shall enter into force upon signature.

DONE at Washington on June 22, 1973, in two copies, each in the Russian and English languages, both texts being equally authentic.

For the Union of Soviet Socialist Republics:	*For the United States of America:*
L. I. BREZHNEV	RICHARD NIXON
General Secretary of the Central Committee, CPSU	*President of the United States of America*

Index

military-industrial complex, 59–60, 148
military strength, 58, 90, 177, 190, 207,
212, 213, 216
   Europe, 54, 111, 120, 121, 161, 190,
212, 221
   U.S. 111, 190, 216
   USSR, 111, 120, 161, 190, 207, 208,
212, 216, 222
Mongolia, 47
Mourousi, Yves, 127

national liberation movements, 34, 38,
42, 47–48, 58, 60, 61, 120, 123,
154, 188, 200
NATO, 50, 58, 90, 108, 109, 111, 120,
121, 122–123, 129, 138, 146, 148,
154, 160, 161, 176–177, 196, 204,
207, 208, 212, 213, 218, 219, 221–
222, 223
Nazism, Nazis, 22, 35–36, 221
neutron bomb, 190, 196–197, 203–204,
206, 215
Ngouabi, Marien, 154
Nixon, Richard M., 11, 13, 14, 16, 17,
18, 19, 20, 21, 22, 23, 24, 26, 28,
29, 31, 45, 70, 74, 77, 78, 79, 107
Non-Aligned Nations' Conference
(Algiers), 51
nonuse of force in international affairs,
45, 53, 112, 113, 121, 135, 138,
143, 147, 171
nuclear age, 5, 16, 52, 113, 134–135
nuclear war danger, 5, 18, 19, 23, 31,
37, 44, 57, 58, 59, 61, 68, 85, 86,
88, 89, 107, 116, 128, 133, 135,
136, 143, 144, 145, 149, 167, 168,
182, 186, 187, 189, 190, 191, 195,
197, 201, 204, 205, 206–207, 209,
214, 218, 221
nuclear weapons, 17, 27, 37, 52, 54, 56,
58, 59, 70, 101–102, 110, 112, 121,
123, 129, 132, 135, 143, 148, 151,
160, 161, 165, 168, 171, 181, 190,
204, 206, 207, 209, 211, 214, 216
   banning of, 91, 110, 111, 113, 121,
135, 138, 143, 148, 165, 168, 171,
190, 209
   nonproliferation of, 59, 110, 135,
144, 151, 168
   reduction of, 54, 77, 111, 115–116,
143, 148, 190
   stopping tests, 59, 71, 77, 110, 113,

115, 121, 138, 143, 147, 160, 165,
168, 171, 190, 196, 206
   Warsaw Treaty pledge, 143, 148,
160, 168, 186–187, 214

Pakistan, 46
Palestinians, 49, 50, 138, 152, 159,
180, 198
Pastorino, Enrique, 35
Patolichev, Nikolai, 81
Peace Program (CPSU), 9, 14, 28, 34,
37–38, 44, 67, 68, 98, 104, 109,
111, 114
peaceful coexistence, *see* coexistence,
peaceful
Poland, 9, 36, 45, 46, 148
Politburo, *see* CPSU
Pompidou, Georges, 30, 32, 69, 104
Portugal, 105, 132
Pravda, 195
Principles of Co-operation Between
the USSR and France, 182
Program of Further Struggle for Peace
and International Co-operation,
112, 121–122

Romania, 46, 137–138, 148
Roosevelt, Franklin D., 22

Sadat, Anwar, 49
SALT (Strategic Arms Limitation
Talks), 4, 16–17, 23, 36–37, 39,
56, 57, 58, 59, 70–71, 77, 85, 86,
90, 107, 110, 113, 116, 121, 122,
132, 135, 139, 144, 145, 150–151,
156, 160, 165, 167, 171–172, 186,
196, 202–204, 206, 213
Scandinavia, 69, 105
Scheel, Walter, 105
Schmidt, Helmut, 69, 105, 195, 223
security, international, 4, 11, 14–15,
16, 18, 25–26, 31, 32, 33, 35, 42,
44, 45, 46, 52, 64, 71, 78, 90,
97, 104, 106, 116, 132, 174
Siberia, 10, 27, 201
Simon, William, 80, 140
Slayton, Donald, 92, 93
socialism, 7, 34, 36, 40, 62, 63, 65, 66,
68, 88, 104, 119, 125, 133, 134,
154, 155, 163, 169, 193, 199, 200
socialist community, 33–34, 38, 46, 56,
89, 125, 154, 155, 188

agencies, the press, radio, and television. Frankly, we are tired of that blather. In the West, too, when serious politicians are asked whether they feel concerned over this alleged Soviet threat, their reply is an emphatic "No."

Of course we are improving our defenses. We cannot do otherwise. We have never yielded, and shall never yield, in matters of our own security or the security of our allies.

However, the allegations that the Soviet Union is going beyond what it actually needs for its national defense, that it is trying to attain superiority in weapons in order to deal "the first blow," are absurd and totally unfounded. Not so long ago, at a meeting I had with a group of leading U.S. businessmen, I said, and today I want to repeat it, that the Soviet Union has always been and remains strongly opposed to such concepts.

Our efforts are directed precisely at averting the first strike and the second strike, indeed at averting nuclear war in general. Our approach on these questions can be formulated as follows: the defense potential of the Soviet Union must be at a level that would deter anyone from attempting to disrupt our peaceful life. Not superiority in weapons, but a course aimed at reducing armaments, at easing the military confrontation—such is our policy.

On behalf of the Party and the entire people, I hereby declare that our country will never embark on the road of aggression, will never raise the sword against other nations.

It is not we, but certain forces in the West, who are stepping up the arms race, particularly the nuclear-arms race. It is not we, but those forces, who are swelling military budgets by throwing money—hundreds of billions—into the bottomless pit of military preparations. It is those forces that represent an aggressive line in international politics today under the false pretext of a "Soviet menace."

Unless this line is duly rebuffed, the threat of war will grow anew. This line is dangerous to the peoples both in the East and in the West. The Soviet Union will do all it can to counter it and expose the danger it presents.

From the experience of recent years we know that the policy of capitalist states can sometimes be determined by other forces—forces which realize the danger of playing with fire and which are capable of reckoning with the realities of the present-day world. We hope that notwithstanding all the hesitations and an inclination toward phrasemongering, which is often dictated by the domestic situation, reasonableness and a sober approach to the problems of world politics will prevail in those states.

Indeed, it is precisely such an approach that made possible a change in the relations between the USSR and France, the conclusion of the well-known treaties between the USSR and the Federal Republic of Germany, the quadripartite agreement on West Berlin, and important agreements between the Soviet Union and the United States and other capitalist countries, and the convening of the Conference on Security and Co-operation in Europe. In other words, détente was set in motion.

What is détente, or a relaxation of tensions? What meaning do we invest in this term? Détente means, first and foremost, ending the "cold war" and going over to normal, stable relations among states. It means a willingness to settle differences and disputes not by force, not by threats and saber-rattling, but by peaceful means, at a conference table. It means trust among nations and the willingness to take each other's legitimate interests into consideration.

Practice has shown that the international atmosphere can be perceptibly changed within a short time. Contacts between countries in the political, economic, cultural, and other fields have been broadened. And the most important thing, comrades, is that the danger of a new all-out war has been reduced. People are giving a sigh of relief and are becoming more hopeful about the future. This is détente; these are its obvious results.

What can the "cold war" generals offer in place of détente? Higher taxes and greater military expenditure? A further cut in allocations for social needs? Building up stockpiles of weapons of mass destruction? A whipping up of war hysteria and of fear of the future? This will not be accepted by the peoples. Definitely not.

A relaxation of international tension, as we all know, has been achieved at the price of tremendous efforts. And it is not easy to preserve the political capital of détente that has been accumulated. But no difficulties and obstacles will make us retreat. There is no task more urgent and vital than making peace lasting and inviolable.

Statesmen who are aware of their responsibility before millions of people, of their responsibility for the destinies of nations, should keep in mind the desire of the peoples for peace. As for the Soviet Union, it will not fail to do its duty in this.

We are prepared to co-operate with the new administration in the United States in order to take a new major step forward with regard to relations between our countries.

First of all, it is necessary, we are convinced, to complete in the nearest future the drafting of an agreement on limiting strategic arms on the basis we had agreed upon in Vladivostok back in late 1974. Some statesmen in Washington now express regret over the fact that such an agreement still has not been signed. But regrets cannot recover lost time, and it is important that practical conclusions should be drawn from this.

In the United States, too, the question is being asked as to what will happen if such conclusions are not drawn. An influential U.S. newspaper recently noted that in such an event the Soviet Union and the United States would start producing a new generation of nuclear weapons which would be practically impossible to control.

Such a prospect does not suit us. I repeat: time is short, and the conclusion of the agreement must not be postponed.

It goes without saying that the Soviet Union is prepared to go further as regards questions of limitation of strategic arms. But first it is necessary to consolidate what has already been achieved and to carry into practice what was agreed upon in Vladivostok, all the more so since the term of the Interim Agreement expires this October. Then we could immediately proceed to talks on more far-reaching measures. Otherwise, should we add new questions to the ones currently under discussion, we might only further complicate matters and delay the solution of the problem as a whole.

The need is urgent to prevent more surely the proliferation of nuclear weapons, to make more effective the nonproliferation rules and regulations defined in the known treaty. We are prepared to hold businesslike talks on this matter.

We would like to come as soon as possible to an agreement also on the reduction of armed forces and armaments in Central Europe. We have no objections to discussing the relevant questions at any level and at any venue—in Vienna, Bonn, Washington, Moscow—anywhere.

Occupying a central place in European politics today is the task of implementing to the full the accords reached by thirty-five states in Helsinki a year and a half ago. We regard the Final Act of the European Conference as a code of international obligations aimed at ensuring a lasting peace. To be sure, all of its provisions must be implemented, and that is our daily task. The Central Committee attaches much political importance to this work. Many of our ministries and agencies are involved in it.

It is quite understandable that at present much has been accomplished in some fields, while in others the necessary measures are being carried out gradually or are only being drafted. Much depends here on the overall condition of political relations between states or, as it is sometimes said, on the level of détente. By poisoning the international atmosphere the opponents of détente are only impeding this work.

In Western countries attempts are often made to single out some elements from the Final Act and launch polemics on them. The purpose here is obvious: it is to obstruct the positive processes started by the European Conference. Judging by everything, those who make such attempts care little about ensuring a lasting peace in Europe. They are concerned with something else. They would like to put pressure on us, to have us live according to rules that are incompatible with socialist democracy, with socialist law and order. I would like to say that this is a lost cause.

In Helsinki, states with a socialist social system and states with a different social system worked together and achieved important results. This was serious, businesslike co-operation based on common interest in making the conference a success. Now this co-operation should be carried forward. We are ready to work toward this and, as you know, have already made a number of concrete proposals, in particular on several economic problems.

We regard it as a big and important task to develop further bilateral relations with France, the FRG, Italy, Great Britain, and other European and non-European states. We have built and will continue to build our relations with them on the basis of the principle of peaceful coexistence. This is a Leninist principle, and we shall preserve and augment Lenin's legacy, all of it, which we hold sacred.

We are for the implementation of the most vigorous measures to eliminate the seat of war in the Middle East. The bloodshed in Lebanon, stopped with such difficulty, has shown once again with what dangers a further delay in reaching a settlement of the Middle East conflict is fraught.

The Middle East needs a lasting and just settlement that would not impinge on the vital rights of any state and any people. Israel, of course, has the right to independence as a state and to a secure existence. But the same right belongs also to the Arab people of Palestine.

The path to a solution of the Middle East problem lies—and we have said this on many occasions—through the Geneva Peace Conference on the Middle East. At present all the interested states appear to favor a resumption of the work of the Conference. And this imparts still greater importance to co-operation between the cochairmen of the Geneva Conference—the Soviet Union and the United States. Given the will, they can do much to help the sides involved in the conflict in seeking mutually acceptable solutions.

Such is our stand on a number of major international issues.

Such are the intentions with which our country has entered the new year, 1977. The Soviet Union will do all it can toward this goal—that the